GRANDI
VINI

GRANDI VINI

An Opinionated Tour of Italy's 89 Finest Wines

JOSEPH BASTIANICH

CLARKSON POTTER/PUBLISHERS

NEW YORK

Library of Congress Cataloging-in-Publication Data

Bastianich, Joseph.
Grandi vini / Joseph Bastianich. —1st ed.
p.   cm.
Includes index.
1. Wine and wine making—Italy.   I. Title.

TP559.I8B368 2010
641.2'20945—dc22   2010008555

ISBN 978-0-307-46303-6

Printed in the U.S.A.

1 3 5 7 9 10 8 6 4 2

First Edition

To my loving wife, Deanna, and my children, Olivia, Miles, and Ethan.

To Tiziano Gaia and Giancarlo Gariglio for their intimate understanding of every aspect of Italian wine. The spirit of our great collaboration permeates every chapter of this book.

To the great *Barolo Monfortino Riserva* Giacomo Conterno, the standard by which all others are measured, a wine that captures the essence expressed in this book yet remains in a class of its own.

~ CONTENTS ~

~INTRODUCTION~

GRANDI VINI: An Opinionated Tour of Italy's 89 Finest Wines not only identifies the most unique and outstanding wines that Italy offers today but also shares everything happening behind the scenes in Italy's dynamic and sometimes mysterious world of wine. This is the present-day story of wine in Italy and, in many ways, my story as well.

In the post–Second World War era, my family members were political refugees and immigrants from the war-torn region of Istria. Although they were people of the earth who produced food and wine, they were forced to leave that life behind and seek opportunities in America. Once settled, they turned back to food and wine in order to earn a living. From positions as cooks, bakers, and waiters, they became restaurant owners, their success predestining my life in food and wine.

Shortly after I was born, in 1968 (a terrible vintage in Italy), my mother, Lidia, and father, Felix, opened Buonavia, their first restaurant, in the Forest Hills neighborhood of Queens, New York. Those early days of the restaurant business were not glamorous; the media-driven frenzy that surrounds top eateries today simply did not exist then. Working in a restaurant was hard, blue-collar work that involved physical labor, lots of hours, and, ultimately, sacrifice. Buonavia wasn't a job; it was a way of life. We worked in the restaurant (all the time), we ate in the restaurant (only between services so no customers could see), we went to the restaurant after school to play and do homework; home was reserved for sleeping only. All my friends' parents were doctors, lawyers, and accountants who belonged to country clubs. My friends went to camp during the summer; we worked in the restaurant.

It wasn't all bad. I always had a lot of grown-up friends as a child, mostly the restaurant employees and neighboring business owners. Sam, the bartender, was always good for a Coca-Cola and some gossip. Salvatore, the salad man (he also plated desserts), was a comrade and resource. Joey "Slice" owned the pizza parlor next door (one can't live exclusively on fettuccini Alfredo), and Lou owned Goldstar Liquors down the block.

The truth is, Lou Iacucci is the person who really introduced New York and America to quality Italian wines in the 1970s. Goldstar was a typical 1970s-style wine and spirits retailer: Wine specials were floor-stacked, and the windows were covered with signs announcing sales and deals on the hard stuff—vodka, gin, and whiskey. While Goldstar sold everything, Lou's passion was for Italian wine. Tucked in the back of the store, Lou's office was crammed with samples from Italy. He would make frequent trips to Piemonte and Toscana, befriending the scene-makers in food and wine. When they in turn came to New York, Lou would reciprocate their hospitality and bring them to meet people in the business of selling Italian wine. One of the places he would always take the Italians to eat was Buonavia.

These were the beginnings of my life in Italian wine. Throughout the years there were many more restaurants and trips to Italy with my parents. Then I began to travel alone, and my passion for Italy and its wines evolved. After graduating from Boston College, I went to work on Wall Street (because that is what you did if you wanted to be successful). I barely made it through the MBA training program at Merrill Lynch and very quickly realized that the culture of office life was not for me. I needed to return to my passion: the food and wine of Italy. I quit my job, packed my bags, and headed out for a two-year viticulture odyssey through the Italian peninsula. I was a cellar rat, grape picker, waiter, cook, private driver—you name it. I met and worked with the people who embodied the very essence of Italian food and wine culture.

While working and traveling in Italy, I came to the realization that I wanted to be involved in the world of Italian food and wine for the rest of my life. That felt completely right.

Twenty years after that seminal trip to Italy, I now own twenty restaurants throughout the United States, three wineries in Italy, and several wine and food shops. It's been a busy yet extremely gratifying run. My business and personal evolution are a direct reflection of the wild popularity of Italian food and wine in this country. I feel lucky to be a conduit or interpreter of two thousand years of food and wine culture, which America is so ravenously consuming. With each new menu, wine list, or, in this case, book, I more clearly define my role not as a creator or innovator but simply as someone who distills the best of what Italy has to offer.

Choosing eighty-nine *grandi vini italiani* was a complex and emotional experience. I handpicked these wines not only for their absolute quality but also for what they represent in the current Italian enological landscape; each wine and its maker tells us a story. Although the wines often speak for themselves in the glass, the details of their journey from grape to bottle are likewise illuminating.

As global trends of sustainable living continue to encourage consumers' interest in knowing the provenance of the food and wine that we consume, this book tells the story of every wine, establishing for the reader a personal relationship with the place, grapes, and people that create these libations. The essays reintroduce wine as an agricultural product, stripping away preconceived notions of ratings (though they are often important) and packaging, bringing wine back to its historical origins as fermented grape juice from a particular place.

The eighty-nine wines included here range from pricey international superstars to recently rediscovered ultra-regional gems. And yet each one has a unique and evocative story that teaches us not only about the wine but also allows us to enter the minds of the best winemakers in Italy today, sharing their aspirations and ambitions.

Enjoy the journey in these pages and in a glass of one of the eighty-nine *grandi vini*. These wines deliver the past, present, and future of Italian wine and will hopefully inspire, inform, and satiate you.

CENTRAL ITALY

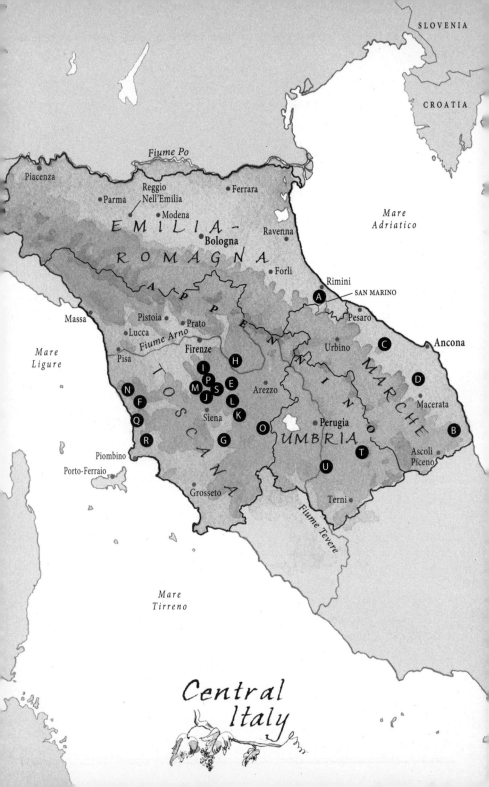

Central Italy

Emilia Romagna

A *Sangiovese di Romagna Superiore Avi Riserva* San Patrignano

Marche

B *Kurni* Oasi degli Angeli

C *Verdicchio dei Castelli di Jesi Classico Villa Bucci Riserva* Bucci

D *Verdicchio dei Castelli di Jesi Classico Superiore Podium* Gioacchino Garofoli

Toscana

E *Alceo* Castello dei Rampolla

F *Bolgheri Superiore Grattamacco Rosso* Podere Grattamacco

G *Brunello di Montalcino* La Cerbaiola

G *Brunello di Montalcino Cerretalto* Casanova di Neri

G *Brunello di Montalcino Tenuta Il Greppo Riserva* Biondi Santi

G *Brunello di Montalcino Riserva* Poggio di Sotto

H *Camartina* Querciabella

I *Cepparello* Isole e Olena

J *Chianti Classico Riserva Castello di Fonterutoli* Castello di Fonterutoli

K *Chianti Classico Riserva Rancia* Fèlsina

L *Chianti Classico Vigneto Bellavista* Castello di Ama

M *Flaccianello della Pieve* Tenuta Fontodi

N *Masseto* Tenuta dell'Ornellaia

O *Nobile di Montepulciano Nocio dei Boscarelli* Boscarelli

L *Percarlo* Fattoria San Giusto a Rentennano

P *Le Pergole Torte* Montevertine

Q *Redigaffi* Tua Rita

N *Sassicaia* Tenuta San Guido

R *Tenuta di Valgiano* Tenuta di Valgiano

S *Tignanello* Marchesi Antinori

O *Vin Santo Occhio di Pernice* Avignonesi

Umbria

T *Montefalco Sagrantino 25 Anni* Arnaldo Caprai

U *Cervaro della Sala* Castello della Sala

EMILIA
~ROMAGNA~

Sangiovese di Romagna Superiore Avi Riserva—
SAN PATRIGNANO

ONE OF ITALY'S most fascinating and forward-thinking wines comes from the most unlikely of places. Yet it couldn't have been any other way, because the beauty and intrigue in every bottle of Sangiovese di Romagna Superiore Avi Riserva is inextricably linked to the people and *terroir* of this winery.

San Patrignano is the largest drug rehabilitation center in Europe. Founded in 1978 by a famous philanthropist from Rimini, Vincenzo Muccioli, San Patrignano now hosts around two hundred young men and women seeking to get their lives back on track. In addition to the classic forms of therapy, San Patrignano requires its residents to work upon arrival, giving them the opportunity to find new self-worth and distracting them from the otherwise uncomfortable position they find themselves in.

Located in the hilly countryside not far from the coast and the region's most famous seaside city, Rimini, San Patrignano is a working farm and home to an avant-garde horse-breeding facility. In fact, some of the horses from the San Patrignano stables have competed in and won the world's most prominent equestrian events. The farm is also the producer of high-quality wine. Thanks not only to the technical staff, which includes some of the top names in Italian winemaking, such as superstar enologist Riccardo Cotarella, but also to the young members of the San Patrignano community, winemaking at San Patrignano has become an exercise in excellence.

Producing wine here came as a challenge, because of certain prejudices against Emilia Romagna wines. In terms of volume, the region comes in fourth in Italy, trailing behind Veneto, Puglia, and Sicilia, producing 600 million liters annually. The majority of the wine is produced in the central part of the region, or Emilia, home to one of the most famous, or perhaps I should say infamous, wines in the world: Lambrusco. Made from the lambrusco grape, this sparkling wine has conquered international markets because of the ease with which it can be drunk and paired with food. Produced for the most part by large companies in Parma, Modena, and Reggio Emilia, Lambrusco has long dominated the local wine industry, adding to the list of regional stereotypes: The people of Emilia are known to love good food (Parmigiano-Reggiano and prosciutto di Parma are made here); classical music (Luciano Pavarotti was from Modena); and fast cars (the Ferrari headquarters are located in Maranello, just outside of Modena).

Romagna residents, however, historical rivals of their Emilian neighbors, are particularly proud of their roots. Sangiovese, the grape of Toscana and a large part of central Italy, dominates the vineyards in Romagna (though the more forward-thinking wineries, like San Patrignano, have planted other cultivars as well). Generally speaking, the sangiovese grown in the subregion is used to make Sangiovese di Romagna, a wine that differs from its Tuscan "cousin" not only because of the differences in *terroir*, but also because of the clonal variety used. Generally, Romangnan Sangiovese is more tannic and, if made well, can withstand long aging periods.

Sangiovese di Romagna Avi is one of the most emblematic red wines produced at San Patrignano. (The "Avi" stands for *"a Vincenzo"* ["for Vicenzo"], the charismatic founder of the community, who passed away fifteen years ago.) The wine is labeled both Superiore, owing to the fact that it has more (far more) than 12 percent alcohol content, and Riserva, because it is not released to the market for at least two years from harvest. Only the best grapes from the 120 acres planted with sangiovese at San Patrignano are used to make this wine. The vineyards are all located within the walls of the community and formed the original nucleus of the center, which has since been enlarged. The members of San Patrignano are responsible for every phase of production, from the vineyard to the cellar. Harvest typically takes place between the end of September and the beginning of October, and the yield of each plant is around 2 pounds of grapes. The vinification process is very traditional, beginning with the use of large (2,800-liter) barrels that bring out the true characteristics of the grape variety.

The wine itself is ruby red with hints of granite. It has a rich and complex nose, with notes of violet, spices, and black fruit. In the mouth, it is elegant and powerful and has a round structure, with a vein of tannins. It finishes with notes of forest fruits and sweet spices.

~MARCHE~

Kurni—OASI DEGLI ANGELI

IF YOU WERE to search the Internet for the word "Kurni," you would be surprised to see just how many websites, blogs, fan clubs, and forums are dedicated to this fairly new wine. I have always loved wines that rise to the top on a wave of mass popularity. For the first time in Italy, the success of a wine can be directly linked to a democratic republic of fans who, in addition to influencing the critics and the ratings of wine guides, gave this wine status by simply spreading the word. Kurni may be the first example of a wine whose popularity was directly propelled by new social media.

In the last decade, Kurni has become an underground favorite able to excite—but also divide—wine lovers like no other. Strangely, this wine is not the product of a celebrated wine area like the Langa, Chianti, or Valpolicella. It is produced in Marche, in a part of the region that until recently had been abandoned because of the poor quality of its agricultural products. But with the arrival of Marco Casolanetti, a young, talented, and motivated winemaker, the area of Marche near Abruzzo, called Piceno, experienced a rebirth. Slowly but surely, Piceno regained the dignity it had lost. Before getting into the details of this wine, it is worth mentioning that, together with his exuberant wife, Eleonora Rossi, Marco expanded their Oasi degli Angeli winery by opening a small hotel and restaurant that allow them to welcome visitors to their paradise. The couple started to grow vegetables, olives, and fruit on their property, serving them to their friends and guests and proving that it was possible to create a new model for agriculture, tourism, and a local economy.

Oasi degli Angeli, however, is even better known for its wine. Or rather, for a specific grape variety. Together with nearby Abruzzo, Marche has the fortune to be home to the great indigenous varietal montepulciano. Traditionally, montepulciano was planted across the region, but farmers were not able to produce wines up to the massive potential of the grape. The Montepulcianos of the past were too austere, lacked focus, and were fairly uninteresting. Marco Casolanetti reignited the local winemaking culture, beginning with an in-depth study of the land and of the reaction of the vines to improvements in the vineyards. He continued by adopting a decidedly modern winemaking style that focused on longevity and extraction.

When the first bottles of Kurni were released, people thought a miracle had occurred. The wine had a dark, deep color; it had an intense nose and an explosive, powerful, almost chewable structure. It certainly could not be a Montepulciano! But it was. In fact, it was a pure Montepulciano, made from grapes carefully tended to, without chemicals, and planted in an extremly dense manner. The wine had also been made to evolve and age like other top Italian reds. And it spoke for itself. Kurni—the only wine produced by the estate until a few years ago—immediately attracted both fans and critics. The wine media praised the wine at the beginning, but in recent years they have paid it less attention because of a renewed interest in less extreme, more accessible wines.

There are two indisputable facts about this wine, one technical, the other geographical. The first has to do with the concept of limits: Before Casolanetti, no one had been able to capture the potential of Montepulciano. Beginning with the vines, he was able to bring out the essence of the grape, of the land, and of its history. The second fact has to do with Marco's influence on the men of Marche: Oasi degli Angeli gave a renewed sense of faith to many young winemakers who had been frustruated to the point of changing careers. Their new faith in the land resulted in the creation of a group of winemakers, called Piceni Invisibili, who work to promote the region of Piceno with their wines. All of this required a pioneer wine, which came in the form of Kurni.

The montepulciano grape is grown in both the Marche and the Abruzzo regions of Italy, but it appears to have found a happier home in the former. Recently, wine producers in Marche have been very active, creating new styles of wine. Some of the best examples of these dynamic winemakers and wines can be found in Piceno, a wonderful, fairly unknown area of the region. Piceno is located along a thin, hilly strip of land, not far from the Adriatic Sea. The position of the area is excellent for growing grapes, and its beauty is worth a detour from the coastal highway. From the water, the land rises quickly to the hills, where you can find many little towns with incredible views. This is a land of history and art. Recanati, for example, was home to the great romantic poet Giacomo Leopardi, and Castelfidardo is the world's accordion center. Amid the olive trees, wheat fields, and fruit trees are vineyards upon vineyards, all touched by the salty sea breezes and protected by the soft hills that recall those of Toscana. The soil is primarily composed of clay—possibly the only defect of an otherwise perfect winemaking zone. The clay gives bold structure to wines made from montepulciano grapes and can often overpower elegance in the glass. This was more of a risk in the past, when winemakers had neither the experience they have today nor the tools to make well-balanced, sophisticated Montepulcianos. Now everything has changed, and elegance reigns in the cellars of Piceno.

The Kurni phenomenon started at least forty years ago, forty being the average age of the grapes in Marco Casolanetti and Eleonora Rossi's vineyard. Their vines cover 25 acres of land, all of which are planted with montepulciano grapes destined to become Kurni. With determination and courage, Marco invested everything he owned in his vineyard. He densely planted his land with a record number of 6,073 plants per acre, using an old training system called *gobelet* (a type of *alberello*, or small-tree style of vine pruning), and lowered his yields to half a pound per plant. The 6,000 bottles of Kurni produced from 25 acres are truly the expression of all of Marco's decisions in the vineyard. The wine is very sensitive to variations in vintages. In addition, Oasi degli Angeli is a biodynamic operation and therefore the grapes that arrive in the cellar are the product of nature and her moods. Once in the cellar, the wine undergoes long fermentation, resting in barriques for fourteen to sixteen months. The wine is then bottled without being filtered.

The results speak for themselves. Even if a bottle of Kurni has been open for days, it retains incredible freshness. Once you move beyond the impenetrable purple color of the wine, you arrive at an explosion of its perfumes: The wine is like a freight train loaded with fruit. When tasted blind, Kurni is sometimes mistaken for an Amarone, or even a Grange Hermitage. Rarely does one shout out "Kurni!" In the mouth, the wine is full and captivating in an almost velvety way. It is elegant and balanced beyond any expectation. Kurni is a wine to drink and enjoy, because beyond its aroma and flavor, it is an expression of a revolutionary territory. Kurni is an anthem of change—of joy, life, and the possibility of new beginnings.

Verdicchio dei Castelli di Jesi Classico Villa Bucci Riserva—BUCCI

AMPELIO BUCCI IS a master of *terroir.* A professor of communications at the IULM University in Milan and consultant to famous Italian fashion houses, Ampelio, at first sight, might appear to be a urban and affluent Milanese who decided to dabble in winemaking. Nothing could be further from the truth.

The Bucci family has ancient roots. Since the 1700s, they have owned property in the town of Montecarotto, one of the Castelli di Jesi, located in the Marche region. Ampelio's father died when he was only thirteen years old, leaving him 988 acres of farmland, tended to by *braccianti* (farmhands) and *mezzandri* (sharecroppers), whose livelihood depended on the productivity of the farm. Having inherited tremendous responsibility at a very young age, Ampelio took over the farm and, thanks to his determination, was able to make it profitable. This was sixty years ago, and since then, the fabric of Italian agriculture has changed dramatically.

During the 1950s, in central Italy and Marche, the *mezzandria* system (the equal division of crops between the landowner and the people who worked the land) was in decline, and by the 1960s, it was replaced with an entrepreneurial system, which obviously came with great risk. By the mid-1970s, the globalization of the food chain led to the devaluation of many Italian crops. Silk, tobacco, and animal husbandry were gradually abandoned altogether. Although Ampelio Bucci led his farm through the transition with success, the changes in the economic climate led him to study economics. He wanted to understand the possible exit strategies for a relatively closed and politically protected agricultural system. He eventually applied his studies of agricultural economy to other fields, including fashion and design, in which he is considered to be one of the brightest minds in Italy.

In the early 1980s, he decided to plant vineyards and olives, at a time when Verdicchio certainly didn't have much appeal. This was true especially in the United States, where the only Verdicchio out there was Fazi Battaglia, which graced the shelves of mom-and-pop pizzerias and which made an appearance on the film *Serpico,* starring Al Pacino. In a few short years, Bucci was able to create a cult around his Riserva, which he did with the help of Giorgio Grai, a celebrated enologist from Alto Adige. Grai was a master of production and blending and is credited with the creation of Italy's first great white wine in those years.

Today, Ampelio is way over seventy, but he carries his years with energy and elegance: a sharply dressed world traveler who loves to visit the global wine and fashion capitals to promote his wine. To those who criticize him for being a fashionista and urbanite, he responds: "I didn't live my life plowing fields, but instead of having blisters on my hands, I have them on my brain from the excruciating mental power needed to come up with new ways to sell my Verdicchio."

Montecarotto is a small village in the hills of Marche, a few miles from the Adriatic Sea. A splendid medieval castle dominates the summit of the town and the surrounding landscape dotted with vineyards cultivated primarily with the native verdicchio grape variety. The area is 1,200 feet above sea level, saddled between the hills that divide the Esino and Misa valleys. The Bucci winery is located between the backbone of the Italian Apennine Mountains and the nearby Adriatic. It is an ideal position for cultivating grapes: The marine winds mitigate the cold winter climate, while the nearby mountains are responsible for the considerable differences in day- and nighttime temperatures, enriching the aroma of the wines produced in this particular *terroir*. Ampelio cultivates his vineyard the way only a great craftsman knows how. In terms of productivity, Bucci has gone against the grain: His vineyards yield half of what is set out in the Verdicchio guidelines, or 15,400 to 17,600 pounds per acre versus the 30,800 pounds permitted by law, which Ampelio considers too lax. His vines are more than forty years old, meaning that they are deeply rooted in the earth and able to fully express the characteristics of the local soil.

Ampelio Bucci has created a wine that is a self-portrait. It is an aristocratic, intelligent, nervous white wine, thanks to its salty acidity. And like Ampelio, it never shows its age. Verdicchio Villa Bucci is, in fact, characterized primarily by its incredible propensity for aging. It is a white that can be aged because of the natural production methods employed and the limited human intervention in the winemaking process. The wine matures for about eighteen months in large oak casks of 4,500 or 7,500 liters that are used for decades and kept in working condition with periodical cleaning and renovation. After carefully tasting all the wines in the cellar, Giorgio Grai and Ampelio Bucci jointly decide which are worthy of being bottled as Villa Bucci Riserva.

Another identifying characteristic of this atypical white wine is that it acts more like a great red, rather than like a classic white. On the nose, it is not overly fruity. Its underlying notes of hazelnut accompany flavors of citrus, chamomile, and lime blossom. In the mouth, it is decisive and powerful, with profound flavor. The finish is salty, minerally long, and rich in juice. One should open a bottle of Riserva Villa Bucci at least a half hour before drinking to enjoy it to the fullest. Surprisingly, the wine is incredibly good a day after uncorking. Even its ideal serving temperature is more similar to that of red wines—never below 57 or 59 degrees Fahrenheit—especially with older bottles.

Verdicchio dei Castelli di Jesi Classico Superiore Podium—GIOACCHINO GAROFOLI

THE HISTORY OF Verdicchio can be divided into two distinct phases. The first spans the large part of the last century, up until the 1970s or '80s, and is characterized by a wine that is easy to drink, fairly inexpensive, and of little quality. I have always been a fan of the wine and an advocate of the verdicchio grape, considering it alongside friulano as one of Italy's most noble indigenous white varietals. Yet it seemed that Verdicchio was destined to remain unappreciated until a handful of winemakers decided that the grape and the *terroir* had much more to give. One such believer was Gioacchino Garofoli, the father of modern Verdicchio. The Garofoli family started making wine in 1871, but it is thanks to Gioacchino's sons—Franco, Carlo, and Gianfranco—that this wine has become one of the most important examples of Verdicchio in recent years.

The winery is located in Marche, a region of central Italy on the Adriatic coast, where the microclimate is perfect for grape growing. The region has a long winemaking history, centered on the city of Jesi, where verdicchio is king. The verdicchio grape has been grown in Marche for centuries, but its origin is unclear: It is believed to be a variation of trebbiano from Soave and Lugana, a lesser grape from northern Italy. For a long time, Verdicchio was known as an easy drinking wine, appealing to a large audience that recognized the wine by its amphora-shaped bottle rather than the wine itself. Since my youth in the 1970s, the green fish-shaped Verdicchio bottle has been carved into my memory as the emblem of Italian white wine. At a certain point during the 1980s, Verdicchio sales were down, and the wine seemed to be nearing its death. Paradoxically, the downturn allowed for wineries like Garofoli to focus on quality, giving the wine a new image. Winemakers studied the territory and verdicchio clones and introduced modern technology to their cellars, such as stainless steel vats and temperature-controlled fermentation. It was difficult to know the true potential of the the grape, yet the results spoke for themselves.

Gioacchino Garofoli produces today about 2 million bottles, of which almost half are Verdicchio dei Castelli di Jesi. Garofoli's Verdicchio has defined a new style for this wine: It has notable acidity and strong aromas, uncommon to Italian white wine. The wine also develops interestingly over time: When the wine is young, it is fresh and easy to drink, not unlike the Verchicchios of the past. After the wine has been aged, it has remarkable power and structure and continues to evolve rather than "devolve." A Verdicchio like Podium di Garofoli should be drunk after a couple of years, when the mineral notes reach their full potential.

Marche is a placid land of about 3,900 square miles situated along the Adriatic Sea, about halfway down the Italian boot. Its landscape is quite varied and can go from sandy beaches to low hills and mountains in a matter of miles. The main towns in Marche are located along the coast, while the inland hamlets are rich in history and natural wonders. Castelli di Jesi is one of the most interesting territories, situated not far from Ancona. The Garofoli winery is found in Castelfidardo, the world's accordion capital. (I fondly recall accordion-buying expeditions with my father, a player and collector during the 1970s.) Castelfidardo is located near the sea, giving the area its dry and ventilated climate. The Verdicchio production area is quite large and spans two different provinces, Ancona and Macerata, but Verdicchio Classico can be produced only in Castelli di Jesi. Podium, a sort of grand cru of the denomination, comes from vineyards located in Montecarotto.

After years of being the clear reference point for the entire denomination, Verdicchio dei Castelli di Jesi Classico Superiore Podium is a rare example of steadfast quality. Thanks to the microclimate of the region and its consistency from year to year, this wine proves excellent across vintages. The vineyard yields in Montecarotto are considerably less than the denomination guidelines call for, making for grapes that are concentrated and rich in pulp. The land where the Podium vines are planted is composed of clay of density. The grapes are harvested once they've reached a proper level of ripeness. They are softly pressed in the cellar, the must is cold-cleaned, and fermentation occurs at a low, controlled temperature. Although the law allows for Verdicchio Classico to contain 15 percent of other white grapes, Podium is made exclusively from verdicchio. The wine ages for fifteen months in stainless steel tanks at 50 degrees Fahrenheit and matures in the bottle for four months in temperature-controlled rooms.

Podium never sees wood, avoiding the sometimes heavy, inappropriate aromas of barrique-aged whites. The wine is golden yellow in color with green tones. It has intense minerally aromas combined with notes of citrus, honey, herbs, and must. It has a seductive flavor and is both robust and full bodied yet acidic and fragrant with a long finish. Verdicchio dei Castelli di Jesi Superiore Podium is a wine you can drink immediately or truly enjoy after six, eight, or even ten years of aging.

~TOSCANA~

Alceo—CASTELLO DEI RAMPOLLA

ALCEO DI NAPOLI was a true prince, not unlike the princes of children's fairy tales, as the story of the Di Napoli Rampolla family is that of an ancient dynasty. In fact, the family has owned their landed estate, Castello dei Rampolla, in Panzano, since 1739, predating the French Revolution. A princely countryman, a great lover of the earth and wine, Alceo would often voluntarily go down into the fields and work, without worrying about dirtying his legendary velvet pants that he loved so dearly. He was open to change and confrontation, even if conservative and traditionalist in spirit. His visceral passion for grapes and wine led him often to visit his French cousins, whom he deeply admired and respected. Visiting the greatest châteaux in Bordeaux and drinking their strong and aristocratic wines, he dreamt of making a miraculous wine in Toscana, on this little estate in Panzano, in the heart of Chianti Classico.

In 1964, Alceo started his winemaking activity and began planting sangiovese grapes, the most important varietal of the area. Later, in pursuit of his dream of making French-style wine, he planted cabernet sauvignon. At the beginning, his best grapes were purchased by Marchese Antinori, who, because of the superior nature of the cabernet grapes, was able to evolve and complete Antinori's flagship wine: Tignanello. This close relationship between the two noble families of Toscana started because they both sought out the consultation of Giacomo

Tachis, the most important Italian winemaker of the time. Consequently, at the beginning, Alceo's top grapes ended up in other wines, and to taste the first bottle labeled Castello dei Rampolla, Alceo had to wait until 1975—an incredible vintage in Toscana. But it wasn't until the 1980s that the winery really took off, thanks to a Super Tuscan the prince named Sammarco, a blend of sangiovese and cabernet sauvignon. The blend was created by both Alceo and Giacomo Tachis, who continued to work as a consultant for the Rampolla house.

Despite the incredible success of Sammarco with the critics and in the market, the prince was still not satisfied and held a dream in his heart: to pit himself against his French counterparts by making a Tuscan wine entirely from native French varietals. In 1990, he decided to plant the most beautiful vineyard on the property with petit verdot and cabernet sauvignon, a heresy in Chianti Classico. But in 1994, before his dream was complete, Alceo passed away, leaving a huge hole in the heart of his estate. His children, Livia, Maurizia, and Luca, despite their loss, continued down their father's path, and the first bottle of Alceo's dream wine was released in 1996. The new wine was named Vigna d'Alceo, a tribute to the vision and hard work of its creator. Needless to say, it was a huge success, and in a few years, the wine acquired legendary status. The top wine critics in the world recognized the importance of Vigna d'Alceo, which for legal reasons had to change its name to the simpler d'Alceo. This wine can probably be considered the most formidable Italian threat to the legendary *premiers crus* of Bordeaux.

Panzano, one of the smallest towns in Chianti, is located in one of the happiest and most fertile winemaking areas in Toscana. The bowl on the southwest side of the tiny, picturesque medieval town is ideal for growing grapes because it is exposed to the sun all day long. The area has even been named the Conca d'Oro ("Golden Bowl"). Here the Rampolla family owns 104 acres of vineyards, cultivated since the end of the 1990s, first organically, and since 2004, according to biodynamic standards. The Alceo vineyard is shaped somewhat like a *panettone,* a cylindrical Italian Christmas bread with a puffy cap, and faces southeast and southwest, with perfect sun exposure. The altitude is 1,200 feet above sea level, and the soil is mainly calcareous and rocky. It is the magical combination of altitude, exposures of the vineyards, and essence of *terroir* that create the perfect situation to make a great Tuscan red wine. The quality of the grapes is stupendous, thanks to the density of the vines, which range between 3,200 and 4,000 plants per acre. The yield, however, is very low and never surpasses 1,600 pounds of grapes per acre. But what makes the Rampolla grapes truly different is that they are grown biodynamically. In fact, the winery even grows its own seedlings, without having to rely on a nursery. It is an exemplary operation, one that is able to successfully maintain extreme respect for the environment with a total focus on quality wines.

Created in 1996, Alceo does not have a long history. Despite its recent entry into the Italian wine scene, it is already considered one of the most important wines in Italy, and perhaps in the world. Ever since I tasted the 1996 vintage for the first time, I've been greatly influenced by the impact it made on me. It represents a delicate balance between restraint and power—the very balance that has propelled it into the global wine scene. Although the wine is made from international grape varieties—85 percent cabernet sauvignon and 15 percent petit verdot—it has deeply *chiantigiano* (local) spirit. The extreme low yield of the grapes results in a very concentrated and powerful wine. If opened young, Alceo will seem closed and strongly wrapped around itself. If you have the patience to wait a year or so, the wine has the ability to impress and surprise even the most seasoned wine tasters, thanks to its fine tannins and aromas. Even with its extreme concentration and intense nose, it is the definition of elegance. There is little technological intervention in the Rampolla cellar, for the winemakers follow the rules of nature and dedicate themselves to the agricultural side of the process. For this reason, the wine does not undergo any physical or chemically invasive treatments. It is aged in Allier oak barriques for twenty-one months, yet the oak is not dominant, because there is already so much substance to the wine.

Alceo is released only in great vintages, and it therefore has consistent characteristics, or few differences from one year to the next. On the nose, it has delicate aromas of blueberry and peony, but also of herbs and juniper, finishing with subtle notes of graphite and gunpowder. In the mouth, despite its immensity, it is alive, multifaceted, and different from one sip to the next, growing in intensity.

Bolgheri Superiore Grattamacco Rosso—PODERE GRATTAMACCO

THE SUBREGION OF Bolgheri, once known for its wild boar and pine trees, is now home to movie stars and jet-setters who have built grand and sweeping estates. The wineries constructed here in the past thirty years turn out wines that have, in a funny way, followed tangentially the lifestyle of the area's posh settlers. This part of Toscana's western coastline has attracted wealth without industry. People come to Bolgheri to spend their money in fabulous restaurants and on luxurious wines. In 1977, when Piermario Meletti Cavallari decided to leave Milano for Bolgheri, Sassicaia (see page 56) was the only wine of quality produced in the area. After meeting and talking to trendsetters of the wine world, including Gino Veronelli, Italy's most important wine critic, Cavallari started traveling to Toscana and Marche with his wife, Laura Loglio, searching for a place to build the perfect small winery and a new lifestyle. When they found an abandoned farmhouse with a small vineyard in Bolgheri, they decided to settle in.

Starting with Sassicaia, the first wines to be produced in Bolgheri were made from Bordeaux grape varieties, giving them sure footing on the international wine market and catering to an international audience of wine drinkers. Cavallari decided to plant cabernet sauvignon at Podere Grattamacco, because of the variety's inherent nobility and because it seemed to prosper in the region. When he realized that the price of wine was rising and that consumers were increasingly interested in quality, he decided to hire consulting enologist Maurizio Castelli. The original "flying winemaker," Maurizio gave birth to a new style of Tuscan wine in the 1980s and '90s. A traditionalist at heart and a smooth operator on the dance floor (I remember a late-night bar scene in Buenos Aires involving Malbec and tango), Maurizio made a name for himself by respecting the innate characteristics of indigenous Italian grape varieties. Presenting Maurizio with the canvas of Bolgheri and a slate of international grapes was like giving Picasso oil paints for the first time. The beauty of the wine made at Grattamacco is inevitably the result of the confluence of Maurizio's experience and the new *terroir* and grape varieties. Charismatic, opinionated, and unrelenting in his pursuit for purity, Maurizio focused exclusively on the winemaking and left marketing and selling strategies to others. To this day, his vision is to make wines that are true to their varietal and that speak of their place of origin. In this case, the winery is small (about 30 acres) and focused—both important attributes.

The soil here is very hard and compact, causing the fruit to be very concentrated in sugar and the grapes to be very small in size—characteristics that lead to high-quality wines. The climate in this area is Mediterranean, with the vines growing not far from the Tyrrhenian Sea. Even the vegetation that surrounds the property is decidedly Mediterranean: There are cypress tress, maritime palms, and pine trees, as well as herbs like rosemary, myrtle, and lavender. The risk in the rapid growth of a wine region like Bolgheri is that many of the wines end up quite similar, with an almost standardized style. Among its Super Tuscan peers, including Sassicaia and Ornellaia, Grattamacco is most directly linked to the land. Grattamacco's profound and clear connection to Bolgheri is a testament to Maurizio's style and conviction as a winemaker who lets the earth speak.

Grattamacco is not necessarily an easy wine to drink. It is a Bordeaux blend with great austerity: When drunk young, the wine has aromas of coastal pine and herbs. From the enological point of view, the secret of this wine is open-air fermentation in large vats made of French oak. Cavallari took this idea from Sassicaia, thanks to the useful advice of Marchese Mario Incisa della Rocchetta. This ancient practice gives the wine its rustic character when it is young. However, if the wine is left to age, it develops notes of blueberries and red pepper, as well as China root and Mediterranean bush, and the tannins become elegant, agile, and juicy.

Brunello di Montalcino—LA CERBAIOLA

GIULIO SALVIONI HAS an eruptive personality. He is a typical Tuscan, genuine and exuberant, never timid about sharing his ideas or convictions. Giulio stands out against other producers in Montalcino, many of whom are either foreigners who were attracted by the beauty of the Tuscan landscape or Italian businessmen who decided to invest in viticulture. Giulio was born and raised in Montalcino and has been making wine in exactly the same way for the past twenty-five years. In the 1960s and '70s, and with Brunello's entrance into the DOC list, many local wine producers started to increase their production volume. The creation of the Banfi estate, for example, owned by the Mariani brothers, American importers of Italian wine, had a revolutionary effect on the region. The vineyard had an important physical impact on the land because of its size (2,100 acres) and also spread the Brunello name throughout the world, especially in the United States.

I have always been drawn to the town of Montalcino. I lived and worked there in the late 1980s, and it always made me feel that I was in the heart of the Italian wine scene. The beauty of the place and the power of the wine are what have positioned Montalcino as a beacon of viticulture. The real success of Brunello came in the 1990s, with the great 1990 vintage and the boom of Italian wine in general. Wine producers began buying up estates and vineyards in Montalcino, involving investors of all types and backgrounds. The area of Brunello planted with grapes went from 160 acres in 1967 to almost 2,500 acres in 1990 and is more than 4,900 acres today. People are beginning to be concerned about the well-being of the soil and the land, as well as about the legitimacy of all this newly found Brunello-worthy *terroir*. There are around 250 producers of Brunello, and a little less than 7 million bottles are produced per year. Despite the considerable increase in production, the price of Brunello has continued to increase as well. At least until a couple of years ago, sales were good, and the prices were sustainable. Brunello, however, has had, and is still having, a difficult time finding its own identity. Many producers have changed their wine to fit the times and market trends, offering easy-to-drink, soft, concentrated fruity wines aged in small wooden barrels. These modern wines are quite different from the original Brunello di Montalcino, which is more austere and rough around the edges.

Giulio Salvioni has witnessed these changes in style but has opted not to participate. Despite the success of his Brunellos—in particular his 1985 vintage—Salvioni has decided against enlarging his estate and against building a larger facility. Instead, he owns 10 acres of land and never produces more than 20,000 bottles a year. This microscopic business model, however, has produced impressive results. By keeping costs low (his only employees are his children, Davide and Alessia) and by producing wines that fetch high prices, he has been able to maintain the quality of his wines and economic viability. Despite being accused of being arcane and overly conservative when it comes to business, he has made Cerbaiola one of the most consistent and impressive wineries in Montalcino.

If you ask Giulio Salvioni the secret to his success in the vineyard and the cellar, he will tell you that it is not all that obvious at first glance. A low yield is certainly important, because the sangiovese grapes—not such an easy variety to grow—risk under-ripeness, which translates into harsh, bothersome tannins in the bottle. Salvioni also has an unmatched ability to coax elegance from the austere and often overly acidic sangiovese grosso. The vineyards are located about half a mile southeast of Montalcino, where Giulio has built two cellars. In the first, located at the center of the estate, he vinifies Brunello and Rosso di Montalcino. He uses the other, which seems more like a bomb shelter because of its small size and general organization, for aging the wine in large Slavonian oak casks. The soil of the vineyards is made up of classic *galestro,* a porous rock that, together with the microclimate, plays an important role in the quality of the grapes. The grapes are planted at an elevation of 1,400 feet on a rocky ridge where there is almost never fog or humidity, which can affect the health of the grapes. The soil is not very fertile, and the cold nighttime temperatures, even in the summer, make for concentrated, very aromatic grapes.

Cerbaiola is the living example of how each step in the winemaking process contributes to the quality of the wine. Both Salvioni's Brunello and his Rosso di Montalcino are made with care, and the main difference between the two is in the type of wooden barrels used to age the wine. The Brunello is placed in new 2,000-liter Slavonian oak barrels for nine to ten years, while the Rosso is put in older, carefully restored barrels for a much shorter period. Giulio Salvioni produced his first Brunello in 1985, a remarkably good vintage allowing him to present the best the vineyard had to offer. Other great years have been 1988 and 1990.

Cerbaiola's unique style of Brunello is neither modern nor completely traditional. On the nose, the wine has a good amount of fruity aromas, including notes of cherry, sour black cherry, chocolate, tobacco, dog rose, and an underlying hint of leather. In the top vintages, the Cerbaiola Brunello is strong and structured, rich in tannins and pulp, showing off the quality of the grapes themselves. The finish is long and persistent, with just the right amount of acid. Although Cerbaiola doesn't have as long a history as other wineries in Montalcino, Salvioni's wines are certain to age with all the great classic wine from Montalcino.

Brunello di Montalcino Cerretalto—CASANOVA DI NERI

THE STORY OF Brunello di Montalcino Cerretalto begins in 1971, when Giovanni Neri, a native of Arezzo, fell in love with an estate in

Montalcino and purchased the property with the goal of producing great wine and distinguished olive oil. However, the real craftsman of the winery—the one who made the wines of Casanova di Neri famous throughout the world—is Giovanni's son, Giacomo, who took over for his father in the beginning of the 1990s. Giacomo led the company through a phase of remarkable growth, both in terms of the number of bottles—180,000 in total—and in the size of the estate, which is now 120 acres.

This growth is emblematic of the incredible revolution that has taken place in Montalcino in the last twenty years. Giacomo was, and still is, an innovator in terms of winery management—from the modern vinification process to the construction of a futuristic cellar, completed in 2005. The cellar is completely underground, so as not to ruin the landscape, and is outfitted with the newest enological technologies. In 1990, and then again in the almost overly praised 1997 vintage, critics and the larger American public fell in love with Brunello di Montalcino. Both wine critic Robert Parker Jr. and *Wine Spectator* gave extremely high scores to these modern-style Brunellos, which were very concentrated and intensely colored, many shades darker than the traditional color of sangiovese. Giacomo Neri's wines were certainly a part of, if not the leader of, this trend. His Brunello Tenuta Nuova of 2001 was actually named the best wine in the world in *Wine Spectator*'s annual Top 100 list. This wine was an extreme example of the Casanova di Neri style, thanks to the ripeness of the grapes, which come from a vineyard located in the most southern part of the Montalcino *comune,* which happens to be the coolest part of the denomination.

Yet a major element is missing from the history of this winery: Carlo Ferrini, one of the most famous enologists in Toscana and in all of Italy. Ferrini's critics like to point out that the many wines he has helped to create are quite similar and express little of the local *terroir.* At the moment, though, Ferrini can count more fans than critics. One fact remains: His wines are much loved on the international market because many people believe that great wines must be rich in color. At Casanova di Neri, to mask the typical characteristics of the sangiovese varietal, Carlo dramatically reduced the grape yield and started to use barriques aggressively.

A pivotal point for the past and future of Brunello came in 2008, with the internationally broadcasted "Brunellogate." Because of internal finger-pointing and whistle-blowing, the Italian government suspected that many producers were using grapes grown outside the DOCG denomination in wines that had this designation. Because sangiovese—the only varietal permitted in the production of Brunello di Montalcino—is typically a grape that does not impart intense color to a wine, the officials and the market as a whole suspected that Brunellos with a deep, fleshy purple brooding color were made by adding grapes other than sangiovese. Fans and detractors will forever debate whether Neri and Ferrini's style of Brunello is the result of skilled vineyard management and superior winemaking or is due to foul play. At the time of this writing (March 2010), Casanova di Neri is still entangled in Brunellogate.

As evidenced by its inclusion in this list of *grandi vini,* Brunello di Montalcino Cerretalto is an atomic bomb of a Brunello, explosive in the glass and resounding in its global impact. In spite of its concentration and color, the wine showcases the best organoleptic characteristics of sangiovese and of the soil of Montalcino. Perhaps this is an opportune time to defend the courageous winemakers who carve their own path and implicate those who prematurely cast guilt based on stylistic association. Great respect is due to Casanova di Neri for valiantly defending its beautiful wine in the face of such fierce opposition.

Although the Brunello di Montalcino denomination is located in a single *comune,* the diversity of the land contained within its borders is broad. There are at least two macrozones that have particularly good climatic conditions, one located at the north end of the DOCG and the other at the south. The southern part includes the towns of Sant'Angelo Scalo and Sant'Angelo in Colle and is dominated by the Banfi estates. In this area, you can feel more of the warm winds that regularly blow in from the Mediterranean Sea. The vineyards located near the Abbazia di Sant'Antimo, in the southeast, benefit from a slightly cooler climate because they are located higher up, but it is still hot. The grapes grown in the north, and especially in the northeast, are quite different. The Neri estate is located in the north at 800 to 1,000 feet above sea level and is bordered by the Asso River. The Neri family bought a well-positioned vineyard here in 1986 and decided to make a special wine called Cerretalto. The winters are definitely rigid, and in the summer there is a considerable difference between day- and nighttime temperatures because of the cold winds coming off Mount Amiata. The land and climate contribute to the particular characteristics of Cerretalto, a wine with decisive acidity and an easily recognizable character.

Cerretalto is Casanova di Neri's signature wine. It is decidedly modern in style and is obviously produced for an international audience. Despite its dark color—an almost impenetrable red—and a nose that reflects the twenty-seven months the wine spends in barriques, Cerretalto is actually a wine enjoyed by people who don't particularly like excessively modern Brunellos. This is due especially to the fact that the sangiovese expresses its best characteristics in this wine. Cerretalto has a rich texture, but Giacomo Neri is able to manage the wine's thickness with the acidity that is typical of this Tuscan variety. There is a balance between the power and the fineness of the wine. In the best vintages, Cerretalto has a nose of chocolate, coffee, vanilla, red fruit, and cherry that blends with more noble and complex nuances of tobacco, leather, and wet earth. In the mouth, it is explosive with a very long finish, thanks in part to an inviting acidity and soft but noticeable tannins.

Brunello di Montalcino Tenuta Il Greppo Riserva—BIONDI SANTI

THE BIONDI SANTI family has been producing wines that have garnered international prestige for generations. Their remarkable foresight has enabled them to stay on the cusp of the changes experienced by the wine scene, and to produce an exemplary Brunello in their Tenuta Il Greppo Riserva.

Ferruccio Biondi Santi—grandfather of the winery's current owner, Franco Santi—made his first bottle of Brunello in 1888, having discovered the organolectic and physical characteristics of a special variety of sangiovese (sangiovese grosso) that grew on the Greppo estate in Montalcino. Ferruccio recognized the potential of the grape and began cultivating it as an experiment. The result was the most structured and long-lived wine made from any sangiovese or sangiovese clone. At the time, in Toscana, wines were made by blending the sangiovese with other grapes at the moment of vinification. You couldn't find wines made from a single grape varietal because in Toscana, and in Italy in general, wine was a beverage consumed for its caloric value rather than its palatability. In the mid-nineteenth century, following the strengthening of the bourgeoisie and the desire of the Italian nobility to serve luxurious meals, Italians began producing quality wine—a transformation that had already taken place in Bordeaux and Burgundy.

Biondi Santi had the force and skill to grasp the historic changes and took commercial advantage of them. The first bottles released by Clemente Biondi Santi, Ferruccio's grandfather, received important recognition at the World's Fairs in London and Paris, in 1856 and 1867, respectively. These wines were still not the Brunello of today, but they were heading down the right path. As previously mentioned, the real father of this wine was Ferruccio, Clemente's grandson. Ferruccio was a highly intellectual and worldly person whose life intertwined with the history of Italy. In his youth, Ferruccio participated in the Italian Risorgimento, or unification, fighting for independence and the creation of the Italian state, which occurred in 1861 with the declaration of the Kingdom of Italy, followed by the annexation of the Veneto region in 1866 and the final unification with Roma in 1870. On July 21, 1866, Ferruccio fought alongside Garibaldi (the heroic general credited with having unified Italy) in the Battle of Bezzecca in Trentino, fending off the Austrian Empire with a small army of courageous soldiers.

After this adventure, Ferruccio returned to Toscana, to the Tenuta Il Greppo, to cultivate grapes and to paint, his two greatest passions. In 1870, Ferruccio had to overcome another difficult period following the plague of phylloxera that destroyed the vineyards in central Italy. He took this as an opportunity to replant all the vineyards on his estate with the sangiovese grosso clone. In 1888, he released the first real Brunello di Montalcino, and from there the denomination continued to grow in both quality and quantity. Despite the company's two hundred years of history, almost one hundred fifty of which have been spent producing Brunello, Biondi Santi has maintained a superior level of intensity and elegance beyond that of most other wineries. (On any given day, you are likely to spot men dressed in tweed jackets and ascots walking around stone castles with purebred German shepherds.) It is important to note that the number of bottles has not increased dramatically and the total per year is less than 70,000. Another important fact is that only 60 of the winery's 370 acres of property are planted with the BBS11 clone of sangiovese grosso, selected by Greppo from the University of Florence in the 1970s. This is because Franco Biondi Santi believes that this grape, grown in Montalcino, can produce incredible results in only very specific places. The vineyards selected by Biondi Santi for making Brunello are south or southeast facing and are located between 980 and 1,600 feet in elevation.

In a time when wines are being made softer, even in Montalcino, Biondi Santi's Brunello is large in structure, aggressive in acidity, and unrelenting in its tannins. This is a linear wine that is unapologetic for the inherent characteristics of the sangiovese grosso clone. The wine has received cult status in Italy because of its longevity: It can be aged up to fifty, or even one hundred, years. It is first aged in 14,000-liter oak barrels, then transferred into smaller 3,000- to 8,000-liter oak barrels. These factors produce a rich, complex wine with nuances of sour black cherry and red cherry up front, followed by more noble notes of rose, violet, wet soil, and leather. In the mouth, the tannins are gutsy, highlighting the *terroir* and the sangiovese, with a sweet, harmonious finish.

Brunello di Montalcino Riserva—POGGIO DI SOTTO

FOUNDED IN 1989, Poggio di Sotto produces the most powerful and resounding example of a new-entry wine in an old category. Much of the success of the winery can be attributed to the carefully selected vineyard sites and the small, focused production of the bottles. Piero Palmucci, the stately yet menacing owner of Poggio di Sotto, is originally from Maremma. A newcomer to winemaking, Piero selected his site for the strong character of the soil and the exposure of the vineyards. The 37-acre estate is at 1,800 feet above sea level and divides the cool, ventilated northeastern area from the hot, Mediterranean southwest area of Sant'Angelo Scalo. The *terroir* of Sant'Antimo, the town the vineyard is near, is unique for its southern exposure in the eastern part of the territory. The climate is therefore mild, thanks also to nearby Mount Amiata (5,700 feet above sea level), which cools off the land during the otherwise scorching summer. The cellar is located in a Tuscan farmhouse, poised high on the top of a scenic hill, not far from the age-old Abbazia di Sant'Antimo.

Piero produced his first Brunello in 1991—an unremarkable year in Toscana. From the very beginning, he recognized the potential of his wines, despite the fact that at the time, more muscular Tuscan reds dominated the market. Piero's goal was to make a Sangiovese without compromise, using no shortcuts in the cellar that modify the character of the climate, the grape variety, and the celebrated *terroir* of Montalcino. His various small plots of land allow Piero to produce grapes with a variety of aromas and maturation levels, giving uniformity to the wine so that less favorable vintages do not suffer as dramatically as those of other wines. The vineyards are cultivated organically, are hoed by hand, and require little irrigation. The yield per acre is quite low and never surpasses 3,600 pounds per acre, which is almost half of the amount given in the production guidelines.

In addition, Piero decided to call on the advice of the well-reputed enologist Giulio Gambelli, who became both a trustworthy partner at the vineyard and a dear friend of Piero's. When the 1995 Poggio di Sotto Riserva hit the market in 2002, it was clear that a star had been born. From that moment on, Piero's wines gained a sort of cult status, aided by the fact that the winery's annual production is limited to 40,000 bottles. This number includes his excellent Rosso di Montalcino, which is often considered a better wine than many of the Brunellos coming from nearby wineries. Another miraculous year for the winery was 1999, which resulted in an absolutely superb Riserva.

However, an inexplicable thing happened to the 2001 vintage. The DOCG approval committee decided that the Poggio di Sotto Riserva did not merit the title of Brunello. The controversial decision rocked the Italian wine world and received harsh criticism from most wine critics and Montalcino wine enthusiasts. Piero Palmucci was forced to change the name of his wine to Decennale 2001 (in honor of the ten-year history of the winery), triggering a major controversy regarding the evaluation criteria during the tasting. The event was also one of the first signs of the impending "Brunellogate" scandal.

In April 2008, during Vinitaly, Italy's most important wine fair, compromising information regarding Brunello wine production was reported by national newspapers. The Sienese prosecutors began investigating many producers of Toscana's most important red wine, because they were convinced that some winemakers were blending cabernet sauvignon or merlot into the sangiovese—a true sacrilege for Brunello lovers. Those who drink Piero Palmucci's wines, however, can rest assured.

The three wines produced at Poggio di Sotto—Rosso, Brunello, and Brunello Riserva—are a focused and pure representation of the sangiovese grown on the property. The Riserva is produced exclusively during top vintages, and for this reason, from 1989 to today, only four vintages have been released. Poggio di Sotto Riserva has a light red color, with aromas that vary from red fruit to more fine and rarefied notes of wet soil, leather, and blond tobacco. In the mouth, it is very easy to drink, with robust yet silky tannins that are never invasive and give the wine lasting flavor.

Camartina—QUERCIABELLA

THE HILLS OF southeastern Chianti are where a wine is produced that is the benchmark for all Super Tuscans. Camartina, first released in 1981, is the product of the legendary Giuseppe Castiglioni, and its outstanding quality is the polestar for every winemaker in the region.

During the 1960s and 1970s, entrepreneurs from northern Italy started to buy up the Tuscan estates and vineyards that were left behind by farmers after the collapse of the *mezzandria,* Italy's sharecropping system. Many of the investors were real wine lovers and had the ambition to improve the quality of the product of these pleasant hills. Giuseppe Castiglioni, known as Pepito or *il messicano* ("the Mexican") to his friends, was one of these investors. Small in stature, but not in enterprise, Pepito was a rich iron and steel manufacturer who spent a considerable part of his time in Mexico. After selling his company and buying taxi licenses for all his workers (allowing Pepito to call upon a reliable driver, or *autista,* anywhere in Italy), in 1974 Pepito decided to purchase a fantastic estate located in the southeastern hills of Greve, in Chianti, not far from the towns of Lamole and Panzano. Besides being an exceptionally refined art collector, Pepito was also a fan and lover of French wine, Burgundy in particular, and is the owner of one of the most important collections of Batârd-Montrachet in the world. Pepito's love of wines from across the Alps led him to plant nonnative grape varieties in Toscana, a novelty at the time. He did not believe much in the potential of sangiovese, especially at the altitude of the vineyards he purchased (980 to 1,600 feet above sea level), and called on the help of Italy's most famous enologist, Giacomo Tachis, known as the father of Sassicaia and Tignanello.

In 1981, the first vintage of Pepito's most important red wine, Camartina, a blend of 70 percent cabernet sauvignon and 30 percent sangiovese, was released. The wine was an immediate success and became the standard bearer for all Super Tuscans. It was sensibly made and showed restraint. It also proved that international grape varieties can grow successfully at higher, more extreme altitudes.

In 1998, Pepito and his son Sebastiano decided to transform the vineyard into an organic operation. At the time, this decision seemed revolutionary because in Italy, and especially in Toscana, there were very few quality wineries that were willing to make such a courageous move. In 2000, Pepito and Sebastiano adopted biodynamic cultivation techniques, giving even more character and distinction to the Querciabella wines. Pepito Castiglioni passed away a couple of years ago, but Sebastiano has been able to maintain, and possibly reinforce, their natural approach to winemaking. Thanks to their top-notch technical team, Querciabella has been able to create one of the most important and successful biodynamic operations in Italy. In recent years, the winery has been developing projects to bring back insects and animals to enrich the biodiversity of their fields and vineyards.

The move toward more natural operations is starting to show in Sebastiano's wines. They have become less adulterated, less strong and muscular, more subtle, and richer in minerality and elegance. In short, they are fresher wines that better reflect the *terroir*. According to winery rules, Camartina is released only in favorable years. For this reason, there are no 1989, 1992, 1998, or 2002 vintages. The wine rests in the cellar for twenty-four months in small French casks, but this fact alone doesn't mean that Camartina can simply be labeled a modern, international wine. It has aromas of mature red fruit, but also of leather and earth, a reminder that the wine is produced in Chianti. Even the flavor, with its strong acidity and sapidity, is a reflection of the unique *terroir*.

Cepparello—ISOLE E OLENA

THE SUPER TUSCAN Cepparello is the flagship of the Isole e Olena estate and is among the top wines of Toscana. Made from 100 percent sangiovese grapes, Cepparello distinguishes itself from the mass of blended, muscular, and extracted Tuscan wines with its great delicacy, elegance, and finesse.

Paolo De Marchi, the producer of this wine, is an atypical Tuscan: He is very measured in his ways, quiet, and understated. This may have something to do with the fact that Paolo is in fact Piemontese. The De Marchi family relocated to the hills of Chianti from Lessona, a small town located outside of Torino, in the mid-1950s and purchased the farm that would become Isole e Olena in 1956. The estate is comprised of 740 acres located in the small town of Olena, a few miles from San Donato in Poggio. Although Paolo is not a native Tuscan, he and his work are ingrained in the evolution of Chianti Classico, and his great estate would not exist without his thirty years of passionate leadership.

Shortly after the arrival of the De Marchi family, however, *mezzandria,* the ancient tradition of Tuscan sharecropping, began to fall by the wayside, as did the agrarian life in general. After World War II, Italians from southern and central Italy (where poverty was felt the most) moved to the industrialized cities, abandoning their agricultural roots for high-rises and higher-paying jobs. This migration was certainly felt in Olena. Almost overnight, the ancient town of 120 people was abandoned almost entirely. Paolo, however, recognized that he had a real treasure in his hands. The city was a time capsule that told the story of postwar Italy. He resisted the temptation of the Chiantshira-zation of Olena (the invasion of wealthy people from Britain and America who scooped up abandoned villas in Toscana when urbanization was spreading across Italy) and hoped to restore the hamlet not only as a beacon of high-end hospitality, but as a living museum of the trials and tribulations of the postwar period. Paolo is convinced that the Tuscan countryside will soon attract a new generation of young winemakers interested in an alternative to the modern lifestyle. Paolo's cellar and the town of Olena have been kept intact and are true jewels of the area. Be sure to take a walk through the vineyards to see the large, dry-stone walls that the De Marchi family have built. The walls are more likely to remind you of Mycenae in Greece than of a Tuscan vineyard. *Ginestra* (broom) plants surround the vineyards. The yellow flowers, the dark earth, and the green of the vines are incredibly striking.

The wines produced in this idyllic setting strongly reflect Paolo's personality: humble and true. I have always maintained that the delicacy of Cepparello distinguishes this wine from others. I've seen it mistaken for red Burgundy by experienced noses on several occasions, and it is that very essence of balancing elegance with structure that continues to distinguish Cepparello. Paolo's style can't be categorized into either the traditional or the modern category. Recently, he has invested significantly in his cellar. In fact, he carved out an underground aging room from the *galestro,* which allows him to age sangiovese in the earth from which it came. Aged in small French oak barrels with the most precise vinification techniques, Cepparello is set apart by its evolution in time and complexity. In its youth, it may not be as obvious of a great wine as its Tuscan counterparts, but over the decades, Cepparello became the most distinguished of them all and a fine example of what sangiovese can yield in the most noble Tuscan *terroir.*

Cepparello speaks eloquently of the story of Chianti and the history of the people of Chianti. The beauty of this wine is that Paolo is able to blend tradition and modernity without becoming a slave to any discipline. Like any great conductor, he combines aspects of each technique and unites them in a harmonious way. Seductive on the nose with the essence of ripe cherries, Cepparello lingers into notes of leather, licorice, and sweet tobacco, with a lingering finale of star anise and cardamom. The palate is fresh and elegant, never muscular and overpowering. The drinkablitiy of this wine is its greatest attribute, thanks to the fresh acidity of sangiovese and its cultivation in the high altitude of these hills.

Chianti Classico Riserva Castello di Fonterutoli—
CASTELLO DI FONTERUTOLI

CASTELLO DI FONTERUTOLI, 1435. The name of the winery and the year it was founded sum up so much of Tuscan enological history. To be more precise, they mark the creation of the subregion of Chianti Classico.

Many centuries ago, the *podestà,* or mayors, of Firenze and Siena were fighting over territorial borders in Chianti, the land that lies between the two cities. To end the age-old battle, they decided to make a wager on a horse race: At the first crow of the rooster, one horse would leave from Firenze, and the other would depart from Siena; the border of Chianti would be defined by where the two horses met. The Florentines chose a black rooster, known to crow well before sunrise, which meant that the horseman from Firenze got a head start. The Florentine horse covered much more ground than its contender, and the two horses ended up meeting near Siena—in Fonterutoli, to be exact. The Republic of Firenze was thus able to extend its border to include the towns of Castellina, Radda, and Gaiole, all renowned red wine zones. Since then, the black rooster, or *gallo nero,* has become the emblem of the territory and is now the symbol of the Consortium of Chianti Classico.

Like many of the large noble winemaking families of Toscana (including Frescobaldi, Folonari, and Ricasoli), the Marchesi Mazzei family, owners of the Castello di Fonterutoli, built their enterprise on farsightedness and avant-garde techniques. They were among the first winemakers to do away with the antiquated *mezzadria* system—a contractual arrangement allowing a farmer *(mezzadro)* to work the land, reserving half of his harvest for the landowner. These noble families are also known for their environmentalism and interest in protecting the Tuscan landscape, including the maintenance and restoration of castles, villas, and country towns.

The Castello di Fonterutoli is located a few miles south of the town of Castellina, in the heart of Chianti Classico, a wine production zone composed of nine *comuni.* Only four *comuni*—Castellina, Gaiole, Greve, and Radda in Chianti—are located entirely within the bounds of the DOCG. Fonterutoli is a small *borgo,* or village, made up of a handful of houses, the ancient church of San Miniato, and the villa of the Marchesi Mazzei family, which was built in the sixteenth century on the site of a former castle. The winery covers 1,600 acres, 300 of which have been subdivided into five zones, and is located between 800 and 1,600 feet above sea level. The soil varies from zone to zone but is composed, for the most part, of sandstone. In fact, the wine of Fonterutoli is referred to as *vino dei sassi,* "wine of the rocks." This particular *terroir* has proved to be good for the production of sangiovese grapes and also of international grapes like merlot and cabernet, which the winery has planted to widen the scope of its production.

Fonterutoli's portfolio is so rich that it is difficult to select a single wine to best represent the winery. Its top two wines in terms of quality are Siepi, a Super Tuscan made from equal parts merlot and sangiovese, and Chianti Classico Castello di Fonterutoli. Of the two, the Chianti Classico best represents the soil and position of the winery. Harvest takes place in the second half of September, after which the grapes are transferred to the winery's new cellar, three floors below. The sangiovese macerate for fifteen to eighteen days and are then moved to French barriques. The final Chianti blend also includes 10 percent cabernet sauvignvon that is aged for eighteen months in small French oak barrels. The resulting 80,000 bottles of Fonterutoli Chianti wine age for eight months before release. This dark red wine gives off aromas of sour cherry, leather, tobacco, and spices that evolve over time. This is a modern Chianti Classico, rich in personality and very representative of the *terroir.* In the mouth, the wine is powerful yet elegant, tannic yet silky, welcoming, and well balanced.

Chianti Classico Riserva Rancia—FÈLSINA

THIS CHIANTI CLASSICO is very different from what most people would expect of a wine labeled as such. Elegant and austere, it can almost take you aback with its bracing acidity—it expresses the beauty of the sangiovese grape with impressive clarity.

The cypress-lined road leading to the Fèlsina winery is a postcard-perfect location, a convincing advertisement for Italy and its beautiful landscapes and architecture. The owner of this idyllic estate is Giuseppe Mazzocolin, son-in-law of Domenico Poggiali of Ravenna, who bought the property in 1966. Giuseppe is a former Latin and Greek instructor who, after thirty years of teaching, decided to join his wife's family's business and make wine. A truly cultured man, Giuseppe enjoys conversing about art, literature, and classical music just as much as, if not more than, about wine. Despite his Venetian upbringing, Giuseppe has a profound connection with Toscana and has created a small oasis of his own in Castelnuovo Berardenga. Housed inside what looks like a medieval chapel, Giuseppe's cellar is possibly the most beautiful in Italy. The large oak barrels are arranged elegantly in rows and are surrounded by a stately colonnade. The aging room is so fantastic that it risks upstaging the wine. However, thanks to the skill of Giuseppe and his family, this has never occurred.

The first great Fèlsina wines were made here during the beginning of the 1980s. From the start, Giuseppe decided to focus his attention on the land and on sangiovese, the reigning grape variety of the area, although other wineries had begun to substitute easier-to-grow international varieties like merlot and cabernet sauvignon. Giuseppe also decided to divide the vineyard into individual crus, leading to the creation of two great wines, Riserva Rancia and Fontalloro. Rancia is a Chianti Classico; Fontalloro drinks like a Chianti but can't be labeled as such because the grapes come from a vineyard located a few hundred yards past the southern boarder of the denomination. Despite all the absurd demands imposed by the archaic regulations of the DOCG—

like the requirement that sangiovese be blended with trebbiano, a white grape variety that does not grow particularly well in Toscana— Giuseppe has made his Riserva Rancia with 100 percent sangiovese since the beginning. This decision was hard to make, but revolutionary and in keeping with the goals of the winery: to make two great red wines that are strong expressions of the land. In addition to Giuseppe Mazzocolin and Giuseppe Poggiali, his brother-in-law, the Fèlsina winery is run by one of Italy's most celebrated enologists, Franco Bernabei, who has been working with the family since 1982.

The winery is located in one of the southernmost *comuni* of Chianti Classico, straddled between Chianti and the Siena countryside. This area has suffered from considerable erosion, first due to the sea that thousands of years ago reached all the way to the Tuscan hills, and later due to rivers. In fact, many of the stones on the bed of the Fèlsina vineyards resemble the round pebbles or shingles typically found on the beach; these stones contribute to the unique character of the wines. The Chianti Classico Riserva Rancia is made from grapes grown at 1,300 feet and protected by a large forest that wraps around the north end of the estate. Fèlsina is around 37 miles from the famous town where Brunello was born (Montalcino), and the climates of both areas are quite similar. As a result, Rancia has many of the same organoleptic qualities.

For first-time tasters, Rancia Riserva generally comes as a surprise. This is not a strong, powerful wine, but a rather lean, austere product with the edgy, tart acidity that only sangiovese can produce. It can be drunk with food but also can be enjoyed on its own for a more meditative experience. If tasted carelessly, this wine may fool you, especially the older vintages. Don't be surprised if after five or six years, Rancia Riserva tastes older than its age; this is normal. The wine evolves precociously but then stops. It almost crystallizes after six years and then continues to age very, very slowly. After ten years, it is surprisingly still full of life. On the nose, it has notes of earth and of minerals like graphite, but also leather, hide, and tobacco. In the mouth it is unexpectedly tart and acidic.

Chianti Classico Vigneto Bellavista—CASTELLO DI AMA

THE STORY OF Castello di Ama begins during the mid-1970s, when a Roman entrepreneur fell in love with the small town of Ama and the surrounding territory of Chianti Classico. At the time, Ama was made up of a handful of stone houses perched at the top of the splendid hills of Chiantishire (the region of Toscana that had been invaded by wealthy Englishmen and Americans during the urbanization of Italy) and a couple of medieval chapels. Everything was pretty much in shambles and in need of heavy restoration. The Roman businessman was able to convince three of his friends to join him in this adventure of renovation. At the beginning, tending to the grapevines was only a pastime and certainly not the core business of the undertaking. Over the years, the hobby became a passion, and winemaking at the highest level became the dream of these Romans. They looked for a top-notch staff and hired two people who would become fundamental to Castello di Ama's success.

The first important person brought on the scene was Silvano Formigli, who gave important marketing input for the cellar but left Ama in the mid-1990s to start Selezione Fattorie, which over the next decade became one of the most important Italian wine distribution companies. The other person was Marco Pallanti, who was hired in 1982 when he was still a very young enologist. In a short period of time, Marco became the technical director for the estate, which at that point included around 120 acres of vineyards. Realizing that he had great potential, the owners of Ama decided to invest in Marco's education, sending him to train with some of the most important winemakers in Bordeaux, such as Léon, Dubourdieu, Glories, Carbonneau, Boidron, and many others. Another important moment in the history of the winery occurred in 1988, with the arrival of Lorenza Sebasti, daughter of one of the owners, an ardent supporter of Ama who later became Marco's wife.

In the 1980s and the beginning of the 1990s, the Ama vineyards grew in quantity and in quality, reaching 220 acres after the purchase of the famous vineyard sites Bertinga and Montebuoni. During the past decade, the goals and intentions of Castello di Ama have come into clear focus, and Chianti Classico has become the central focus of Lorenza and Marco's work. In a time when all the big-name Tuscan winemakers were producing Super Tuscans, Ama was creating great Chianti wines: Bellavista in 1978, San Lorenzo in 1982, Casuccia in 1985, and Bertinga in 1988. In addition, Ama made a few bottles—10,000 max—of a pure Merlot called Apparita, which was more an exercise in style than a symbol of a winery that has remained faithful to Sangiovese in its various forms. However, among all of Ama's successes, their best move was to create a "base," if you can call it that, its super Chianti Classico in 1996. With 150,000 bottles of the wine per year, they were able to change the worldview of Chianti Classico. It is not a simple, easy-drinking wine, but a product able to impress even the most demanding palates.

Thanks in part to his magical intuition and his ablility to change the face of an entire denomination, Marco Pallanti was elected head of the Consortium of Chianti Classico in 2006, and again by unanimous vote in 2009. It is also important to note the real work of patronage that Castello di Ama has undertaken over the years, whereby it made the small Tuscan town into a cultural retreat for contemporary artists, especially young artists. Thank to Marco and Lorenza, the artists can spend time on fertile land where they can express their individual creativity. In fact, there are dozens of art installations on the property, created by some of the most well-known names in international contemporary art, including Daniel Buren, Carlos Garaicoa, Kendell Geers, Cristina Iglesias, Anish Kapoor, Michelangelo Pistoletto, Nedko Solakov, Chen Zhen, Giulio Paolini, and many more.

Gaiole in Chianti is located at the center of the Chianti Classico region and contains some of the most important and historic vineyards in the entire Chianti area. It was not by chance that some of the most internationally celebrated wineries are located here. Castello di Ama is without a doubt the shining star of an already rich cast of characters. The Ama vineyards are positioned at a high altitude for classic sangiovese standards. Almost all the vines have been planted between 1,400 and 1,800 feet above sea level. Bellavista, planted between 1967 and 1975, is the top cru of the estate and covers almost 54 acres. Its soil is composed primarily of clay and is quite pebbly. One of the interesting characteristics of the operation is the shape in which the vines are trained, called a *lira aperta* ("open lyre"), implemented in 1982 by Marco Pallanti after his sojourn in Bordeaux. This method allows the quality of the grapes to improve by increasing the surface area of the leaves exposed to the sun. Like a solar panel, the leaves capture the sun's energy and pass it on to the bunches. Among the 54 acres in the Bellavista cru, only 20 acres have been converted to this innovative system. Besides sangiovese, malvasia nera grapes, used in a small percentage to make Chianti Classico Vigneto Bellavista, are also grown in this vineyard.

The Vigneto Bellavista is the pure expression of the *terroir* of Ama: the true flagship of Marco Pallanti and Lorenza Sebasti's cellar. It is an austere and powerful wine, full of personality and classic style. It is a strictly territorial wine, made from two native grape varieties, of which 90 percent is sangiovese and 10 percent is malvasia nera. Over the years following the release of the previously mentioned 1996 Chianti Classic "base," the Vigneto Bellavista has gone through dramatic stylistic changes. Before this new label, Bellavista was a wine that was released to the market almost every year. After the birth of the "base," Bellavista became a super selection, released only during top vintages; in the past fourteen years, therefore, only seven vintages have been released (1995, 1997, 1999, 2001, 2004, 2006, and 2007). The wine is aged in French oak barriques, 60 percent of which are new wood, for about fifteen months. The wine has great potential for aging, and if tasted young, it may seem a little closed and not so explosive. However, if you have the patience to wait at least five years from the harvest, the wine will reward you with unique sensations. Its fruity aromas transform and develop into notes of hummus and cigar box, star anise and graphite. In the mouth, it is fleshly and juicy, with elegant, almost silk-like tannins.

Flaccianello della Pieve—TENUTA FONTODI

FIRST PRODUCED IN 1981, Flaccianello della Pieve is one of the finest wines of Toscana. This wine is made by Giovanni Manetti, who, despite his young age, is one of most important wine producers in Italy. He successfully maintains the strong Tuscan winemaking traditions while creating a sustainable model for the future, based on a complete traditional farming and winemaking style.

For centuries, the Manetti family, owners of the Fontodi estate since 1968, was in the tile-making business. Handmade in the town of Impruneta, Manetti clay tiles can be found in many of Toscana's more beautiful homes and monuments: Brunelleschi's dome, atop the Firenze cathedral, is covered in their tiles, as is the floor of the Botticelli Room in the Uffizi Gallery. The family's artisan spirit, passed down for generations, contributes to their skillful winemaking. This legacy is certainly carried by Giovanni, who shifted his attention entirely to wine at the end of the 1970s. Over the course of only thirty years, Tenuta Fontodi has become one of the most revolutionary wineries in Chianti, thanks to Giovanni—a charismatic and dashing fifty-something-year old, who was able to increase not only his family's business, but that of the entire region of Panzano.

Many things make this estate truly special. To begin with, the 200 acres of adjoining vineyards constitute one of the most important enological areas in Italy. Tenuta Fontodi is located in the Conca d'Oro ("Golden Bowl") region, known as a natural amphitheater of vineyards. The vines tenderly frame the small, picturesque town of Panzano and its eleventh-century castle, built by the Firidolfi family. Panzano is located on the ridge of the string of hills that divides the valley from the Pesa River on the east and the Greve on the west. This is the true geographical heart of Toscana and Chianti Classico, just a few hundred yards from the border that divides the provinces of Firenze and Siena. A large part of the Fontodi vineyards is planted between 1,100 and 1,500 feet above sea level, an ideal location for growing sangiovese. The soil is composed primarily of *galestro*—a crumbly schistlike rock—and a lesser amount of clay. The grapes destined to become Flaccianello are grown on land that is 1,300 feet above sea level and that has excellent southern exposure.

Giovanni Manetti was one of the first winemakers to believe in the potential of pure sangiovese wines produced without the addition of international grape varieties like cabernet or merlot or native varieties like colorino and canaiolo. With his understanding of the land, good vine density, and vines that are at least thirty years old, he is able to fully mature his grapes. Giovanni beat the odds, proving that wines made exclusively from sangiovese are able to compete against the best wines in the world.

And then there is Giovanni's courageous commitment to work organically—not for recognition or as a marketing tool, but because he is convinced that his wines simply taste better that way. No chemical fertilizers are used in the vineyards, and to take things a step further, Giovanni decided to breed his own herd of Chianina cattle (famous for their white coats and buttery rich, yet gamey meat, typically served as *bistecca alla fiorentina*). In the lower part of the estate, he built a small, wooden, ecofriendly stall, where he raises the animals. Because of his vision and determination, Giovanni was able to modernize the tradition of Chiantigiano winemaking and to give sangiovese worldwide appeal.

Flaccianello della Pieve is the perfect example of Giovanni's achievement as a winemaker. At the beginning of the 1980s, there were only a handful of quality Tuscan wine producers, and even fewer of these had the great courage demonstrated by Giovanni Manetti, who made the uncommon choice to produce pure sangiovese wine. In all truthfulness, he also benefited from the good fortune of meeting one of the most talented and capable Italian enologists, Franco Bernabei, who knew how to tame a wild breed like sangiovese. The first few vintages had a closed nose, but the wine later opened up, developing elegance and rare grace. The wine is characterized by fruity notes, but also leather and hide. One can sense warm notes of pepper and pipe tobacco on the finish. In the mouth, the wine bounces between sensations of hot and cold, with robust tannins present when the wine is young, but that smooth out over time.

Masseto—TENUTA DELL'ORNELLAIA

MASSETO IS one of the most sought-after wines in the world and also one of the best to be drunk immediately—even if I only have twenty years of history to support my argument. Like Pomerol, the small denomination in Bordeaux, and Saint-Emilion, Masseto has become synonymous with great Merlot.

Ornellaia was founded by the Antinori family in the early 1980s and was later sold to the Frescobaldi clan, another century-old Florentine winemaking family. At the beginning of the twenty-first century, the Frescobaldis established a joint venture with the Mondavis from California, creating one of the first, and certainly the most famous, Italian-American partnerships in the wine world. Tenuta dell'Ornellaia returned to Italian ownership in 2005 after the joint venture with Robert Mondavi came to an end at the time of Mondavi's involvement in Constellation Brands. The American wine and spirits producer, capable of generating revenues equal to those of a small country of eastern Europe, was "turned away" by the Frescobaldi family, who were intent on keeping Ornellaia far from the globalized wine circuit. Thanks to a purchase agreement, the Frescobaldis took over the winery, whose wines were already marketed on five continents, giving it the spirit of an Italian dynasty that has six centuries of history producing wine in Toscana.

In the past, winemakers believed that the production cycle of wine was directly connected to the rhythms of nature. Making wine took time and patience. However, with the arrival of modern technology and a general increase in technical skills, production times were reduced, allowing vineyards that were utterly unknown twenty years ago to stand alongside the most ancient, noble, Italian winemaking areas. Today, Bolgheri is like California's Napa Valley or Australia's Barossa Valley: For the wine lover, each is simply known as a top wine region, a place where winemakers have been able to create great wines, thanks to modern winemaking techniques.

The top wines at the *tenuta* (estate) are Ornellaia, primarily a Cabernet Sauvingon, and Masseto, a pure Merlot that was released for the first time in 1987. Thanks to these bottles and those of another superstar of Bolgheri, Sassicaia of Tenuta San Guido, the subregion of Bolgheri is recognized internationally. The success of Masseto came as more of a surprise than that of Sassicaia, because Masseto became popular so quickly and because it is made from a grape variety that had not yet produced good results in Italy. Masseto surpassed every expectation: International wine critics unanimously declared it one of the greatest Merlots in the world. On more than one occasion, Masseto came in ahead of Merlots from Bordeaux in the rankings. Both the Italian and the French territories are fairly flat and close to the sea—the latter of which is a key element for understanding the success of the merlot grape in these areas and the wine made from it. In the case of Masseto, the vineyard is only 17 acres in size and is located close to the company headquarters. This is precisely where the Frescobaldi family has found that the merlot grapes express themselves the best.

Experienced agronomists are able to distinguish the grapes grown on the various parcels of this cru: The harvest is not based entirely on the selection of the healthiest grapes, but on keeping the grapes from the different microzones of this vineyard separate—all the way to the cellar. The quality of the grapes is controlled twice, both before and after the stems are removed. The fermentation occurs at 77 to 83 degrees Fahrenheit, after which the must macerates for ten to fifteen days at 83 degrees Fahrenheit. Malolactic fermentation takes place in 100 percent new barriques, and aging lasts twenty-four months in a cool and damp cellar. After the first twelve months, the wines from the single parcels of Masseto are blended and then transferred to barrels for another year of aging. The last twelve months of the wine's life at Ornellaia occur in the bottle, and then it is off to market.

The wine has aromas of dark black fruit, smoke, tobacco, and minerals. The perfumes are well matched, yet individually recognizable. Thanks to the mild climate, the wine has remained fairly consistent throughout the years. For example, 2002 was much less disastrous here than it was for the rest of Toscana, and 2003 was not particularly harsh compared with the rest of Italy. In the mouth, the tannins seem velvety. The wine has an incredibly pleasant level of alcohol and power. This is a big Bolgheri wine. It is international by definition, modern by nature, and yet very Tuscan. Masseto has redrawn the map of excellence that the winemakers of Pomerol, the masters of Merlot, have come to know and respect.

Nobile di Montepulciano Nocio dei Boscarelli—
BOSCARELLI

A FANTASTIC EXAMPLE of a pure sangiovese wine, Nocio dei Boscarelli is a gem. Already a masterful wine, it will be exciting to see how it continues to develop, as the available vintages are all still quite young, and the wine clearly will age extremely well.

Born into a family of renowned blacksmiths and artisans from Montepulciano, Egidio Corradi did not become a winemaker until later in life. Even as a child, he was a quick learner, prompting his parents to send him to school rather than train him in the family business. He graduated with a degree in business and economics and became a wheat broker, with one office in Montepulciano and another in Milano. In 1962, after a long time spent scoping out the market, Egidio purchased two fantastic estates in Cervognano, on the southeast side of

Montepulciano. The fields were originally planted with wheat and tobacco, but he decided to replant them with sangiovese grapes. Two years later, he built the cellar.

Sadly, Egidio wasn't able to enjoy his wines for long because of his early death in 1967. His daughter, Paola, and her husband, Ippolito De Ferrari, took over the family company while living in Genova, more than two hundred miles away. At the beginning, the couple traveled back and forth as commuting winemakers. The distance was not easy, especially because the Italian roadways were not as well developed at that time as they are today. But in the end, they decided to move to the hills of Paola's youth. Ippolito also ended up dying fairly young, in 1983, leaving Paola to depend on her own strong character and business sense. Seven years later, in 1990, she invited her eldest son, Luca, to be a part of the business. At the time, Luca was a tall, thin blond boy with an extremely elegant style. If it weren't for his thick Genovese accent, one might easily take him for a Tuscan nobleman straight out of the Renaissance. For more than ten years, Luca and his mother Paola have worked together with Niccolò, the youngest of the Boscarelli clan.

The De Ferrari family generally prefers to work quietly, out of the limelight, and it therefore took some time before the critics recognized the wines of the Boscarelli vineyard. Since the mid-1980s, Boscarelli has benefited from the advice of Maurizio Castelli, an enologist who has always opted for minimal intervention in the cellar. Together they are able to make wines that best express the characteristics of the land.

Located at the top of a rocky hill at 2,000 feet above sea level, the view of Montepulciano is known to amaze visitors who arrive from the Val di Chiana or the Val d'Orcia. In recent years, Montepulciano wines have been going through an identity crisis, partly because the regulations allow for an exaggerated use (30 percent) of other grape varieties, like cabernet and merlot. You can find a wide variety of Montepulciano wines, some seeming extremely international in style, while others, like Nocio, are a real expression of the denomination. This area is blessed with a decidedly hot climate, compared with Chianti Classico. In 1989, the De Ferrari family purchased the Nocio vineyard from a farmer who had been selling them grapes for years. The cru covers around 7 acres total. The soil, made from alluvial deposits, contains an excellent amount of gravel and sand, allowing for good drainage and giving life to an elegant, complex wine.

The De Ferrari family had always wanted to make a wine from 100 percent sangiovese grapes (here called prugnolo), but DOC regulations established in 1997 did not permit this. Therefore, for the first years, 1991 and 1993, the Boscarellis produced a wine called Riserva Vigna del Nocio, blended with complementary native grapes like canaiolo, mammolo, and colorino. In 1997 and 2000, they added a small amount of merlot, which didn't really seem to affect the austere, territorial nature of this wine. In 2001, the winery finally got its chance to make a pure sangiovese when the regulations were changed to allow it, and they began labeling it as Nocio dei Boscarelli.

Nocio dei Boscarelli is a wine that in its best years is not easy to read because it is made for aging. The best and most celebrated vintages are 1995, 1997, 2001, 2004, and, among the more recent, 2006. Its aromas recall leather and wet soil, graphite, and the nobility of mature red fruit, in particular cherry and cassis. In the mouth, it has the stuff of champions, with silky tannins, excellent acidity—typical of sangiovese—and deepness and length from the beginning. It is a great wine that speaks the language of its land.

Percarlo—FATTORIA SAN GIUSTO A RENTENNANO

FATTORIA SAN GUISTO A RETENNANO functions on the basic principle that a winemaker must be directly connected to the land to produce the best wine. Percarlo is a clear example of the truth of this statement, for it is one of Italy's finest wines.

The San Giusto a Rentennano winery is a former Cistercian abbey at the end of a winding road that passes through the scenic hills of

Chianti Classico. In 1204, Rentennano marked the border of the Florentine and Sienese republics. The Guelfian crenellations are testament to the town's history, as are the underground cellars used to bottle and barrel-age wine. For centuries, the estate—which starts at the castle of Brolio in Gaiole and includes all the significant landholdings in this southern part of Chianti Classico—belonged to the Ricasoli family. In 1957, the property was purchased by Count Enrico Martini di Cigala— a distinctive and handsome man with white hair and a passion for making great wine and playing chess. Enrico had a multitude of sons— nine in all. The sons shared his lively spirit and love for winemaking. At the beginning of the 1990s, three of his children took over the company: Francesco and Luca look after the vineyards, while his daughter Elisabetta is in charge of the administration and accounting.

The beauty of the Martini di Cigala family is that they are men and women of the earth, not afraid to get their hands dirty and be a part of the agricultural process. Luca, for example, is a true vigneron, with callused hands and a friendly yet ill-tempered spirit. His life is a juxtaposition of his responsibilities and duties as both a noble landowner and a farmer. Although he may dress in fancy suits, Luca would rather walk you through the vines than sit and taste wine in the cellar. He is critical of the Tuscan tradition of bringing in highly paid consultants rather than being personally involved in every aspect of the winemaking process. He insists, with good reason, that the Tuscans are lacking the attachment to the soil present in other great wine regions, such as Piemonte or Burgundy. His winemaking style is most similar to that of those other regions. Light-years ahead of other Tuscan winemakers and wine critics, Luca has committed fully to organic cultivation.

Percarlo is a wine that speaks of one man's commitment to this ancient *terroir*, as it is able to manifest the essence of sangiovese and Chianti. The land and climate are similar to those of Castelnuovo Berardenga, with a rich soil of clay and calcareous and alkaline rocks. The vineyards that produce Percarlo are situated in an area with Pliocene origins. The soil is composed of layers of sand and pebbles that vary between 7 and 16 feet in depth and are supported by banks of clay. The average altitude is about 890 feet in a natural environment with very little development or human intervention. As far as the eye can see, there are rows of cypresses and oaks and pastures for the regal white Chianina Tuscan cattle.

The farm is a mixed holding of around 400 acres: 77 acres of vineyards, 27 acres of olives, 99 acres of forest, and some 200 acres of open field and pasture. Because of the altitude and the great amount of surrounding forest, the daytime and nighttime temperatures vary considerably, which is perfect for the cultivation of sangiovese and for making wines of great structure and quality. About half the vineyards are over thirty-five years old and are comprised of native clones like sangiovese and canaiolo, which the family uses to proliferate clonal selections. Luca made the choice to clone his own plants rather than purchase new ones from nurseries. In 1990, 42 acres were planted at a density of 2,000 plants per acre. In recent years, the entire estate has been converted to biological farming.

It is almost redundant to describe the character of this wine because it is such a perfect reflection of the man who made it. Percarlo is a wine of power and austerity, not inclined to make an impression with its muscle, but rather with its elegance, nobility, and, at times, rustic yet engaging character. In its youth, three or four years after the vintage, the wine can still be closed and show notes on the nose of its long barrel aging and scents of cocoa and coffee. As the wine ages, it becomes one of the most elegant and complex wines in the entire world of Tuscan viticulture. Percarlo is made exclusively from sangiovese grapes and is macerated for a minimum of eighteen days. After alcoholic fermentation, the wine is left to age in small French oak barrels for twenty to twenty-two months, depending on the vintage. After a year and a half of bottle aging, the wine is ready to be placed on the market. Percarlo opens up on the nose with nuances of raspberries and cherries, then turns to notes of red licorice, finishing with charcoal and leather. On the palate, the wine is explosive, with a tannic structure that is uncommon and truly great.

Le Pergole Torte—MONTEVERTINE

LE PERGOLE TORTE is one of the first Super Tuscans made from pure sangiovese grapes. The wine has a cult status both for its amazing quality and for the bottle label, which was designed by the gifted painter and engraver Alberto Manfredi.

Montevertine is a small estate that has been inhabited since the eleventh century. Once a defensive fortress, the building was converted into a rural home during the Renaissance. When Sergio Manetti arrived in 1967, the villa was not in livable condition, and he quickly began restoring the property. He also planted 5 acres of sangiovese (known here as sangioveto) and other complementary native varieties, such as canaiolo and colorino, on the property. His vision was clear: no cabernet, no merlot, and no pinot noir. Having spent most of his professional life in the iron industry, Sergio Manetti proved to have surprising foresight in regard to wine. He was an atypical entrepreneur, a sort of Renaissance man, interested in literature, the arts, and even winemaking history.

In 1971, Manetti released his first 4,000 bottles, debuting his wine at Vinitaly, Italy's most important yearly wine fair. It was an immediate success. In 1997, Manetti decided to stop blending his sangiovese with other varietals—a very bold move in the eyes of others. The Consortium of Chianti Classico stridently rejected his wine because Chianti Classico DOCG was defined as a blend, as documented in the famous formula created by Baron Bettino Ricasoli at the end of the nineteenth century. Profoundly frustrated by what he considered to be a myopic, conservative rule, in 1981 Sergio decided to break away from the denomination. In just a few years from its initial release on the market, Le Pergole Torte was a success. From then onward, the wine developed a considerable following, to the point of becoming in a very short period one of the most prestigious wines produced in Italy.

Over the course of his winemaking career, Manetti came to be known as an intellectual of the land, as he espoused great theories of agriculture as they pertain to the human condition. For a few years, he wrote a column called "Vino e cucina" in *La Repubblica,* one of Italy's most important newspapers. He was a tireless collector—of paintings, of men's tiepins, of walking sticks, of modern sculpture, and even of art catalogs—and he carefully ordered his finds chronologically, a silent testimony to all the exhibits he had attended through the years. Later in life, he even published a book on Tuscan culture, which he wrote and compiled, with written tributes from his friends. He had the rare ability to bring out the natural curiosity in anyone near him, thanks to his own genuine curiosity and interest in people and culture. Sadly, in 2000, Sergio Manetti died, leaving the company and the winery to his son Martino. Wisely and humbly, his successor decided not to change a grape in his father's winning recipe. Martino continues to follow the valuable advice of enologist Giulio Gambelli, the true and renowned *signore* of sangiovese.

Giulio has participated in over sixty-seven harvests and has become an icon for Tuscan wine lovers. He has worked alongside other big names in winemaking, such as Tancredi Biondi Santi. Known as Bicchierino ("little glass") by his close friends, Giulio was able to bring new respect to the sangiovese variety with a few simple changes at Montevertine. After the harvest, the grapes are placed in concrete containers without any sort of temperature control, but the wine is repumped over the cap to keep it wet. Malolactic fermentation occurs with the wine still in the cement; the wine is then put into wood—first, small casks, then larger ones, for about two years total.

Le Pergole Torte is a very strong expression of the land: It is sangiovese through and through. The Montevertine vineyards are located high in the hills of Radda in Chianti, an area where the altitude makes it considerably difficult to mature sangiovese grapes. Here, only the hillsides with good sun exposure are able to produce grapes of worth. Le Pergole Torte is made from a 5-acre, north-to-northeast-facing vineyard planted by Manetti between 1968 and 1982. In recent years, the vineyards have been restored with care and dedication by restructuring the unproductive zones. The grapes are grown using the Guyot system in the older vineyards and the *cordone speronato* system in the newer vineyards.

For far too long, wine critics confused the elegance and depth of Montevertine wines for leanness and lack of structure. The climate and the soil impart deep complexity to the wines, both in terms of aromas and in terms of flavor. However, these are certainly not the best wines for lovers of big, fruity wines. Le Pergole Torte, as mentioned before, is a wine of the land: Its aromas are refined and elegant, but not invasive. There are hints of sour cherry, cigar, and wet soil. In the mouth, the wine is fresh and spiced, with noble tannins. It has the structure to age for a long time. Collectors should look into the 1981, 1985, and 1988 vintages, and especially the 1990.

Redigaffi—TUA RITA

REDIGAFFI IS one of the great Merlots of the world and has even competed in tastings alongside Pétrus, one of Bordeaux's most famous wines. A modern wine, made from relatively young grapes, Redigaffi is nonetheless an outstanding example of a pure Merlot.

In Italy, merlot has had its successes and failures. In places like the Veneto, this French variety has practically found a second home and has been grown there for more than a hundred years. In other regions, especially Toscana, winemakers have decided to plant merlot grapes because they grow more easily than other varieties, and the wine is much loved by consumers and critics for its rich, fruity flavor. In France, merlot grows best in Pomerol, and, thanks to Château Pétrus, this variety has become legendary. In Italy, however, the results have not been as good: Merlot risks flattening or masking the flavors of many Italian wines. The variety, however, is quite flexible and blends nicely with sangiovese, which is known for its rough tannins and pale color. Merlot is the exact opposite: opulent, creamy, high in alcohol, and impenetrably dark.

In 1984, Rita Tua and her husband, Virgilio Bisti, decided to buy land in Suvereto, an area without any real winemaking tradition. Located in a rocky part of the fertile plain of Venturina, just a few miles from Pombino and the Tyrrhenian Sea, Suvereto benefits from a coastal climate. Even during the summer, the nighttime temperatures drop considerably, helping the grapes to mature. Mount Capanne, a 3,300-foot mountain on the island of Elba, acts as screen, protecting the coast of Venturina and Suvereto from major wind and weather. Also, the hills generally experience little rainfall. The summer is quite arid, and the soil—composed of clay, silty sand, and small pebbles—is lacking in nutrients. Sangiovese and a couple of other local varieties of grapes had been planted here without much success.

When Rita and Virgilio arrived, they decided to take a road less traveled, planting their vineyards exclusively with merlot grapes. Their desire was to make a unique wine with great personality that would stand apart from everything that had been produced in Suvereto thus far. Over the course of a few years, the wine became famous throughout the world, and its price increased significantly. Tua Rita is a relatively small operation, which allows the two owners to dedicate great attention to the land and the winemaking process. The vineyard is no more than 45 acres, 30 of which are currently in production. Each year, the winery produces a little less than 40,000 bottles. Many winemakers, including those who work just miles from Suvereto, have tried to replicate Tua Rita's secrets without success.

Redigaffi has, in fact, nothing in common with the fruity Merlot that you can find elsewhere. The company looked to the French as a model and imported the practice of barrique aging. On the nose, Redigaffi has strong but not excessive aromas of mature fruit, like prune, and more subtle notes of rust, leather, wet soil, and graphite. In the mouth, the wine is fleshy and juicy, with a good acidity and well-measured tannins. The finish is elegant, full bodied, and long lasting. The wine is undeniably modern, but it could be no other way, given that this area is lacking in tradition.

Sassicaia—TENUTA SAN GUIDO

TENUTA SAN GUIDO is the birthplace of the legendary Sassicaia, and it still produces world-famous wines to this day. Though it has a relatively short history, it is absolutely a pillar of Italian wines.

Sassicaia is the creation of the Piemontese aristocrat Marchese Mario Incisa della Rocchetta. In 1930, after marrying a Tuscan noblewoman, Clarice della Gherardesca, he decided to plant cabernet sauvignon grapes on the land he had received as a dowry. The marchese, a debonair racehorse breeder, revolutionized winemaking in northern Maremma by selecting the French grape variety over sangiovese because of the similarities he had noted between the Les Graves and the Sassicaia vineyards in the course of his travels in the Bordeaux area. Unlike the noble Tuscan winemaking families, the house of Incisa had never produced wine in the region. It was the marchese's brash and nonconformist spirit that gave birth to a whole new category of Tuscan wines.

At first, Sassicaia was kept close to the vest, and production was limited exclusively for private consumption and for gifting to fellow landed gentry. However, as rumblings of this superb, innovative wine spread among the wine society of Toscana, the Incisa family decided to begin selling Sassicaia to the general public, beginning with the 1968 vintage. Giacomo Tachis was the winemaker whose vision and collaboration thrust this new wine firmly onto the scene. Italy's most celebrated enologist, Giacomo is the spirit and brains behind some of the country's most prestigious wines: In addition to Sassicaia, he was responsible for Solaia and Tignanello for the Antinori family, and for Santadi Terre Brune in Sardegna. It was the marriage of intentions between Tachis and Incisa that generated the legend of Sassicaia. A Bordeaux in Tuscany? Who had ever heard of such a thing? The fact is that, since 1968, Sassicaia has been the talk of the wine world. Though its debut was received with some trepidation from the more staid, old-school Tuscan set, it attracted fans and accolades from the outset. In

1983, Marchese Mario died and was succeeded by his third son, Nicolò, who raised the wine to even greater international acclaim.

Sassicaia was the first wine in the region to be christened a Super Tuscan—a term coined by the American wine writer Nicolas Belfrage that is now common terminology. In 1985, Sassicaia achieved global positioning with a vintage that has since become a legend in world winemaking. Sassicaia has become the bellwether for great Italian wines. Its auction pricing sets the standard and the market for Italian wine values, and it continues to outscore Clarets from California and France in blind tastings. Although getting on in years, Nicolò still has the swagger of a true Tuscan nobleman who perhaps shot two wild boars and broke a horse before his morning coffee. This Tuscan bravado, along with Nicolò's family lineage, makes itself apparent in every bottle of Sassicaia.

The San Guido estate is situated in one of the loveliest corners of Toscana, just inland from the Tyrrhenian Sea in an area of Mediterranean scrub and cypress trees. This unique landscape was immortalized by Giosuè Carducci, winner of the 1906 Nobel Prize in Literature, in his poem "Davanti a San Guido." Thanks to the sea breezes, the climate here is temperate, typically Mediterranean, and the soil is particularly stony. The highest point on the estate is 1,300 feet above sea level. Two-thirds of the grounds are covered by woodland; the rest is occupied by the training stables for Dormello-Olgiata thoroughbred racehorses—a breed selected and developed by Marchese Mario—and about 222 acres of vines. The vineyards dedicated to the cultivation of the cabernet sauvignon and the cabernet franc grapes used to produce Sassicaia are found in the southwest area of the estate.

What makes Sassicaia reminiscent of its French cousins is, above all, its elegance, while its scent and flavor are quintessentially Mediterranean. This is a wine that ages superbly—so much so that celebrated vintages of the past, such as 1978, 1985, and 1988, are still as quaffable and as exciting as ever. The wine is aged for twenty-four months in French oak barriques, then for six months in the bottle. The result is a wine that is deep ruby red in color with nuances of Mediterranean herbs such as rosemary and bay leaf. The bouquet, redolent of red berries, is potent and dense with very fine tannins. Notwithstanding the use of barriques, Sassicaia is neither modern nor traditional in style. Sassicaia is simply Sassicaia, a wine that has created a school of its own, with lots of devotees keen to imitate its unmistakably aristocratic elegance. Its best vintages hold unique sensations in store; in a tasting organized by international wine authority and author Hugh Johnson for *Decanter* magazine in 1978, the 1972 Sassicaia was named Best Cabernet in the World. A distinctive feature noted in the wine is the cyclical nature of its taste potential: In other words, it seems to give off its best in the winter, only to close up again in spring and then bloom magnificently in summer.

Tenuta di Valgiano—TENUTA DI VALGIANO

A NATURAL WINE through and through, Tenuta di Valgiano is a masterful example of the fact that organic farming practices can and do produce world-class wines. This wine's story is that of an iconoclastic blending of two seemingly disparate ideologies: Milanese fashionistas and traditional biodynamic farming.

Moreno Perini, the son of a reputed businessman in the footwear industry, and Laura di Collobiano, a descendant of a noble Piemontese family, purchased Tenuta di Valgiano in the mid-1990s. The two city slickers decided to hire another cosmopolite, Saverio Petrilli, as their consultant. Having an educated understanding of the environmental issues plaguing the world, the team chose ecological sustainability as their battle flag. They began by obtaining organic certification, and then became biodynamic in 2001. Together they created an oasis in Valgiano, where forty-something-year-old Saverio works together with a team of talented and innovative young people. Nowhere else in Italy can you find so many youngsters working the harvest, sharing ideas and building lasting relationships. The result is a cultural phenomenon that has positive effects on the wine.

Tenuta di Valgiano turns out perfect wines in terms of aroma and taste, without using chemical fertilizers or yeasts created in laboratories. They have a perfect synthesis. The recipe is simple: "The soil and the sun make wine without compromises," as Saverio loves to say. Nothing else, just nature and her slow, constant rhythms. There are no magic tricks: It is not a question of philosophy, but simply one of high-level agriculture, without the sort of ideological superiority that many biodynamic producers often adopt. Here at Valgiano, people challenge themselves every day and are willing to face what each day brings them.

Until just a few years ago, the countryside outside Lucca was completely undervalued and considered ill suited for making quality wines. There were few wineries, and their wines were poorly received by the critics and poorly valued by the market and consumers. Few people saw any potential in the land. As this area is located halfway between the Tyrrhenian Sea and Chianti Classico, the climate is influenced by both the sea and the land, with dramatic changes in temperature between night and day.

Tenuta di Valgiano is hidden in a valley spared from the excessive cement paving that much of the outlying areas of Lucca suffered during the 1970s. The villa of the estate is also located in this unpolluted area of the region, which is covered with grapevines and olive trees that provide some particularly memorable extra-virgin olive oil. The area is truly shell shaped, positioned about 800 feet above sea level and surrounded by tree-covered hills that rise up to 3,300 feet in altitude. The soil is dense with clay and has a strong presence of alberese, a compacted calcareous rock. The soil is therefore poor in nutrients, but perfectly fit for making high-quality wines. The vineyards range from six to forty years old.

The sangiovese grape always does well in the alberese soil, which gives Sangiovese wines great aromatics while allowing them to maintain their complex structure. Merlot grapes, on the other hand, when farmed in clay soil, produce wines with great finesse and elegance. It is only the merlot grape that when grown in sandstone pebbles will result in a wine with strong notes of perfume and a complex composition. The nature of biodynamic farming, in which farmers seek to acknowledge and respect the preference that certain grape varieties have for certain soil types, allows the organic nature to come through in the glass. These techniques even allow international varieties to integrate themselves into the local profile of sangiovese. They complement the local varieties by bringing their own bells and whistles to a great wine that speaks of its *terroir*.

Tenuta di Valgiano is a blend of native and nonnative grape varieties: In addition to sangiovese, it is made with merlot and syrah. However, despite its two international parents, the character of the wine is undoubtedly Tuscan: In the mouth, it is acidic, edgy, and rugged, but at the same time rich in juice, fruit, and grand elegance. How is this miracle possible? It is probably the biodynamic approach in the fields and the hands-off approach in the cellar that make this wine less artificial and constructed, more pure and more linked to the *terroir*. The use of invasive technologies has been reduced to the bare minimum, and the wine is left to ferment in wooden vats for six to eighteen days, depending on the vintage. The grapes at Tenuta di Valgiano come from single vineyards, and the wine is not made from grapes selected in the winery. The wine is then aged in barriques, where malolactic fermentation occurs during the winter. To initiate the fermentation, no chemical yeasts or enzymes are used. Everything happens naturally, leading to a wine that is rich in aroma.

When tasted young, Tenuta di Valgiano is dominated by mature red fruit, such as cherry, but it then develops aromas of stone, dry leaves, tobacco, and leather after aging in the bottle. In the mouth, it is edgy and reactive, though neither quality weighs down the structure or good body of the wine. The finish is long lasting, with sweet, pleasurable tannins. Some of the top vintages include 1999, 2001, 2004, and 2006. Despite its short history, Tenuta di Valgiano has all the necessary elements of a wine with great aging potential.

Tignanello—MARCHESI ANTINORI

PRODUCED IN the heart of Chianti Classico, Tignanello defies tradition and is in a class of its own. The wine has always been magic for American wine drinkers. It is a name that has the same gravitas as Brunello or Barolo but which is even more powerful in the United States. The popularity of this wine dovetailed with the boom of authentic Italian cuisine in America and created a whole new market for modern Tuscan wines.

After six hundred years of making wine in Toscana, the Antinori family revolutionized the way wine was made in Chianti. In 1970, Piero and consulting enologist Giacomo Tachis released a single-vineyard Chianti Classico Riserva that had been aged in barriques. This modern approach was unheard of in Toscana at the time. In fact, the following year, Piero had to declassify Tignanello and label it as a *vino da tavola:* The wine contained international grape varieties like cabernet, rather than a majority of sangiovese grapes with some lesser-quality grapes like white trebbiano toscano, as was required by the Chianti Classico regulations. Although Tignanello never returned to being a Chianti Classico, it certainly sparked a revolution in the Chianti area and in Toscana in general.

Although the headquarters of the Antinori empire is located in Firenze, in a beautiful downtown palace, the soul of the company has always been in the green sea of the gently rolling hills of Chianti. Tignanello comes from a vineyard of the same name, situated 19 miles from Firenze, between the small towns of Montefiridolfi and Santa Maria a Macerata—in the heart of Chianti Classico. The estate covers 870 acres, 360 of which are planted with grapes. However, it is the quality of the grapevines that is really impressive: Some of the top crus in Toscana, like Tignanello (120 acres) and Solaia (25 acres) are located here. The soil is composed of sea marl from the Pliocene period and is rich in limestone. The altitude of the vineyards varies between 1,100 and 1,500 feet. The microclimate is fantastic for winemaking: During the most important part of the ripening process, there are long, hot days, often with a little breeze and an ideal difference between night- and daytime temperatures.

Tignanello became the vineyard the Antinoris used to express their creativity and their desire for experimentation. They planted cabernet sauvignon and cabernet franc back in the 1920s. The vineyards were abandoned during World War II—during which time the estate was used to protect the family and their staff while their home in Firenze was being bombed—but they were slowly revived in the 1950s and blossomed in the 1960s. Together with sangiovese, these two vineyards led to great change in the region. And speaking of sangiovese, in recent years, the Tignanello vineyard has been home to interesting research dedicated to this native Tuscan grape: Pieces of white rock called al- berese, already present in the area, were placed at the base of each row of vines. The reflection of the sunlight off the white rocks, along with the absence of infested plants and the density of vineyard, help the san- giovese grapes ripen perfectly here.

The magic formula for Tignanello is 85 percent sangiovese, 10 per- cent cabernet sauvignon, and 5 percent cabernet franc. The wine is uniquely modern, part of a general trend during its inception, but it has unashamedly maintained this style. The wine is released only during top, or at least very good, vintages. The wine was not released, for ex- ample, in 1972, 1973, 1974, 1976, 1984, 1992, and 2002. In 1982, the Antinoris established which vineyards would be used to make the wine—but only after much trial and error. The three grapes are har- vested between September and the beginning of October. Much atten- tion and care is given to the fermentation and extraction stages, which involve *délestage* and the pumping over of the must. Alcoholic fermen- tation occurs at temperatures between 81 and 88 degrees Fahrenheit for all the grapes. After drawing off the lees, the wines are placed in new, small wooden casks, where malolactic fermentation occurs. Only then are the wines carefully blended and then left to age for twelve months in barriques. The wine is then bottled and left to age for an- other year.

Traditionally, Tignanello has a very intense ruby red color and fragrant notes of red fruit, spices, wet soil, and licorice. In the mouth, the wine is rich, sapid, round, and elegant. It is famous for its aromatic and long finish, which seamlessly recalls the wine's olfactory notes. The noticeable tannins and high acidity level add to the longevity of this red wine.

Vin Santo Occhio di Pernice—AVIGNONESI

EVERYTHING ABOUT this wine and winery is special and classically Italian. No other wine in the world speaks so clearly of the history of Toscana. The story of the Avigonesi di Montepulciano winery is woven together with history, politics, and the Catholic church, or, more specifically, the popes.

Vin Santo Occhio di Pernice is tied to the history of the Catholic church in the early fourteenth century. Serious tensions were brewing in the Roman court, and King Philip IV of France was strongly anti-pope. The cardinals decided to meet in conclave to elect a French pope, transferring him to Avignon until the situation in Roma calmed down. What was supposed to be a temporary arrangement lasted almost seventy years, during which seven popes were elected, and three antipopes were named by the European kings. It was a time of intrigue, civil unrest, and theological and political disputes, recorded by historians as the Western Schism. By 1377, the political situation in Europe had changed, allowing for the definitive return of the pope to Roma. Back in Italy, Pope Gregory XI brought many French families from Avignon with him who settled in the Eternal City, Siena, and Montepulciano. The Avignonesi family (a name given to them because their original French last name was too hard to pronounce) started a winery that, over the centuries, became a reference point for the winemaking in the region.

Montepulciano is an area of great red wines made from sangiovese grapes (locally referred to as prugnolo gentile). However, the Avignonesi family was destined to make a sweet wine generally served at parties and special occasions. The origins of the wine's name—Vin Santo (holy wine)—are veiled in local legend, but the name may relate to the similarly sweet wine then used in the Catholic Mass. The Avignonesi winery came to produce a Vin Santo, which became the reference point for Vin Santo production, named Occhio di Pernice. After various generations within the family managing the winery, including the thirty years in which the Falvo family spread the Avignonesi brand worldwide, the winery was transferred to the hands of Victrix, a Belgian maritime company, in 2008.

Until a couple of decades ago, Vin Santo di Montepulciano was considered a wine too good to be sold. Bottles were saved for special occasions like weddings or the arrival of an important guest. Almost every family living in the countryside made it, but no one dared sell it. It would have been too difficult to set a price for an elixir of this rarity. After the grapes were dried out (the *appassimento*) and after the pressing—which may occur in November, or is sometimes pushed back until the following spring—the wine is placed in small, 50-liter wooden barrels called *caratelli* (small barrels) in farmhouse attics. And there they remain. The winemaker doesn't have to do anything, only wait for seven to eight years before opening, with some trepidation, the small casks. Out comes a honeylike liquid with almond and hazelnut aromas. In the mouth, the wine is sweet and welcoming, but not cloyingly so. Vin Santo Occhio di Pernice is a wine made with time.

To make wine according to the rules of Vin Santo may seem crazy or impossible, but in the Avignonesi cellar, the traditions have not changed. The winemaking and aging processes are too long and laborious for most producers, and therefore Avignonesi is the only winery to produce this wine. The Vin Santo room, where the hundreds of *caratelli* are kept untouched for eight years, is a sight to see. The secret of an excellent Vin Santo is the "mother," or starter—the hundred-year-old liquid that initiates the fermentation process and that is reused after the barrels are opened. This starter makes a significant difference in the quality of the wine, setting it apart from the more industrial types of Vin Santo available on the market, which are often sold as a souvenir to tourists together with a box of Tuscan *cantucci* (almond biscotti). I find the rich, oxidized style of this wine spiritually uplifting.

The color of this wine is shady yellow to light brown, with a rim that glows like bricks awash in sunshine. On the nose, it's a symphony of dried fruit, dominated by sun-baked figs. On the palate is where this Vin Santo steps ahead of other wines, as it is of such density and viscosity you can practically chew it. All this concentration and power is focused by an overriding sensation of classic elegance.

~UMBRIA~

Montefalco Sagrantino 25 Anni—ARNALDO CAPRAI

IN THE MINDS of most Italian wine lovers, Arnaldo Caprai's 25 Anni represents the birth of the sagrantino, a grape variety of surprisingly good quality that has existed in Montefalco, and nowhere else, for at least four hundred years. When Arnaldo purchased his estate in 1971, sagrantino was experiencing a slow, inexorable decline because it was considered unable to produce great wine. Caprai arrived with the determination and dedication to find out its real potential. Thanks to his work, and that of his son Marco, not only did sagrantino survive, but a vast movement of small producers and important investors, even from outside Umbria, has been created around the grape.

With Marco at the wheel, the company dramatically improved the quality of its wines, as well as its image. The winery became a leader in clone research on the sagrantino variety and was one of the first to effectively promote both the wine and the territory. The company was probably the first to truly believe in the potential of the Internet as a communication tool and even came up with a wine—the Nero Outsider—that could be purchased exclusively online.

Tradition, innovation, and territory: at Caprai, bringing together these three ingredients has become an art, and the definition of their style. And since every project should have a powerful symbol to explain its importance, better than words could do, Caprai selected the Montefalco Sagrantino 25 Anni as its symbol. Created for the company's twenty-fifth anniversary, this wine quickly became an exemplary wine in Italy and abroad, winning over thousands of wine lovers and proving the potential of grape varieties closely tied to their area of origin. The 25 Anni project, part of the winery's far-reaching undertaking, is today one of the best examples of high-quality enological entrepreneurship. But this is an unconventional company, and with someone like Marco Caprai at the helm, there is no saying what we can expect next.

Montefalco is full of historical and literary references, beginning with its name. Emperor Frederick II renamed the small town immersed in the green countryside of Umbria that had previously been called Coccorone. Frederick was known as a passionate falcon hunter, a hobby that is now uncommon, but that will always be connected to this town because of its name, which means "falcon mountain." Montefalco is not located in a particularly great territory in terms of winemaking. A few miles away, you can find the source of the Clitunno River, which captivated the likes of Pliny the Elder, Byron, Carducci, and Goethe. The hills around the town are mostly dedicated to cultivating other plants, and to find an area densely planted with vines, one must travel many miles toward Roma to the area of Orvieto, or northward to the tiny winemaking enclave of Torgiano.

Montefalco is Sagrantino, and Sagrantino is still, despite the development of other wineries, Caprai. But the elements described above have another effect. In the case of Caprai and of Sagrantino, it doesn't seem sensible to talk about cru in the strict sense of the word: The celebrated 25 Anni was created out of careful attention to selecting the best grapes available at the winery, from more than one vine, and yet it is the perfect expression of the complexity of the territory of Montefalco. Here, the land can vary from deep, fresh soils to others composed predominately of clay-calcrete, and can rise to 1,500 feet in altitude. The area benefits from a unique microclimate, thanks to the fresh winds that slip down into the valley from the nearby hills.

When Montefalco Sagrantino 25 Anni was released for the first time in 1993, few would have guessed it would have such an incredible success—that is, except for its creators, Arnaldo and Marco Caprai, who were convinced from day one that they had created a true enological phenomenon. Today, after many years and infinite tests in terms of the market and its image, 25 Anni still shines as bright as ever. The wine is the fruit of a harvest of only sagrantino grapes from the best vines on the property. The production per acre never exceeds 2,000 pounds. After a very soft crush, the must is continuously repassed over the cap to extract the essences contained in the skins. The maceration goes on for up to thirty days. Next, the wine is aged in barriques for two years, then spends another eight months in the bottle before being released on the market. Today, production has reached around 30,000 bottles a year.

The 25 Anni is particularly fascinating because it is the essence of the world of sagrantino. It has aromas of spices, red and black fruit, earth, and leather, perfectly paired with vanilla notes derived from the wood. A powerful yet velvety soft flavor makes the wine incredibly rich without seeming too big and gives it a decisive character and unquestionable personality. I remember the first time I tasted this wine: The weblike tannins were so gripping that it felt as if my tongue had been wrapped up by them. However, after the wine is left to age, the gripping tannins smooth out and become the epitome of elegance.

Cervaro della Sala—CASTELLO DELLA SALA

CERVARO DELLA SALA—the singular wine from the Antinori family's storied estate, Castello della Sala—has been historically the beacon for great Italian white wine. Although the Antinori name immediately reminds one of the great red wines of central Toscana and twenty-six generations of winemaking in Chianti, this story is about a central Italian white wine that forever changed what the world would think of Italian white wine. Although I don't think that Cervaro may be the "best" white wine in Italy, I do believe that few rival its impact and significance.

The winery itself is a medieval castle, with guard towers, thick walls, and a strategic defensive location atop a rocky hill. The fortress was built in 1350 by the Della Vipera family, who came to Italy with Emperor Charlemagne. In 1518, the property was given to the Opera del Duomo, a charitable organization based in Orvieto, a town known for its beautiful striated cathedral. With the unification of Italy in 1861, the estate, along with the Orvieto cathedral and many other works of art, passed from the the hands of the Catholic church to the state. In 1940, after the Vipera estate had witnessed a series of owners, Marquese Niccolò Antinori decided to purchase the property to be able to add a good white wine to the family's wine portfolio: Until then, the Antinoris had been dedicated to making red wines in their native region of Toscana.

An enormous amount of effort went into turning Castello della Sala into a winery: In addition to the main building, the Antinori family bought and restored some twenty-nine farmhouses, or *cascine,* and almost 1,200 acres of land. It took a decade before the wine produced on the estate made a leap in quality, which it did with the help of one of the top Italian enologists, Renzo Cotarella. Having arrived at Castello della Sala in 1979 at a very young age, Renzo—currently the director of the entire Antinori house—started by carrying out Niccolò's dream to produce a white wine capable of aging and competing against the top wines in Italy and abroad. This was a difficult challenge for various reasons: The region was not known for its quality wines, so there were no other locally produced white wines to use as a benchmark. At the beginning, the technical skills and technological applications needed to reach this goal were simply not available. Renzo was also lacking the right grape variety to launch this project. It took a trip to Burgundy in 1981 to change his outlook.

A lover of the world's greatest white wines, Renzo Cotarella was inspired by the power, evolution, and nobility that the combination of chardonnay grapes and Burgundian *terroir* could realize in the bottle. He returned from Burgundy with the understanding that even in Italy, and specifically in Umbria, he could make white wines at the level of his more storied Burgundian contemporaries. After four years of nonstop experiments, tests, hopes, and failures, Renzo started planting chardonnay, as well as grechetto, a native grape variety. Another major development—not only for the winery, but for Italian white wine makers in general—was Renzo's decision to use only new barrels to age the wine. Perfectly managed cold maceration and malolactic fermentation in barriques complete the picture of this innovative, if not revolutionary, approach to making white wine in Italy.

In 1985, the first bottle of Cervaro della Sala was released, and it was a smash hit. Since then, the wine has seen good and great vintages, but it has remained the same. It is, arguably, Italy's most famous white. And what's more, Renzo Cotarella, "the father of Cervaro," mapped out a new road in Italian wine, demonstrating with authority the role of the enologist as interpreter of the grapes and *terroir*, and inspiring generations of winemakers. Today, Renzo oversees the entire Antinori group, while his brother Riccardo has followed in his footsteps, becoming another one of Italy's most acclaimed enologists. As for Castello della Sala, it has never shone so strong.

Ficulle, the town where Cervaro is produced, is certainly not known as one of Italy's or Europe's top wine zones. Like most areas of Umbria, however, it has a long-standing winemaking history, and thanks to its vicinity to the thirsty market of Roma, demand for local wine has never been a problem. Over the years, these hills have been witness to some strange occurrences: With Toscana directly to the north, Umbrian winemakers used to blend, or "cut," their full-bodied reds with Tuscan grapes. But with Roma to the south, the same winemakers had to produce easy, inexpensive wines (mostly whites) to meet the demands of foreign tourists and city sippers. It took a fair amount of time before this Umbrian "middle land" came into its own, revealing the intrinsic value of its products and the clearer, more precise character of its wines. The Umbrian hills have a rare beauty and are made up of lush valleys that are sheltered from the wind, with ample water supply, and that have been left unharmed by industrialization. It is an area almost "destined" for enological success. The region is made of various soils, all of which are suited for wine production. In the case of Ficulle and its neighbor Orvieto, the land is composed of rocky sediment, with large stones dotting the landscape and shaping the vineyards. There are several native white varietals here, including trebbiano, toscano, and grechetto, while the reds include sangiovese, canaiolo, and ciliegiolo.

The name Cervaro della Sala comes from two branches of the family that feuded over the castle during the Middle Ages—the Della Cervara family and the Della Sala family. This wine was first released in 1985, but according to Cotarella, it was the following vintage, 1986, that truly defines the unmistakable style of the wine. Typically made of 85 percent chardonnay and 15 percent grechetto, this wine does not have a strict formula, and the amount of grechetto may increase (it rarely decreases) depending on the year. The grapes come from fifteen- to twenty-year-old vineyards located around the castle, at 660 to 1,300 feet above sea level. The soil is composed of rock and clay. The two grape varieties are vinified separately, with respective musts sitting on the lees for eight to twelve hours at 50 degrees Fahrenheit. Both alcoholic and malolactic fermentation occur in new 225-liter French oak barriques (Allier and Tronçais). After six months in the wood, the two wines are blended and aged in the bottle for another ten months before being released on the market.

Cervaro della Sala has intense aromas, with classic notes of citrus, fruit, and flowers, balanced with a note of vanilla. In the mouth, it is full, round, and minerally, with a long finish. The wine is exceptionally complex and is able to withstand long aging—an unusual characteristic of whites from this latitude.

THE ISLANDS

The Islands

Mare
Tirreno

SARDEGNA

Olbia
Tempio
Pausania
B
Sassari
Nuoro
Oristano
Lanusei
Sanluri
C
Cagliari
A
Carbonia

Mare
Tirreno

Messina
F

Palermo

Trapani
G
SICILIA
D
I
Enna
Caltanissetta
E
Catania
MONTE
ETNA
Agrigento
Siracusa
Ragusa

MARE
MEDITERRANEO

H Pantelleria

Sardegna

A *Carignano del Sulcis Superiore Terre Brune* Cantina Sociale di Santadi

B *Tenores* Tenute Dettori

C *Turriga* Argiolas

Sicilia

D *Rosso del Conte* Tasca d'Almerita

E *Etna Bianco Pietramarina* Benanti

F *Faro Palari* Palari

G *Marsala Superiore Riserva 10 Anni* Marco De Bartoli

H *Passito di Pantelleria Ben Ryé* Donnafugata

I *Santa Cecilia* Planeta

~SARDEGNA~

Carignano del Sulcis Superiore Terre Brune—
CANTINA SOCIALE DI SANTADI

THIS SIGNATURE WINE of the renowned Cantina Sociale di Santadi is a strong, earthy wine that developed out of years of researching the native varieties of Sardegna. All the hard work of study has paid off, as Carignano del Sulcis Terre Brune is quite a winning wine.

Cantina Sociale di Santadi was the first winemaking cooperative established on the island of Sardegna. Santadi is located in the heart of Sulcis, an area of incomparable natural beauty in the southwestern corner of the island. We are talking the antithesis, both geographically and culturally, of the glamorous Costa Smeralda, a favorite summertime destination for the rich and famous. In Sulcis, time seems to stand still. The landscape is not unlike that of Arizona: deep canyons and desert sands. In fact, many of filmmaker Sergio Leone's famous spaghetti westerns were inspired not by Utah's Monument Valley, but by his visits to Sardegna. The area was once a top-ranked mining center, and many villages were built nearby. When the mining stopped, the small towns were abandoned, much like the towns in the American West were when the gold rush ended.

The Cantina di Santadi came as a wake-up call for the region, something concrete in an otherwise unstable environment in a difficult moment in history. The cooperative offered an economic alternative to many of the people living in the area when the mines began to close. In addition, the creation of the winery led to an important study of the territory and the discovery of native grape varieties with great potential. Mineral sediments were found just yards beneath the soil in Sulcis, allowing for traditional viticulture that didn't depend on American rootstock because the vines were resistant to aphids and phylloxera. The farmers of Sulcis, with their steadfast faith and determination, are responsible for having reversed the gloomy economic situation on the island and for paving the way for quality Sardinian wines. The cooperative also made a wise decision in collaborating with legendary enologist Giacomo Tachis, the father of Sassicaia and Tignanello, who helped to create some of the most important wines in the Santadi portfolio. Today the co-op has around 250 members who tend to more than 1,500 acres of vineyards. Collectively, the producers make just less than 2 million bottles of wine per year, divided among full-bodied reds, mineral-rich whites, and warm, welcoming dessert wines.

Sulcis is located to the west of the Sardinian capital of Cagliari, situated between the flatlands of Campidano and the southwestern coast of the island. The 66 square miles of territory are dominated by arid, desertlike landscapes of remarkable beauty. The beaches directly in front of the islands of Sant'Antioco and San Pietro are dotted with white sand dunes and dramatic rocky cliffs overlooking the deep sea. Moving inland, you arrive at the rural part of Sulcis, where the mineral mines were once located. Agriculture and mining existed side by side for years, but when the coal ran out, farming came to dominate the local economy. Naturally, the land is rich in minerals, with sandy topsoil. In fact, some of the grapes that go into Santadi wines come from vineyards built on costal beaches—areas that are quite difficult to farm. In this corner of Sardegna, the climate is mild year-round, with the exception of the summer months, when it is decidedly hot and dry. The vegetation that grows around the vineyards is referred to as *macchia mediterranea,* or Mediterranean scrub. There are oak, olive, and strawberry trees, not to mention the cork oaks used to make the famous Sardinian corks.

Sulcis and Sardegna owe a lot to the work of the Cantina Sociale di

Santadi, and to Giacomo Tachis. The area and the island are home to native grape varieties that were saved from extinction and relaunched onto the market by the cooperative. Nuragus, nasco, and vermentino are all native Sardinian white wine grapes, but the greater renaissance was based on the main red grape of Sulcis, carignano. The signature Santadi wine, Carignano del Sulcis Terre Brune, was made possible by clonal research, the choice of the *alberello* training system, and the use of both traditional and modern winemaking techniques. The grapes for this wine come from the old vineyards in southern Sulcis that still have old rootstock. The soil in these vineyards is loose and soft, composed of sand and some limestone. During the summer, the climate can be scorching. Harvest takes place between the end of September and mid-October. Alcoholic fermentation occurs in steel vats and lasts fifteen days, during which the maceration of the must on the skins allows for the complete release of the polyphenols. The secondary fermentation happens after the wine is transferred to barriques, at the beginning of December. Terre Brune ages for sixteen to eighteen months in new French oak barriques, followed by a year in the bottle.

This is an earth-driven wine that is dark ruby red with granite-colored hues; the bouquet is intense, with aromas of jam, hay, dry sage, rose petals, and aromas of Mediterranean bush. In the mouth, the wine is exuberant, dense, and rich in tannins, which give the wines its elegance and finesse. The pronounced acidity signals a long-lasting wine, which Terre Brune has proved to be. At seventy or eighty dollars on a wine list, this is one of my go-to wines.

Tenores—TENUTE DETTORI

MADE FROM A grape that has flourished in Sardegna, specifically, for centuries, Tenores is a unique wine. The particular frangrances of Tenores come from the ancient land and the unique care of master winemaker Alessandro Dettori.

The Dettori family has ancient roots but has only a recent history when it comes to making wine. Alessandro Dettori founded the family winery in 2000 and began producing wines that reflect his strong personality. Over the course of a few years, he became the big new thing in the Sardinian wine world, competing with names like Argiolas and Santadi.

Alessandro Dettori didn't really become a star overnight. His success should be attributed in part to his family's history of working the land, growing grapes, and tending to fruit trees. In addition, Alessandro is an excellent communicator and is a champion of natural processes. He is one of a small group of Italian winemakers who try not to intervene with the natural cultivation and vinification processes. Alessandro treats his vines only twice a year with sulfur to protect the plants from humidity. Alessandro owns 45 beautiful acres of land in Sardegna, but his production never exceeds 45,000 bottles. His approach has produced wines that on first taste may seem surprisingly lean, at times rough, and often overevolved. The wines need to oxygenate for a long time before drinking but become something really special. Alessandro is also proud of the fact that his farm is self-sustaining. In addition to wine, he produces wheat, vegetables, fruit, and extra-virgin olive oil. His property is located in a dry and unknown part of Sardegna, far away from the Emerald Coast frequented by international VIPs. Alessandro's wines taste strongly of the soil of inland Sardegna, a place cloaked in mystery. Wine lovers and critics were quick to fall in love with Alessandro's wines because of their perfumes and ancestral flavors.

One of the most distinctive elements of Alessandro Dettori's vineyards is that the grapevines are all planted using the *alberello* training system and that some of these magnificent plants are almost 120 years old. These plants are still alive thanks to the local farmers who invested their lives in the vineyard. *Alberello* is the only type of training system that would work here because *cordone speronato* or Guyot would be threatened by the strong winds that whip through the vineyards during the winter. The town of Sennori, home to the Dettori winery, is located in Romangia, an area named after the Romans, who introduced grapes and olives here. Romangia is covered with hills and has an altitude of 820 feet. The soil is composed primarily of limestone and is creamy white in color. In addition to grapes, the land is planted with olive trees, *macchia mediterranea* (Mediterranean scrub), and pear-producing cactus. The vineyards have been left unchanged—trained in the *alberello* system, without irrigation, and with a density of 2,000 to 2,800 plants per acre. If you do a simple calculation, you will arrive at a surprising fact: If the yield per acre is only 2,700 pounds for 2,000 plants, this means that each plant produces no more than 21 ounces of grapes per plant, a trifling amount.

Tenores is made from cannonau, an grape variety that is practically considered indigenous, though it was brought to Sardegna by the Spanish in the seventeenth century. Cannonau adapted extremely well to the island and has come to represent Sardinian wine as a whole. Alessandro Dettori's interpretation of the grape is very different from what you find in the majority of cannonau available on the market. Alessandro and his father hand-select the grapes. Dettori does not use industrial yeasts or enzymes in this wine, nor does he allow a gram of sulfur dioxide *(solfo)* to be used during vinification (for the majority of the wines, it is not added later either). Tenores is neither clarified nor filtered and is not even stabilized with tartaric acid. The wine is simply racked two, or a maximum of three, times. There is no wood in the Dettori cellar; the wines are kept in steel and cement. Alessandro bottles his wines by hand together with a crew of family members. The only technology used in the cellar is cold air. The grapes, must, and wine are moved from place to place by gravity. Wood, wood chips, added tannins, various aromas, and all the things commonly used to make wine more approachable are forbidden here.

Tenores has a sequence of very complex and unique aromas. At first, the wine smells like blueberries and currants, followed by licorice, orange peel, chocolate, lavender, and star anise. In the mouth, it is strong and muscular with firm tannins. The alcohol is balanced by a fresh acidity. This wine is truly unique.

Turriga—ARGIOLAS

FOR MOST, Argiolas is synonymous with Sardinian wine. Although there are now many excellent Sardinian wine producers, this winery, located at the gates of Cagliari, is still considered throughout the world as Sardegna's gold standard.

For over seventy years, the history of the Argiolas family has centered around Antonio, the unforgettable, charismatic founder of the company. Today, Antonio is no longer with the Argiolas family: He passed away in 2009, at the age of 102, leaving behind a story of intuition, courage, and passion. Antonio's children and young grandchildren carry on his spirit and his dream of blending tradition and history with innovation and modernity. Antonio played a fundamental role in reintroducing a countless number of indigenous grape varieties to the market and importing barriques into his cellar—a novelty at the time. He also created an important commercial network for his wines, both in Italy and abroad. Antonio was a great man who, thanks to his wine, brought Sardegna into the modern world.

At heart, Sardegna is a savage, rural place. The mountainous zones have nurtured legends of people living between reality and fantasy, legality and lawlessness, solidarity and solitude. The essence of Sardinian winemaking can be found here: where the sun beats down on the hard, dry soil; where towns are still linked together by unpaved roads; where farmers tend to their fields on horseback; and where sheepherding is still commonplace. (There are 7 million sheep in Sardegna.) If Sicilia has culture, Sardegna has nature.

Perhaps the person who could best attest to this axiom is Giacomo Tachis, the legendary Italian enologist. Giacomo brought decades of experience working throughout Italy—first Piemonte, then Toscana, then Sicilia—to Argiolas. Here in Sardegna he was able to carry out his mission of making a wine capable of expressing the spirit of an entire region. The Turriga project became such a mission. This red wine is not an expression of a single vineyard or cru, but the quintessence of a land, a climate, and a tradition. Turriga could not have been made were it not for the combination of Tachis, Argiolas, and Sardegna.

The Argiolas winery is located in Serdiana, a few miles north of Cagliari, in the southernmost part of the island. The Serdiana area is actually a contradiction of the classic image of inland Sardegna: It is green and fairly rich in water. Over the centuries, this region has been occupied by the Phoenicians, the Carthaginians, the Romans, the Spanish, and the people of Piemonte, during the period when the Kingdom of Sardegna was ruled by the Savoy dynasty. However, prior to all this, the island was home to the Sardinians, a population of the second millennium B.C. that decorated the territory with nuraghe, or cone-shaped stone towers. These megalithic monuments were the center of the social life of the ancient Sardinians to the point of becoming the name of the civilization: the nuragic civilization. The nuraghe are the largest and best-conserved monuments in Europe today and are considered the symbol of the island. The 620 acres of Argiolas vineyards are set against this magnificent backdrop. The vineyards are divided into five estates, the main one located in Serdiana. Here, the fertile soil is primarily calcareous marl and sandstone. Three of the estates are in Trexenta, an area of vineyards and olive and fruit trees. The fifth property, and the most recently purchased, is located in the arid zone of Sulcis and is dedicated to the cultivation of the carignano grape.

The Turriga estate is situated just north of Serdiana, near the town of Senorbì. This area has a rich archaeological imprint that is depicted on the bottle with an image of mother earth. The soil is calcareous and fairly dense, dotted frequently with stones. Turriga is a blend of cannonau, carignano, bovale sardo, and malvasia nera: an extraordinary representation of the island's ampelography. The climate is Mediterranean, dry and subject to drought, with hot, windy summers. After the harvest, which is done by hand between the end of September and mid-October (depending on the grape), the fruit is pressed and fermented at a controlled temperature between 82 and 90 degrees Fahrenheit. Maceration takes sixteen to eighteen days, after which the wine is transferred to new French oak barriques, where it rests for eighteen to twenty-four months, and where malolactic fermentation occurs. The resulting wine is deep red in color, both strong and elegant at the same time. On the nose, the wine has strong notes of ripe fruit and dried flowers, as well as Mediterranean brush. The wine is easily recognizable in a blind tasting. Tobacco, leather, and chocolate notes develop in the wine as it ages. In the mouth, the wine has a splendid balance of structure and silkiness. It is round and tight. Its tannic structure gives the wine its long, well-balanced finish. Turriga is an immortal red wine that will carry on the spirit of Antonio Argiolas for another hundred years.

~SICILIA~

Rosso del Conte—TASCA D'ALMERITA

AS A TWENTY-TWO-YEAR-OLD, I had done all the time I'd wanted to on Wall Street and had come to Italy to find myself. Instead of discovering the "inner me," I lost myself in the world of Italian wine and the wonderful people who inhabit that magical place. By the time I arrived in Sicilia I had been on the move for the better part of a year. I had worked a harvest in Piemonte, fallen in love with a Tuscan baroness in Montalcino (she had no idea), had my skis stolen from the roof rack of my car in Napoli (while I was stopped at a red light), and had come to realize that Italian wine would guide me through the rest of my life.

When I boarded the ferry from Calabria to Messina I imagined that Sicilia would be the Wild West of Italy, with crazy, passionate people running around eating lots of fish and spicy pasta. What I discovered quickly changed my plans, my ideas about the region, and in a lot of ways, my life. On my first morning in Messina, I awoke from an itchy, sweaty sleep in a cut-rate, one-star hotel on the central piazza to two sullen gunshots. I was sure it was a car backfiring or a secretive Sicilian two-gun salute, but when I approached a small crowd in the center of the piazza, I saw a small man lying still in a widening halo of blood radiating from his head toward the feet of the people encircling him. I could hear the soles of Ferragamos shuffling against cobblestones as the bystanders backed away. I almost got a glimpse of the dead man's face, but an onlooker took off his overcoat, covered the body, and walked away, as did everyone else in virtually the same instant, until I was left standing alone. Never before or since have I felt so scared and isolated in my entire life. After my complete sensory immersion in death, I turned and walked into the heart of Sicilia and experienced the true essence of life with the people who must have invented living.

Some weeks later, I arrived in Palermo to meet some big-shot tasters of a new big-deal guide to Italian wine called *Vini D' Italia*. We met at a restaurant on a long pier and had lunch for five hours; by early evening, our table was heatedly discussing the merits of pairing pure bitter chocolate with fifty-year-old solera Marsala. For dessert, we drove to another town, fifty miles away, because it had the best pistachio *gelato en brioche*. Finally, sometime before midnight, we arrived at the Tasca d'Almerita estate in the center of Sicilia to get a good night's rest before the next day's vertical of Rosso Del Conte. At the time, Sicilia was known for bulk industrial white wine, volcanoes, beaches, and the Mafia. The concept of a world-class red wine that evolved over time and was made from indigenous grapes was inconceivable, but apparently that is what we would taste—and not only that, but vintages dating back to the mid-1970s. In the late 1980s there was a lot of buzz around Rosso del Conte among the in-the-know Italian wine people. The word was that the sleeping giant had awakened, and that Sicilia, with its powerful and expressive Nero d'Avola, would take the rest of Italy by storm with red wines that were like the African sirocco, a Sicilian sunset, and Sophia Loren in the glass.

The Tasca d'Almerita (Regaleali) estate was like going back to another time. An agricultural property that has been cultivating grain since the sixteenth century, it is located in the province of Caltanissetta, an arid area in the geographic center of Sicilia. Now, a lot has been said about Nero d'Avola since those early days: Some even call it the Sicilian savior or a mutation of syrah, grown in the California of Italy. I think we tasted a dozen vintages of Rosso del Conte (90 percent nero d'Avola and 10 percent perricone), and my palate and my mind were opened to the world of evocative and soulful southern Italian wines. The wines that were a decade old showed leather and earth mixed with forest fruit and tar while evolving and changing in the glass. Although more extracted, the younger vintage exhibited persistence and complexity on the palate that took me straight to Alba. If this is what nero d'Avola could produce in its native *terroir*, then the future of Sicilian wines was being tasted at that very table.

The tasters were clearly impressed with the wines. They shouted expletives and spoke with their hands. Being a youngster, I may have been short of opinions at that moment, but the impact of that tasting resonated in my wine consciousness for decades. As lunch approached, servants butlered *pannelle* with *spada agro dolce* (chickpea fritters with swordfish in a sweet and sour sauce), and cool, lean Catarratto was poured from sweating bottles as the midday heat began creeping in. I stood in the medieval courtyard as the midday sirocco wind gained momentum and lifted waves of leaves in the surrounding vineyards. Sicilia is the jewel of the Mediterranean, desired by many, but ultimately conquered by none.

Etna Bianco Pietramarina—BENANTI

OFTEN PEOPLE THINK of Sicilian wines as products of a single *terroir*, characterized by high temperatures and strong sunlight. People also tend to associate Sicilia and its surrounding islands with a limited number of grape varieties: nero d'Avola, chardonnay, and moscato. These would be legitimate associations were it not for Mount Etna. The mountain divides the island into two distinct worlds: There is Sicilia, and there is Etna.

The volcano is an immense cone with a diameter of 28 miles, located 10,000 feet above the Ionian Sea. The tallest active volcano in Europe, Etna erupts regularly, spewing hot lava and destroying nearby homes and agricultural land. Humans have lived alongside Etna for millennia, thriving because of both their courage to dominate the mountain and their deep respect for its disastrous force. The ancient

Greeks arrived on the coasts of Sicilia a few centuries before Christ and upon discovering Etna, began circulating stories of the evil spirits contained inside the volcano. Over the centuries, Sicilians learned that the power and unpredictability of the volcano also had its good aspects: For example, they discovered that the slopes of the mountain were extremely fertile. Although the mountain is steep and hard to climb, it is ideal for viticulture. Astonishingly, the grapes planted on Etna were not destroyed by phylloxera, and you can easily find plants with their original rootstock, not grafted like most grapevines had to be after the phylloxera epidemic.

The Benanti family are the winemaking pioneers of the Etna area, and they discovered that there are still other benefits offered by the mountain. The Benanti winery has been in operation since the late 1800s, but it didn't begin producing quality wine until two generations later, with the arrival of Giuseppe Benanti, the founder's grandson. A high-ranking viticulturist and gifted entrepreneur, Benanti called on the help of one of Sicily's top winemaking consultants, Salvo Foti. Together the two men carefully studied the *terroir* of Etna, and because of their work, we now know that the mountain is home to the largest patrimony of native grape varieties in Sicilia. Their research also revealed that the mountain soil changes dramatically depending on the location, and that certain grape varieties grow best in specific areas.

More as a cultural experiment than as a commercial one, Benanti began vinifiying lesser-known grape varieties like nerello mascalese, nerello cappuccio, minnella, and carricante at the beginning of the 1990s. At the time, most Sicilian winemakers hadn't even heard of these grape varietals, while the elder generations of islanders knew them well. Benanti first created a line of wines called *monovitigni* ("single varietal") and then launched an equally ambitious line of cru wines, made from grapes from specific vineyards on Etna. When his white wine Pietramarina, made from carricante grapes, was released to the market in 1991, neither Benanti nor Foti imagined that the wine would be the forerunner to a new local winemaking style and create an "Etna mania" throughout the region and beyond. The eighty-year-old vineyard had all the qualities necessary to become legendary in the wine world. Today, Benanti is a focused company that has maintained its interest in extreme vineyards. Recently, it has invested in the area of Noto, home to the Sicilian grape nero d'Avola, and in the island of Pantelleria, once a volcanic zone and known for its wonderful sweet wines.

Etna is such a geographically significant structure that it is a microcosm in and of itself. The area of vineyards stretches from the lower slopes of the mountain, some 700 feet above sea level up to 3,300 feet. Most of the vineyards are located on the south-facing part of the volcano, which also happens to be the most densely populated. The southern slopes are primarily covered in forest. The most picturesque and typically volcanic sides of the mountain are the western and eastern slopes: The western slopes are bare and dry because of the long expanses of petrified lava, while the eastern slopes are where you'll find the lunar Bove Valley, a three-mile-wide bowl formed thousands of years ago where rivers of hot, molten lava flow down from craters above and collect. The Benanti cellar is located in the Bove Valley. The high mineral content in the soil of the eastern slopes and the intensity of the sunlight make for waxy, nutty, almost oxidized wines. The grapevines are trained primarily using the *alberello* system, and it is still common practice for farmers to bury offshoots of the vines to produce new plants, a technique known as *propaggine* in Italian.

Despite the emergence of other great white and red wines in Etna, Pietramarina still remains the most expressive example of a specific grape variety, of a *terroir,* and of the best possible combination of the two. The Etna denomination, to which this wine belongs, was established in 1968, only a couple of years after the creation of the legislative system of wines. This proves how popular winemaking had already become on the volcano. The Superiore label, which has also been given to Pietramarina, is a further recognition of the quality of white wines produced exclusively in the *comune* of Milo, located on the eastern slope of the mountain. The vineyard is located in a part of the *comune* called Contrada Caselle, 3,100 feet above sea level. The soil of this ancient land is sandy and rich in minerals from the volcanic rock. Carricante is a grape native to this side of Etna, and its name is derived from the verb *caricare* ("to load"), referring to the fact that the plant is loaded with grapes.

The vineyard is planted densely at 3,600 plants per acre, and the plants are trained using the *alberello* system on French rootstock. The harvest occurs late in the season because of the altitude and the mountainous climate. The grapes are collected in the second half of October, after which the entire bunches are lightly pressed. The must is left to ferment at 64 to 68 degrees Fahrenheit in steel tanks. The wine ages in steel tanks for a year before bottling, and then left to age for another year in the bottle. Pietramarina has a rich straw-yellow color and a fresh nose of citrus fruit, flowers, and minerals. In the mouth, it is dry and acidic, with a bitter note on the otherwise well-balanced finish. The persistence of its aromas is remarkable, and it has an aftertaste of anise and almond. It is a white wine to be drunk in its youth or after aging it for many years.

Faro Palari—PALARI

FEW PEOPLE in the United States have heard about or read the detective stories of Andrea Camilleri. His books are set in Sicilia and written, for the most part, in Sicilian dialect. Since the mid-1990s, each new Camilleri release has sold like hotcakes in Italy. The author recounts the beauty and complexity of the island, and the unique people who have a strong sense of honor and history, a love of eating and good company, and an appreciation for heated conversation and social elegance. Salvatore Geraci—Turi to his friends—could easily fit the role of one of Andrea Camilleri's protagonists. Dressed head to toe in pressed linen, with his Panama hat resting on his head, Andrea is the iconic country gentleman, zipping through winding vineyard roads in his vintage red Jaguar.

Of course, Turi didn't grow up farming. He first made a name for himself as one of the most sought-after and renowned architects of Messina. He was even given a position as the cultural councilman of the city. Later in life, he developed a love for winemaking and the countryside when he decided to take over his family farm. The property included a splendid eighteenth-century villa in the Messina countryside. When Turi arrived, the vineyards were in very poor condition. The plants were trained in the *alberello* system and not well cared for. But Salvatore understood the land's potential and invested heavily in the property. He even convinced his younger brother, Giampiero, to work in the cellar and help him revive a denomination—called Faro—that had practically fallen out of existence.

Wine production in this area can be traced back to the Greek colonization and the thousands of years of exchange between Sicilia and the rest of the Mediterranean countries: Spain, France, Greece, Libya, Egypt, and Turkey, just to name a few of the important ones. In the past fifty years, because of poor political decisions, Sicilian agriculture shifted away from focusing on high quality to low-cost mass production. The wine industry followed this path, and many of the grapes grown in Sicilia are now sent to northern Italy to give additional alcohol and color to important wines like Barolo, Barbaresco, and Chianti Classico. Consequently, many of the historic Sicilian denominations suffered tremendously, and the most difficult wine regions—even if they were of the best quality—were abandoned. Faro, a very respected historical denomination, risked dying out and becoming a DOC only on paper.

In the mid-1990s, Salvatore decided to restore his vineyards, choosing to produce his first wine bottles without the help of technology, armed instead with a strong will. He sent the wine from his first vintage to his friends and acquaintances, one of whom just happened to be Gino Veronelli, one of the most important Italian wine critics of the twentieth century. Veronelli fell in love with the wine and told the Geraci family that they had gotten it right. From then on, thanks in part to the invaluable advice of winemaking consultant and friend Donato Lanati, Salvatore continued to evolve his little masterpiece. He decided not to build a new winery, but to convert the eighteenth-century villa into the cellar. He put the fermentation vats in the ballroom and the bottles in what had been the guest quarters. He made an unconventional decision, combining the winemaking and architectural history of the area: a decision that could only have been made by an architect who is as romantic and eccentric as Salvatore Geraci.

Santo Stefano Briga, where the estate sits, is located halfway between the *comune* of Messina and Taormina—one of the most famous and captivating cities on the island, with spectacular Greek theaters that dominate the highest part of the town. This is the eastern side of Sicilia, an area characterized by the presence of the dark and mysterious Mount Etna. The volcano is almost 11,000 feet high, making it the highest point in Sicilia. It is also the most active volcano in Europe. The Geraci vineyards are positioned in a place of rare and incomparable beauty: perched directly above the blue sea, with a view of the peaks of the Calabrian Aspromonte mountain range in the distance. The extreme beauty here is hard to match: In only 3 miles, the altitude rises from sea level to 1,600 feet. Salvatore was faced with the enormous undertaking of terracing the vineyards.

The estate is at the very bottom of Italy, just a couple hundred miles from Africa. The climate is hot, and extremely hot during the summer, when the scorching winds of the sirocco blow up from the Sahara. To deal with the heat, the old Faro Palari vines were planted and trained using the *alberello* system, which is a time-consuming method but the one best suited for the Mediterranean climate. The soil of the vineyards is mostly sandy and fairly loose, poor and unproductive. This, together with the old age of the vines (twenty years and up) results in low yields.

Forget any preconceived ideas you have about Sicilian wines. We are all accustomed to thinking of them as products of the sun, super-concentrated with notes of jammy red fruit. This is not the case with Faro Palari. Salvatore Geraci has created a Burgundian style wine on Sicilian land. In a blind tasting, it would be hard to place the wine so far south, not because it doesn't reflect the land or the *terroir*, but because the prejudices and preconceptions about Sicilian reds are hard to overcome. The wine is a blend of grapes native to Sicilia, dominated by the excellent and still relatively unknown nerello mascalese grape. This variety has grown on the terraced hillside since the Greeks arrived on this coast almost three thousand years ago.

Faro Palari is certainly not a concentrated wine; rather, it is rich in nuance and complexity. If you leave it in the glass, it will change quickly, revealing its many faces. The first aromas to emerge are those of red fruits such as plum and cherry. Next are notes of spice and leather, slightly animal, but softened by notes of incense and cacao. In the mouth, the wine is sapid, well balanced, delicate, and at the same time robust and muscular. It is at once tannic and smooth, subtle yet persistent. It is rich in contradiction, just like Sicilia. Faro Palari takes getting to know to appreciate its unique, celestial balance.

Marsala Superiore Riserva 10 Anni—MARCO DE BARTOLI

THOUGH THE MARKET is unfortunately still dominated by a sea of ill-tasting Marsala, this bottle from the famed vigneron Marco De Bartoli is set firmly on a pedestal above the fray. A true Marsala in every way, Marsala Superiore Riserva 10 Anni will shatter any preconceived notion of what this type of wine can be.

Although Marsala has been made for centuries, most sources associate the introduction of this wine on the global market to John Woodhouse, an adventurous merchant from Liverpool who came to the town of Marsala in the 1770s. Vincenzo Florio, the first Italian to arrive on the Marsala scene, was a brilliant Sicilian businessman and founder of various well-known wineries. He revolutionized the production and distribution of Marsala. Florio discovered that the key to success for Marsala depended not only on the quality of the product but also on the quality of its distribution. He immediately purchased as many boats as he could: ninety-nine in all. He would have bought more, but he was forbidden to acquire more ships than Regia Marina, the Royal Navy.

Thanks to Florio, Marsala became Italy's most famous and exported wine. Money-hungry imitators quickly followed suit, damaging not only the quality of the wine but also its image. During Prohibition, Marsala became popular in the United States because its strangely shaped bottle could often pass for medicine. From the 1950s onward, sadly, the quality of Marsala dropped, and the bottles available on the market had nothing to do with the noble wine of the past. Nowadays, there are very few Marsala producers who are making quality wines.

Marco De Bartoli, a former racecar driver, stands out for his courageous decision to produce high-quality Marsala. At the beginning of the 1980s, Marco decided to try his luck at the family tradition of winemaking. He decided to make Marsala the old-fashioned way, using the solera method, and he named his first wine Vecchio Samperi in honor of the land from which the grapes came. I love this man, and I love his wine. He did more to influence me as a winemaker and wine lover than any other single person. I lived with him in the late 1980s when I was studying wine in Sicilia. Every day after lunch, we would go for a swim. This man knew how to live. Marco seemed able to make everything right in the world. He adopted a misfit wine that for time had been bulk made and mistreated, and he developed an art form out of how it is made and consumed. It is incredible how someone's commitment to a wine can transcend inherent difficiencies in its marketability.

Known by the Arabs as the gate to heaven, Marsala is located in Sicilia's westernmost point. The nearby island of Mozia, an ancient Phoenician city and archaeological treasure, is located directly off the coast of Marsala. The territory is dotted with salt beds and white windmills that appear almost rose colored at sunset. Here, the climate is decidedly Mediterranean, with very hot summers and little rain. The vineyards are located near the coast, allowing for the salt to deposit directly on the grapes, especially during stormy weather. In fact, the white wines from this area have a salty, sapid character. The sea breezes that constantly blow through the vineyards help to defend the plants from disease, while the *alberello*-style training system protects them from the stronger winds like the libeccio, the mistrals, and the sirocco. The grapes practically cook in the summer heat (with temperature exceeding 100 degrees Fahrenheit) and are harvested in mid-September.

Marco De Bartoli's Marsala Superiore 10 Anni is made using the solera method, commonly used by Spanish Sherry, or Jerez, producers in Andalusia. Spanish terms are used by Marsala producers in order to correctly explain the winemaking process. The solera system was created to maintain the quality and character of wine over time. In fact, products made with this system are never identified by vintage. The *solera y criaderas* method is based on the principle that the young wine should acquire the character of the older, more developed wines. In practical terms, rows of barrels, each called an *escala* ("ladder"), and each containing a wine of a specific age, are stacked into a pyramid. The oldest *escala*, identified as the *solera* ("support"), is located at the bottom of the tower in contact with the soil (*suelo* in Spanish). The *escalas* above the *solera* are called *criaderas* ("nurseries"). The number of *criaderas* varies according to type of Sherry or Marsala to be produced, but normally there are five to fourteen rows. In the case of Marsala Superiore 10 Anni, there are ten, one for each year. Each year, wine from the *solera* is removed—an action referred to as *saca* ("extraction")—and bottled. The wine that was removed is replaced with wine from the first *criadera*, and so on and so forth, until arriving at the last *criadera*. The wine in the top barrel of the pyramid is topped off with wine from the *sobretablas*, the barrel on top of the pyramid that contains the youngest wine. The action of topping off the wine is called *rocio*. One must perform the *saca* and *rocio* in small quantities to ensure the quality and characteristics of the entire system.

Another detail in the production of this Marsala is that while the must of the grillo grapes ferments in oak barrels, the pressed inzolia grapes are enriched with aquavit. This liquid, called *mistilla*, is added to the wine during maturation. The result of the entire process is a Marsala of unique aroma and flavor. It is reductive and fiercely acidic. On the nose, the wine has woody notes of sandalwood, walnut, and incense. There are also notes of dried fruit, candied figs, and licorice. In the mouth, the wine starts off sweet but is nicely balanced with acidity adding to its persistency. The finish is characterized with notes of hazelnut and bitter almond. I would drink this Marsala with mushroom barley soup or bitter chocolate or a Sicilian marzipan.

Passito di Pantelleria Ben Ryé—DONNAFUGATA

ONE OF the few wineries with vines that date before the phylloxera plague that destroyed practically all grapevines across Europe, Donnafugata is unique. Ben Ryé is a magical wine that is a clear expression of the land and the searingly hot winds that blow through the vineyards.

The name of the Donnafugata winery comes from a town in central-western Sicilia that was immortalized in Giuseppe Tomasi's 1958 historical novel *Il gattopardo (The Leopard)*, which is set in the time of the Sicilian unification with the newborn Kingdom of Italy (1860–1861). In the book, Donnafugata is the name of the vast estates of the the main character, the Prince of Salina. The novel was later made into a film directed by Luchino Visconti, which won the Palme d'Or in 1963 at the Cannes Film Festival. Giacomo Rallo can be credited for naming his new winery Donnafugata in 1983.

Born into a very well-known dynasty of entrepreneurial winemakers, Rallo had the bright idea to focus his company not on the generic concept of quality, but on its close tie to the *terroir*. At the time, Sicilia was not yet seen as a particularly attractive winemaking area, and people were unaware of its potential. Giacomo Rallo, with the support of his wife, Gabriella, started a sort of revolution. He took over the historic family winery in Marsala, where they had been producing wine grapes since 1851. Renaming the winery Donnafugata in 1983, it became the center of his new project. Rallo began purchasing vineyards in the top territories in western Sicilia—particularly in Contessa Entellina, which, in 1994, became the first DOC comprising a single producer. In 1998, the company decided to shine a light on itself, in the literal sense: Donnafugata decided to start nighttime harvesting, a practice recommended by Pliny the Elder in A.D. 60 to save the grapes from spoiling under the scorching sun. The cooler nighttime temperatures kept the grapes from needing to be refrigerated before pressing, while also saving energy and producing excellent organoleptic results. In 1999, the company expanded to Pantelleria, a beautiful volcanic island in the middle of the Mediterranean. This windy island is located at the same latitude as Tunis, whose lighthouse you can see in the distance on clear nights. On this island, Donnafugata gave life to a true masterpiece, bringing back a lost winemaking tradition based on the clever technique of using stone walls to terrace the steep hills and the cultivation of a symbolic grape variety, moscato d'Alessandria, or zibibbo. From the top of the 820 acres of vineyards—where the native grape varieties of inzolia, nero d'Avola, and zibibbo are grown together with international varieties (chardonnay, syrah, merlot)—Donnafugata looks out into the distance, well beyond the horizons of its own island, and into the future.

Donnafugata's vineyards on the island of Pantelleria are situated on what is a large, dark volcanic rock budding out of the smooth Mediterranean Sea. Seeing this land allows you to fully understand the essence of the winery's mission. Only the smell of the sea in the wind, the sparkle of the sunlight reflecting off the rocks, and the dryness of the land can explain the irresistible attraction one feels on visiting the island. However, Pantelleria only became known for its wines after Rallo's arrival. In 1999, Donnafugata started to develop a small estate planted with zibibbo grapes called Khamma (an Arabic name). From research conducted on the plants and grape bunches, the winery learned that the vines were around one hundred years old. This area had been left unharmed by the destructive phylloxera plague that destroyed a good part the European vineyards at the end of the nineteenth century. Reeling with excitement about this discovery, Rallo decided to commit himself to making quality wine on the island. This was certainly not an easy undertaking: The whipping wind, the merciless sun, the hostile soil, and the almost vertical slope of the vineyards were tough obstacles. But Rallo succeeded, and today, there are acres upon acres of vineyards on Pantelleria, of which Donnafugata owns sixty-eight. The main grape variety is zibibbo. The vineyards are located between 70 and 1,300 feet above sea level on terraced hillsides with fertile, volcanic soil. To protect them from the wind, the vines, which grow like little individual trees or bushes, are planted inside holes in the ground. Due to the extreme landscape, the density of the vines can't exceed 1,200 plants per acre, and the annual yield is generally around 8,800 pounds. The majority of the work can only be done by hand. The harvest of the best grapes, which will be dried to make passito, begins in mid-August. The heat of the island, and its surrounding sea, are responsible for the rest.

The island of Pantelleria is famous worldwide for its extraordinary sweet wines made from the zibibbo grape. Many of them have overtones of Moroccan spices and have a unique palate of flavors: dried fruits, overly steeped teas, and prunes. At Donnafugata, the harvest of the grapes for making passito begins immediately after August 15. The natural drying process (appassimento)—during which the grapes are place on straw mats and dried out by the sun and wind—lasts up to a month and is what gives the grapes their high concentration of sugars and aromas. In September, after a second harvest, must is made from the fresh and very mature grapes. During fermentation, the dried grapes, picked off the bunch by hand, are added to the must, releasing their sugar and incredible bouquet of aromas. In November, the "miracle" of Ben Ryé is completed when the wine reaches its ideal balance, which it will keep way beyond the ten to twelve months of aging in vats and in the bottle. Drinking Ben Ryé is the closest thing to a trip to Pantelleria. Its bright yellow amber color shines like the sun. After the intense notes of apricot and peach, the aromas vary from dried fig, to honey, to broom (ginestra) and the essence of the Mediterranean. In the mouth, the wine is elegant, complex, and soft. The name Ben Ryé means "Son of the Wind" in Arabic, and in this wine you can certainly taste the heat of Africa that blows in with the sirocco.

Santa Cecilia—PLANETA

SANTA CECILIA HAS been one of the most important 100 percent Nero d'Avola wines in Sicilia since its release in 1997. It comes from one of Italy's largest and most respected wineries: Planeta.

If you were to ask one hundred Italians to name a Sicilian winery, ninety-nine of them are certain to respond, "Planeta." And if you were to ask one hundred foreigners, the result would likely be the same. Volumes have been said and written about the impact of this winery on the increasing popularity of Sicilian wines in the past decades. Planeta has helped not only the Sicilian wine industry, but the image of Sicilia in general. The young Planeta cousins—Alessio, Francesca, and Santi—are in a position of tremendous responsibility. In fifteen years, they have constructed an enterprise of five wineries in five separate areas of Sicily. Their estates total 990 acres of vineyards and produce 2 million bottles of wine annually. These numbers, however, may be misleading. The company is focused on producing quality wines. Back in the early 1990s, the young cousins established their goal of reawakening Sicilian wine production by making wines that reflect the warmth of their land and that would appeal to the new generations of wine consumers, in Italy and abroad.

The cousins started off on their mission with their family's history supporting them. The Planeta family has lived in Sicilia for four centuries, and Diego Planeta, father of Francesca and uncle of Santi and Alessio, is the current president of Settesoli, the largest wine cooperative in Italy. The cousins decided to make a departure from the Sicilian wineries of the past by focusing on international grape varieties, which would allow their wines to enter foreign markets more quickly. Merlot and, especially, chardonnay were the first grapes to put Planeta on the map. After making a name for themselves, the cousins started researching native varietals, starting with nero d'Avola, then moving on to carricante, frappato, nerello mascalese, grecanico, and moscato bianco. This experiment proved quite fruitful.

Research, experimentation, knowledge of the land, and family history have been the keys to the winery's success. We must, however, add the age and youthful approach of the Planeta clan to this list. Since their first public appearances at wine fairs and tastings, the cousins have grabbed attention with their liveliness and creativity. Their debut in the formal, at times stuffy, world of wine was a welcome addition to the scene, proving that young people were capable of producing great wines. Their winemaking style, focused on freshness and simplicity, also captivated the wine world. Planeta wines are simple, but not banal: Making "simple" wines has actually become difficult. Wine enthusiasts seek out simplicity, or wines that are a simple expression of a *terroir,* a grape variety, or a typology. In just a few years, Alessio, Francesca, and Santi Planeta have achieved such wines. They built a new image for Sicilia based on proven agricultural and winemaking techniques, but using a more modern language. They created a sense of mystery around their wines, making Planeta one of the most famous brands in Italy.

The Planeta headquarters are located in, and the family resides in, Sambuca, which is not far from Agrigento. On the banks of an ancient river, now a lake, the cousins constructed the first buildings of the Planeta winery. Inside, they produce the main whites of the estate, including their celebrated Chardonnay. Planeta's main vineyards are located in nearby Menfi, where you can visit two of their cellars and over 380 acres of vineyards, planted primarily with international red grape varietals. Moving east, you will find two other estates and their respective cellars: one in Noto and the other in Vittoria. Noto, known throughout the world for its Baroque art and architecture (the town and its cathedral are a UNESCO World Heritage site), is home to Planeta's production facility for Moscato and Nero d'Avola for Santa Cecilia. In Vittoria, Planeta produces Cerasuolo, a red wine made from nero d'Avola and frappato. The estate most recently acquired by Planeta is on Mount Etna. Referred to as "the mountain" by Sicilians, as if there were no others in the world, Etna has a unique climate and growing environment. The mountain, an active volcano, has attracted all the top Sicilian winemakers, who have eagerly bought up parcels of land there.

Santa Cecilia is a pure Nero d'Avola made from the grapes grown in Noto. The company produces 100,000 bottles a year from vineyards located 170 feet above sea level, with 2,000 plants per acre, trained using the *cordone speronato* system. A portion of the estates had already been planted with grapes when the Planeta family arrived, and these vines are now over thirty years old. The grapes are harvested at the end of September, and after being crushed, they are left in contact with the lees in stainless steel tanks for twelve days. The wine is aged in barriques—a third of these are new wood, and the remaining barrels have been used once or twice before—for twelve months before bottling. Santa Cecilia has a dark ruby red color and an intense nose recalling the forest floor, red fruit, sweet spices, and graphite. In the mouth, the tannins do not overpower the elegance and balance of the wine but give it a structure and fullness. It is a perfect example of a modern Nero d'Avola, a sunny and joyful wine with a long potential for aging. It is nero d'Avola vinified for the first time in a very unapologetic and extracted style.

NORTHEAST ITALY

Alto Adige

A *Alto Adige Terlano Pinot Bianco Vorberg Riserva* Cantina Terlano

B *Alto Adige Sauvignon Sanct Valentin* San Michele Appiano

C *Alto Adige Valle Isarco Kaiton Riesling* Peter Pliger Kuenhof

D *Alto Adige Valle Isarco Kerner Praepositus* Abbazia di Novacella

E *Alto Adige Val Venosta Riesling* Falkenstein

Friuli–Venezia Giulia

F *Ribolla Gialla* Josko Gravner

G *Collio Bianco* Edi Keber

H *Vintage Tunina* Silvio Jermann

Trentino

I *Giulio Ferrari* Ferrari

J *San Leonardo* Tenuta San Leonardo

Veneto

K *Amarone della Valpolicella Vigneto di Monte Lodoletta* Romano Dal Forno

L *Amarone della Valpolicella Classico* Giuseppe Quintarelli

M *Amarone della Valpolicella Classico Vigneto Monte Ca' Bianca* Lorenzo Begali

L *Recioto della Valpolicella Classico TB* Tommaso Bussola

N *Soave Classico Calvarino* Leonildo Pieropan

O *Soave Classico Monte Fiorentine* Ca' Rugate

~ALTO ADIGE~

Alto Adige Terlano Pinot Bianco Vorberg Riserva—CANTINA TERLANO

IN RECENT YEARS, Alto Adige has become synonymous with high-quality white wine, and Pinot Bianco will always be the calling card of the region. With its impressive longevity, the Vorberg Riserva is an outstanding example of the great potential to be tapped in the pinot bianco grape.

The Terlano cooperative was founded by a handful of farmers who amassed the fruit from their small mountain vineyards. There are now 105 members of Terlano, cultivating a total of 350 acres of land and producing 1 million bottles of wine a year. Seventy percent of the wine is white and is made, in large part, from pinot bianco and sauvignon grapes, both planted across 70 acres of land. The basic ingredients for making top-quality wines in Alto Adige are the meticulous care of the vines, incentive-driven management, technological innovation in the cellar, business-minded politics, and a well-orchestrated image. But do not overlook the *Kellermeister,* literally, the cellar master. In the cellars of Alto Adige, the *Kellermeister* is not simply an enologist; he is the link between the member grape growers and the management. He is the face of the winery, "the one who arrives first and leaves last," said perfectly by Sebastian Stocker, the *Kellermeister* at Terlano for forty years before passing on the baton to the young, talented Rudi Kofler. Another important name in Alto Adige winemaking worth mentioning here is Giorgio Grai, a well-known enologist and wine blender with an extremely refined palate and unparalleled knowledge of Italian and other European vineyards. Called an "artisan-composer winemaker" by the *New York Times,* Grai established a winemaking style at Terlano that has spread throughout the region.

So much about Alto Adige can be understood by looking at a map. The region is dominated by a sunny central valley that splits off into ten smaller valleys surrounded by some of the most beautiful mountains in the world. Many of Italy's top skiers grew up on the slopes of Ortisei, Selva di Val Gardena, and Corvara Alta Badia. Stelvio National Park, with its 990,000 acres of government-protected land, and the granite peaks of the Dolomites add to the beauty of the local landscape. Although it may come as a surprise to some, grapes grow well in the rocky soil and cold climate. The longevity of the Terlano wines, however, is due primarily to the strong presence of porphyry in the soil of the Terlano vineyards. Porphyry is a light, friable rock that allows water to penetrate deep into the soil, causing the vines to root down to reach it. Historically, grape growers have trained their vines using the pergola system, but recently many winemakers have converted to the simpler Guyot system. At Terlano, however, the pergola system is still used and continues to pay off year after year in extraordinary grapes. Terlano is located halfway between Bolzano and Merano. In many ways, it is the heart of the region and is certainly the heart of Alto Adige winemaking: Nearby are roads leading to Appiano, Caldaro, and other top winemaking *comuni.* Farther away, near the Austrian border, you will find the Isarco Valley, the last frontier of Italian wine and the source of top white wines.

Recent tastings of older vintages of Terlano wines have confirmed the surprising longevity of their white wines. We are talking about wines produced in the 1970s that are perfectly drinkable. In response to a question posted on the winery's website suggesting that the only factor influencing the life of white wine is acidity, *Kellermeister* Kofler wrote that there are many elements that must be balanced to have long-lasting whites, including the soil and the grape variety. Long-lived wines come from vineyards "in harmony," to use his expression, meaning vineyards with low yields and biologically vital soil. Kofler believes that the quality of the Terlano whites is due to the quality of the vines that produce them. The Pinot Bianco Vorberg Riserva is a good example of this balance. The wine has been made exclusively from grapes from this grand cru since 1995, and today production is about 50,000 bottles. The vineyard starts at 1,600 feet above sea level and extends to 3,000 feet: a true mountain. The soil is composed of porphyry, and the yield is about 7,100 pounds per acre. The grapes are vinified at complete maturity and fermented in temperature-controlled large oak barrels. The malolactic fermentation occurs in the barrels, and the wine is left to rest for twelve months on the lees. The rest of the process is a waiting game: Time must play its part. Most often, the resulting wine has a nose of mature apple and pear, chamomile, yeast, and light spices. In the mouth, the wine has good, full body and is at the same time elegant, with crazy sapidity and extremely rich minerality. The incredibly long finish of this wine is likely to leave an even longer-lasting imprint on your palate. This wine speaks to the beauty of the area and emulates the aesthetic appeal of the region.

Alto Adige Sauvignon Sanct Valentin—SAN MICHELE APPIANO

THERE ARE NAMES that when said aloud evoke feelings of fascination in the listener—or in this case, in wine lovers. One such name is undoubtedly Sanct Valentin. These two magical words are worth more than any sensory description of a wine whose popularity has surpassed even that of the cellar from which it was produced: Cantina Produttori San Michele Appiano.

The path to success was long and tedious and began precisely one century ago, when all the main cooperative Alto Adige wineries were started. San Michele Appiano is a co-op based in the Sanct Michele area of the municipality of Appiano, just a bit south of Bolzano. The co-ops were created to help the small local winemakers who were too poor and unskilled to support both the production and the commercial activity on their own. The fruit of the small vineyards that cling to the steep slopes of the Alto Adige mountains at dizzying heights was brought to the cellar of the cooperative for vinification. Until the middle of the twentieth century, life at San Michele Appiano, like that at the other co-ops, was calm and uneventful. The local wine production made no noteworthy jumps in terms of quality—until the arrival of *Kellermeister* Hans Terzer.

Acknowledged internationally as a master white wine producer, Terzer cemented this image with his work in the Appiano cellar. By taking advantage of the location and position of the Appiano vineyards, by cultivating indigenous grape varieties with greater care, and by implementing more modern technology, Terzer was able to create a new name for San Michele Appiano. In just a few years, Appiano became the most well-known winery in Alto Adige. Terzer worked exceptionally well with sauvignon, considered one of the lesser-known and least cultivated white grapes in Italy, possibly because of its difference in flavor from the more common Italian whites. And yet for San Michele Appiano, sauvignon worked wonders. Native to Bordeaux, sauvignon produces the best results in its home region, where it is made into wines of immense character, recognizable for their classic olfactory notes of sage or "cat piss," structure, and longevity. Sauvignon produced in Appiano gained the approval of wine lovers thanks to less "invasive" aromas, extraordinary minerality, freshness, and drinkability. Given the large annual production size and the moderate price, people describe Sanct Michele Appiano Sauvignon as "miracle" wine. While the Sanct Valentin line contains wines made from a variety of grapes, the Sauvignon is the most exceptional. It has almost become a brand, or a symbol of quality, thanks to the hard work of Terzer and the vineyard itself.

In recent years, Alto Adige has affirmed its position as a great wine region of Italy. Today, only some red wines are limited to local consumption and purchased in taverns, where they are often still sold in liter bottles. The white wines are being drunk around the world, rivaling the great whites of Bordeaux, Burgundy, Germany, California, and New Zealand. The 350 members of the Appiano co-op cultivate an average of 2.5 acres of land per head, supplying the cellar with the fruit from 910 acres of vineyard. On the steep slopes of the Adige mountains, pergolas are used to plant vines in the rocky soil. Nowadays, the Guyot training system is being used more and more often— a more modern and quality-oriented approach. Alto Adige was one of the first regions in Italy to map the vineyards, defining individual parcels as crus. San Valentino, along with Schulthaus, Gleif, and Monticolo, are crus where some San Michele Appiano grape growers own property.

Sauvignon Sanct Valentin is produced from grapes grown in the San Valentin cru. Appiano is located at the heart of the classic white wine making zone, on vineyards that are 1,600 feet in altitude. The orientation of this large cru is south to southeast, and, in addition to sauvignon, gewürztraminer, pinot grigio, and pinot bianco are grown here. The key to the success of sauvignon Sanct Valentin is its balance, a characteristic that is likely to surprise first-time drinkers and to impress the connoisseur. Vinified solely in stainless steel, this wine has all the classic notes of Sauvignon, from sage to pepper to tropical fruit. Thanks to the mastery of Hans Terzer, the aromas are held under control, unlike many of the Sauvignons produced elsewhere. The main characteristic of the wine remains its freshness and drinkability, and minerality in later life. (Sanct Valentin has proved to age well.) In the mouth, the wine has a solid structure. It is round and even strong, but Terzer has also been able to maintain a certain "lightness" while also supporting the alcohol content, which is currently at 13.5 percent. The finish is extraordinarily well balanced and remains fixed in your memory.

Alto Adige Valle Isarco Kaiton Riesling—PETER PLIGER KUENHOF

IN ITALY and in the rest of Europe, winemakers often profess thier production methods to be biodynamic or "natural" even if just years before they were treating their vineyards with synthetic fertilizers and pesticides. Worse yet, some of these producers once uprooted vineyards and reshaped entire hills and mountains before turning "natural." By calling their methods "biodynamic," people have discovered a new way to position themselves in the already crowded wine market, even if their key selling point is a mere marketing ploy. Thankfully, substance generally outlives appearance. That is the case with Peter Pliger and his truly all-natural wines, of which this Riesling is the best example.

Peter Pliger and his wife, Brigitte, have built their winery step by step, following the pace of nature. They believe that if you try to speed up or force natural processes, you understand nothing about good viticulture and, perhaps, nothing about life in general. There are no tricks to the trade. Peter is an active practitioner of biodynamic agriculture. Better, he listens to nature and believes in the wisdom of old farmers, who rely on less-invasive homeopathic treatments to care for their vines. Over time, synthetic products and chemicals were eliminated from the soil of Pliger's vineyards and were replaced by earthworms and colorful fields of flowers. The grapes—and ultimately the wine—benefited immensely from this change.

In 1990, Peter Pliger decided, after faithful devotion to the Abbazia di Novacella winery, to purchase his own land and vinify his own grapes. He started off producing only 1,500 bottles, but the results were promising. Beginning in 1991, he began restoring his magnificent *maso*—fortified farmhouses from the Middle Ages—and built a small but modern cellar. Peter and Brigitte's house was built in the eleventh century and is known as Kuenhof. Until two hundred years ago, the property was owned by the bishop of Bressanone and has been in the Pliger family for five generations. The couple now owns around 15 acres of vineyard, from which they produce 25,000 bottles of wine a year. The yields are low because biodynamic farming does not permit pushing the plant to extremes. But this yield is in keeping with the Pliger philosophy. They would never release a bottle that they didn't believe in 100 percent. Their decision to use less invasive and more sustainable techniques was not in the least a marketing ploy.

The Pliger vineyards are truly beautiful, spread across the sunny slopes facing the Isarco Valley a few miles south of Bressanone, also known as Alto Adige Brixen. The grapes are planted between 1,800 and 2,300 feet above sea level. The view from the vineyards is fantastic, and even if this doesn't improve the quality of the grapes, it certainly improves the quality of the lives of the people who work there. Here you can feel that nature, and the earth is alive. The 15 acres of vineyard are as beautiful as they are difficult to work, owing to the impervious location and the steepness of the slopes. A term often used to describe the viticulture at Kuenhof is "heroic." The soil is composed of clayey sand with a large amount of shale. The vineyards are almost all supported by dry rock walls. The Isarco Valley together with the Venosta Valley represent an area of great growth in terms of quality winemaking. Here, white wine grapes like riesling, sylvaner, and kerner are king, because of the cold climate.

After harvest, and once the work in the vineyard is completed, the grapes are quickly transferred into the cellar housed inside the Pliger's farmhouse. The use of technology is limited here as well: The wines do not undergo malolactic fermentation, but rather a simple clarification process before they are ready to be bottled. Peter doesn't believe in physically concentrating the must. He has the maximum respect for the climatic variances from harvest to harvest and does not want to shape the end result in any way. Next to the stainless steel tanks, Peter keeps large acacia wood barrels, used to mature the wine. The winery produces a total of four wines. The wine that best represents the essence of Kuenhof is without a doubt Riesling Kaiton. Depending on the vintage, the personality of the wine may change slightly. Some elements, however, have remained constant over time: There is no doubt that this is an elegant and austere product. Initially, the wine appears edgy, then dynamic, and finally it settles in. Light, yet complex, it has a rich aromatic and flavor profile, yet it is at the same time easy to drink, with a long, sapid finish. This is an uncomplicated wine, created from the great imported varietal riesling, that when combined with the noble alpine *terroir* is destined to create a world-class white wine.

Alto Adige Valle Isarco Kerner Praepositus—
ABBAZIA DI NOVACELLA

ABBAZIA DI NOVACELLA is more than just a winery. The property has special significance for the Alto Adige region, and, moreover, it has spiritual and economic significance for all of northern Italy. It's one of the most prestigious and historic religious institutions in all of continental Europe. Situated in one of the most extreme *terroirs*, Abbazia di Novacella produces one of the world's most beautiful wines: the Kerner.

The first written testimonies of the presence of this abbey date back to A.D. 1142. The abbey was founded by Bishop Hartmann of Bressanone, and since then it has been the seat of an order of Augustinian monks. The most important tasks of the monks were, and still are, to give spiritual guidance, educate children and adults, and conduct scientific studies in various fields, including viticulture. Actually, winemaking at Novacella dates back to the birth of the abbey itself. The monks of the Abbazia di Novacella also left a significant impact on the region. They planted fruit trees, as well as grapes, which contributed to both the local economy and that of the abbey. Today, the Abbazia di Novacella owns over 173 acres of vineyards and produces an average of 600,000 bottles per year. The wine is no longer made exclusively for the consumption of the monks, but is a way for them to finance important philanthropic activities.

Bressanone is a small town in Alto Adige, rich in history and charm. The center of the town is surrounded by medieval walls, from which you can see the tall alpine peaks in the near distance. At first sight, this area appears unsuitable for making wine; however, a number of cold-weather indigenous and international varieties of grapes grow here. Kerner is one such grape. Created in 1929 in the laboratory of a then young German grape breeder, August Herold, kerner is the result of a cross between schiava grossa and riesling. After much work and experimentation based in Lauffen, Germany, Herold finally presented kerner to the scientific world in 1969. The grape was named after Justinus Kerner, a famous German poet who wrote extensively about wine. In Germany, kerner is the eighth most planted grape and covers about 9,880 acres of land. For the moment, in Italy, kerner is found exclusively in Alto Adige, where the cold climate is ideal for this variety. The vineyards at Abbazia di Novacella benefit from dramatic differences in day- and nighttime temperatures, which brings out the aromatic characteristics of this grape. The poor, pebbly soil also contributes to the limited productivity of the plants, and therefore green harvesting is not as essential as with other types of grapes.

Every important winery in Alto Adige is overseen by a resident enologist or *Kellermeister,* and at the Abbazia di Novacella, that person is Celestino Lucin. Beginning in 1994, the wines produced at the abbey have been named, in chronological order, after the abbots of the abbey. The first wine in this new line was called Praepositus ("prior"), in honor of the founder of the abbey, "Beatus Hartmannus," Bishop Hartmann of Bressanone. In 1995, a wine was named after Henricus Primus, the first abbot of Novacella. The monk who is currently in charge of the abbey will have to wait for the 2049 vintage before a wine is named after him. The Kerner is vinified exclusively in stainless steel so that aromas from the wood do not mix with the intrinsic perfumes and flavors of the grape. The wine is rich in aromas of tropical fruit, green tea, and fennel, as well as peach and yellow melon. In the mouth, the wine is sapid, with good structure and alcohol, and has a fruity and aromatic finish. This wine is very food-friendly and appeals to our sensibilities and palates.

Alto Adige Val Venosta Riesling—FALKENSTEIN

AMONG THE profligate apple orchards of the Alto Adige, the glorious vines of Falkenstein are entwined. But rather than the expected local grape varieties, this winery has made its name, and made history, with Germany's fabled riesling.

Franz Pratzner was never supposed to be more than an apple farmer, like his countrymen in the Val Venosta and their parents before them. If he had adhered to the traditions of the region, he might well have lived out his years putting on his lederhosen each morning to chase the crows from his orchards. But Franz is a dreamer, and in 1995, at the young age of thirty-four, he looked around at his land, optimally insulated by the surrounding mountains, and decided to plant grapes among the trees. The soil was perfect, and so was the climate, he reasoned. But once again he bucked tradition, and rather than planting vines of schiava, a varietal popular locally for beefing up the color and structure of lifeless wine, he followed his whimsy and palate to plant riesling vines.

Riesling, which comes from the magnificent Rhine Valley in Germany and finds itself most at home in Austria or the French region of Alsace, has the capacity to develop a fascinating complexity in aroma and taste. When young, it offers scents ranging from lemongrass to citrus fruits, while when aged, it develops the singular fragrance of petroleum. It is a versatile varietal and can result in vastly different wines, from dry whites to passito, ranging from just a little residual sugar to late-harvest bottlings. In Alto Adige, however, Riesling has a unique set of characteristics totally independent of its counterpart in Germany, where the latitude cuts summers short and hampers temperatures from reaching the Mediterranean highs of neighboring Italy. The opulent warmer-climate Rieslings of Alto Adige don't need added sugar to increase their alcohol content.

In fact, the land stretching from Alto Adige's capital, Bolzano, westward to Merano and Silandro has characteristics of both the mountains and the Mediterranean, as evidenced by the cypresses and larches growing side by side. Both trees thrive in the wind currents that travel from the north to the south. The Val Venosta, which begins at Merano and runs east–west, terminates at glaciers in the Alps. The area is predominantly given over to apple cultivation on Mount Mezzodi. In recent years, however, between the villages of Pracines and Silandro, and especially with the creation of the Val Venosta DOC, grapevines are returning to areas that, while once widely planted, have long been neglected. Today, nearly three hundred growers cultivate an area less than 170 acres—a ridiculous figure in relation to other Italian winemaking regions. The valley has an excellent climate for viticulture: There is less precipitation here than in any other region in Italy. In the autumn, the valley is visited by a curious phenomenon: hot, dry winds that dry the grapes while allowing them to mature perfectly, making this region ideal for late-harvest wine. The pronounced difference between daytime highs and nighttime lows further facilitates the growth of high-quality grapes. Finally, the poor, inherently arid, and rocky soil here results in strong mineral intake. And whereas the riesling vineyards of Germany—especially in the Mosel—are planted on gravity-defying slopes, Italians have found that the varietal does just as well on a slightly gentler incline.

It is on just such an incline that Franz Pratzner has built his modern winery, a minimalist structure clinging to the side of a mountain at 2,300 feet above sea level. Somehow, his little nest of stone and cement, visible even from the valley floor below, does not disrupt the harmony of the landscape crisscrossed with grape vines and orchard rows. And Franz—a calm, reserved, almost phlegmatic man with a deep love of the region he calls home—would have it no other way. The winery is overseen solely by Franz. He and his wife, Bernadette, who helps him in the vineyard to allow him more time in the cellar, make Riesling that sings of the land on which it is raised. He does not attempt to impose characteristics on his wines or to force a preconceived typology; instead, he applies the criteria of natural winemaking. After a short maceration, the wine ferments with carefully selected yeasts in wooden barrels—acacia for whites and oak for Pinot Noir. None of the wines undergoes malolactic fermentation, and *bâtonnage* is employed until March.

As a result, the Val Venosta Riesling is a powerful wine, extracted and high in alcohol, yet subtly expressive of its mountainous pedigree. Indeed, the wine is reactive and nervous, with intense acidity, yet it is balanced beautifully by a full body. Similarly remarkable is the longevity of this wine: Despite having been in production for a scant fifteen years, the Falkenstein Riesling—like a fine Italian woman—has demonstrated its ability to mature without showing its age. While young, the wine offers nuances of smoke and peach, then in time it develops notes of flint and petroleum. Its mouthfeel is juicy and harmonious, with a very long, clear finish. Franz's respect for the Val Venosta has been returned to him in spades as he has risen through the ranks to reach critical acclaim in a relatively short time.

FRIULI— VENEZIA ~GIULIA~

Ribolla Gialla—JOSKO GRAVNER

JOSKO GRAVNER'S Ribolla Gialla is a fascinating, very full-bodied white produced using methods and traditions that reach back five thousand years. This wine is an extreme example of tapping in to ancient winemaking history to cull time-tested practices that when paired with modern techniques make for a truly groundbreaking product.

The journey of Josko Gravner has led him from regional pioneer, to antiestablishment rebel, back to iconoclastic oracle. In the culturally and politically fragmented eastern reaches of Friuli–Venezia Giulia, Gravner has drawn and redrawn the parameters of what defines great wine. If asked, he will sidestep the overt issues of greatness and dive headlong into the more conceptual discussion of the very essence of wine: The earth brings forth grapes and humans, who ever so gently guide the natural process of alcoholic fermentation. Josko's quest has been to find truth and purity in the world's oldest created beverage. The road has been filled with challenges, dissenters, and economic uncertainty, and, of course, the most powerful uncontrollable variable of all, Mother Nature.

In Friuli, the northeastern corner of Italy, the gently rolling foothills of the Julian Alps meet the warm, brackish lagoon of the northern Adriatic (Venezia is a noted island in this lagoon), and the magical mixture of the respective cool and warm breezes—along with the *terroir*—create the climatic magic necessary to make long-lived, structured yet aromatic white wines. As a young winemaker, Gravner found himself on the edge of a technological revolution during the 1970s. Temperature control, stainless steel technology, and strict cellar discipline were paving the road for world-class white wines. Gravner blazed his own trail from the advent of this cellar technology, creating varietal wines that screamed of technique and purity, but the elation of this technovinification was short lived. Gravner's quest then turned to creating wines that could live longer—ten, twenty, thirty years—and for that, he took inspiration from the time-honored Burgundian technique of small-barrel fermentation, maceration, and aging. Once again leading the trend, Josko created wines of great complexity and massive structure, infusing the power of new and almost new oak into the minerality, complexity, and finesse that the native soil also imparted on these wines. The resulting white wines took the enological world by storm in the mid- to late 1980s.

Although the world took notice, the achievements in the barrel left Josko Gravner empty. The separation between the wine and the earth created by the interference of the heavy-handed and dominant oak pained his soul. Gravner delved even further into the very origins of wine and fermentation and found himself immersed in the five-thousand-year history of winemaking in Georgia (the former Soviet republic), the cradle of civilization. Josko observed the locals who still imitated the five-thousand-year-old tradition of fermenting and macerating wines in giant clay amphorae that had been lined with beeswax and buried in the earth. Being in the earth, the wine became one with it, and the porous clay facilitated a direct communication between the two as the wine developed in the very *terroir* that gave it life. These wines have been on the forefront and have impacted winemaking in the entire world. I like them because they are whites that walk, talk, and act like reds. You can get the best of both worlds.

Josko's Ribolla Gialla has a golden amber color that reflects the tones of sun-baked grape skins. On the nose, the wine shows candied orange rind, raw honey, and oversteeped tea. On the palate, the wine is tannic and has a powerful grip; it is waxy and bracing, with lingering flavors of dried fruits and nut oils.

Collio Bianco—EDI KEBER

LABELED BEFORE 2007 as Collio Tocai (before European Union legislation required all Italian Tocai to be renamed Friulano), this wine changed the course of winemaking for—as well as the reputation of—this region's now famous grape: tocai friulano.

In Cormòns, the wine capital of the Collio, Edi Keber and his family have vinified tocai for over three hundred years. Beginning in the Austro-Hungarian Empire through several border changes, this family relied on tocai friulano as the most important local varietal to make delicious wines that were always sought after in the marketplace and could distinguish the Keber family through their quality. In the past twenty years, Edi Keber has made his Tocai stand out from the pack, so much so that he's now known for producing what many say is the best Tocai Friulano.

In the 1970s and '80s, during the white wine revolution in Friuli, tocai was largely abandoned for international varietals like chardonnay and pinot grigio. In 1990, Edi left behind the trend of using these international varietals and focused his efforts on only two wines. Tocai would certainly be the focus of the winery and would be vinified both on its own and as the principal base of a blend called Collio. The Collio blend project was to be the future of his winery and the entire DOC region known as Collio. There was certainly nothing new about a blended wine based on tocai (with smaller percentages of ribolla and malvasia istriana). This was the wine of Edi's ancestors and the wine that spoke most clearly of the Collio *terroir* and its people. For twenty years, Edi made Collio and Tocai Friulano. Edi Keber is a man of vision and determination, and it all came together in 2008, when Tocai and Collio Bianco were joined to create one wine with the name Collio. Edi will tell you that the future is to distinguish his *terroir* to the world, rising above the varietal to give the utmost prominence to the specific geographic area that gives birth to this world-class white wine named Collio. Just as Champagne or Barolo say everything about a wine, referencing only a place-name, Edi, and 80 out of 120 producers in the Collio, believe that a wine named simply Collio, crafted from historic and native varietals, is the only future for this tiny border wine region making the best white wines in Italy and perhaps in the world.

This border area has been under the control of the Austrians, Slavs, and Italians. Despite what language was spoken here, the name of the area has always remained Collio. The winemaking tradition in Collio dates back to the Romans, who found that farming grapes was more rational and lucrative than other crops. Wine production was so widespread here that Emperor Maximinus I of Thrax purchased enough wooden barrels and vats from the region to build a bridge over the Isonzo River to transport his troops. This anecdote shows just how important viticulture was to Collio centuries ago. Nowadays, the town of Cormòns is made up of numerous small winemakers, unlike anywhere else in Italy. The two most important areas of the *comune* are Plessiva and Zegla, the latter being where the Keber winery is located. In Zegla, the climate is characterized by intense sunlight, resulting in higher temperatures, which are good for growing Tocai Friulano.

Edi Keber has a very interesting approach to winemaking. He has the utmost respect for the land and cares for his vineyards attentively. Although he has never applied for organic certification, his land is completely natural. Edi's son Kristian joined his father in the vineyard and in the cellar after obtaining a degree in enology. This is good news, because the winery had reached its limit with 25 acres of land to tend to and just one person to do so. In addition to his vintage Collio Bianco, Edi makes a Riserva from the same wine by aging it in barriques for various months and then bottling it exclusively in magnum bottles.

Returning to Collio Bianco, after fermentation, the wine is transferred to cement vats, where it matures slowly. Keber's wines have a decidedly strong and distinctive character. On the nose, Collio Bianco may seem slightly less expressive than other Friulian whites. If you are willing to wait, your patience will pay off: The wine develops notes of carbon, elegant white flowers, and flint. In the mouth, the wine is deep and linear. It leaves your palate very clean, with the desire for another sip. The finish is long, thanks to its refreshing acidity.

Vintage Tunina—SILVIO JERMANN

PRIOR TO 1975, and the emergence of Silvio Jermann, the color of wine for all Italians was red. White wine was for quaffing out of dewy pitchers in Roman trattorias or downing cheap, cold, and fast with linguini and clam sauce while on beach vacation in Campania. In the tradition of his Austro-Hungarian ancestors, Silvio blended five common white varietals to create not a simple farmer's field blend, but a world-class white wine that could stand at the table with all the great whites of Europe and the world. Vintage Tunina—dedicated to Antonia ("Tunina"), Casanova's only non-noble lover—demonstrated the power and potential of Italy's greatest white *terroir,* the Collio Friulano. It was Silvio's unrelenting belief in the ability of his land that gave birth to Italy's first "super white" (blended white wines of fruili), Vintage Tunina.

Field blending was a common practice for the *contadini* (farmers) of eastern Italy, the Austro-Hungarian Empire, and the western Baltic reaches. A father would pass to his son the knowledge of what percentage of which varietals planted all together would make a hardy, tasty, and, most important, annually consistent white wine. In the case of Vintage Tunina, the recipe was mostly chardonnay and sauvignon blanc, with some ribolla gialla, malvasia istriana, and a touch of picolit. These varietals were planted side by side, farmed together, and harvested together to make the *vino della casa* (house wine). Although

Tunina was born in the spirit of this tradition, Silvio took it to another level. He planted the perfect dense vineyard for each varietal, seeking out the perfect exposition and microclimate for each. The varietals were farmed to grow fruit of maximum expression and ripeness, then cofermented with indigenous yeasts. The Tunina field blend is fermented and aged in stainless steel. Neutral and hyperclean, the stainless environment coaxes the nuances of *terroir* and varietals as brushstrokes in a masterpiece. Tunina is not a wine that speaks of the varietals that compose, it, but a wine that screams of its birthplace and Italy's greatest white wine region, Friuli–Venezia Giulia.

Indigenous Italian varietals like arneis, vermentino, and trebbiano can make beautiful, simple, and regionally significant wines throughout the Italian peninsula. Only in the hillside vineyards of the Carnian Alps do both indigenous (friulano, ribolla gialla, malvasia istriana, picolit) and international (chardonnay, pinot grigio, sauvignon blanc) varietals give birth to white wines of massive structure, cellar evolution, and complexity. Vintage Tunina announced great Italian white wine to the world and now serves as its beacon.

The Collio vineyards hug the foothills of the Italian Alps and drain into the ancient floodplain of the Isonzo river basin. The highly porous, claylike marl of the hills gives way to the more fertile soil of the gravel-laden river plains. Millions of years of snowmelt and mountain erosion have brought the mountainous minerality ever closer to the northern Adriatic lagoon. As the damp air and warm humidity fill the Isonzo river basin and crawl up the Collio hills every day, the Adriatic Sea brings the hot Mediterranean climate always closer to the alpine mountain peaks. At nightfall, the pendulum swings again, as the northern alpine winds charge down the Carnian mountain valleys and drive toward the seas. This daily climatic struggle creates the high thermal diversity (hot days and cold nights) that is essential to crafting aromatic, structured wines that will live for decades. The harmony and dissonance created by the interaction of *mare e monte* ("sea and mountains") creates the perfect climatic conditions to make world-class white wines.

It has been said that the greatest wines in the world are white. A vintage Champagne offers delicacy and refinement, Rieslings bring us power and spectrum, while a white Burgundy is the essence of balance, giving everything and little all at the same time. Vintage Tunina, in its almost four decades of evolution, encompasses important elements of all these great white wines while remaining uniquely Italian. The nose, when young, is pure minerality accented with white flower and chamomile aromatics that in time evolve into clover honey, tangerines, wet straw, and apples. Having tasted some examples from the early 1980s, I can say that the nose in perfect maturity will give sweet notes of ripe pears, piecrust, and caramel candy. The palate is a study in balance, beginning with laserlike focus and persistence and evolving into broad palate viscosity and glycerin. Again, in full maturity the palate becomes almost waxy, with the perfect determination to support delicate and evolved flavors.

~TRENTINO~

Giulio Ferrari—FERRARI

IN THE WORLD of sparkling wine, Champagne rules supreme. Champagne drinkers often are not even willing to consider non-French sparklers. The Ferrari sparkling wines made in Trento, Italy (no connection to the famous car maker in Modena), however, can be compared with the greatest Champagnes of Marne and Reims and are, in my opinion, the greatest sparkling wines made in Italy.

The history of the Ferrari winery dates back to 1902, when Giulio Ferrari, at the young age of twenty-three, started producing sparkling wines in his hometown of Trento. (It is interesting to note that Trento, until 1918, the end of World War I, was part of the Habsburg Empire. So in effect, the winery was born under the rule of the Austro-Hungarians.) Guilio was a well-rounded, determined young man, who spent time in various French wine regions and studied enology in Montpellier— a rare decision for his time. Returning to his native Trento, Guilio applied the knowledge and skills he learned abroad to growing chardonnay, a typical French grape variety, in Italy. His intuition and understanding led him to plant the noble varietal in the mountainous areas of Trentino, which allowed him to make wines with great breed and character. It was these early efforts of vinification and careful selection of varietals that began to cause Trentino's star to shine in the enological world.

Giulio's intuition did not stop at the chardonnay grape, as he also had a vision of the future and began looking for a partner who would be able to sell wines from an unknown area in a commercial market. That man was Bruno Lunelli, an important wine salesman who had become enchanted with Ferrari and the wines from Trento. Beginning the collaboration in the 1950s, Bruno was able to develop this little prewar winery into a modern, prolific, state-of-the-art wine company. Bruno was also able to place the wine throughout the *enotecas* (wine cellars) and restaurants of Italy by creating the new category of Italian sparkling wines. Ferrari wines, branded and molded after their French counterparts, were until recently referred to as *champenoise*—a term that has been replaced with *metodo classico* because of conflicts with European branding laws.

The Ferrari winery is now in its third generation, managed by Bruno's sons, who have entered into the family fold and continue the tradition of making great sparkling wines. In just fifty years' time, Ferrari has gone from a small family winery to a global leader with its products, thanks to the winery's obsessive commitment to making quality sparkling wines at all price points. In fact, Ferrari is one of those rare examples of an Italian winery that owes its overall success to a confluence of many factors. It is omnipresent and clearly the market leader; it has high production (7 million bottles in 2009) but maintains a high level of value. Ferrari has also become a beacon for wine production for the entire region of Trento because of how it manages relationships with grape farmers. In contrast to the traditional buy-sell market driven by grower-buyer relationships, Ferrari's philosophy is to become intimately involved with the grape growers, providing them with technological and viticultural expertise but, most important, paying them above-market prices, as they recognize that the farmers are the foundation of any great winemaking ambition.

Giulio Ferrari Riserva is made of 100 percent chardonnay grapes, and if we were in Champagne, it would be called a *blanc de blanc.* The chardonnay grapes that are used to make "Il Giulio," as the wine is affectionately called by its many admirers, are grown in one select vineyard called Maso Pianizza. This cru is located in the *comune* of Trento, at an altitude of 1,600 to 2,000 feet, with a south-southwest exposure. With this altitude and exposure, the vines are able to bask in the gentle late-afternoon sunsets, which offer intense luminosity and a gentle, extended day of sunshine. The harvest begins in late September when the grapes have the proper level of acidity and aromatic peak. The challenge in growing chardonnay for great sparkling wines is the inherent balance between retaining acidity and achieving maturity. Acidity gives sparkling wines their structure and backbone, but ripeness contributes delicacy and finesse. The unique alpine microclimate of Trento allows these grapes to achieve both these targets. The grape-growing regions of Trento, located on the foothills of the northern Italian Alps, benefit from temperature variance. In the day, you have a continental climate with daytime highs, and at night, you have an alpine cooling effect. The dramatic changes in the temperature result in chardonnays that are aromatic, yet highly structured and complex. The soil is rocky, unfertile, and unproductive, allowing for viticulture of great concentration and depth of flavor.

In the Italian enological landscape, Giulio Ferrari stands alone. Inspired by the long-standing tradition of Krug and Cristal, Giulio Ferrari is released only after ten years of slow aging, with the longest contact with the lees of any Italian sparkling wine. The base wine for *metodo classico* is chardonnay that is fermented then aged in barriques, after which it is bottled to await secondary fermentation, which takes place in the bottle. The second fermentation is the defining moment for a *metodo classico*, when residual sugars, acted upon by yeast, continue to ferment in the bottle until the wine becomes completely dry (all the sugar is fermented in alcohol). The bubbles *(bolicini)* captured in the wine are a by-product of the in-bottle fermentation. At this point the wine is disgorged (opened to removed dead yeast sediment and add the dosage) and corked with a final closure. It's then ready for additional aging. Extended cellar time allows the wine to come to completion and harmonizes its many olfactory and tactile sensations. It is amazing that a wine of such power, structure, and vigorous vinification can also express such delicacy and finesse.

The wine has an elegant perlage (tiny bubbles) with delicate mousse. On the nose, the wine shows notes of honeydew melon, ripe peaches, hazelnuts, and bergamot, but also hints of yeast, lavender, orange blossoms, and musk. It is fresh and creamy on the palate and draws you in for a second taste with its delicacy and harmony. The true essence of Giulio Ferrari comes to fruition after time in the cellar, where the more obvious sensations develop into subtleties of a world-class sparkling white wine. It is certainly worth tasting some of the legendary vintages, such as 1983, 1986, and 1989, which might convince even the most skeptical Champagne lover of Italy's ability to produce great sparkling wine.

San Leonardo—TENUTA SAN LEONARDO

AN ANCIENT ESTATE, Tenuta San Leonardo is where a wine was first successfully made in the Bordeaux style—a wine that yet manages to be an utterly clear expression of what can only be Italian *terroir*. A fascinating creation, San Leonardo wine is a surprise for an Italian wine and is truly a gem of Italian winemaking.

The Italian city of Avio isn't much more than a pit stop on the busy autostrada that leads from Lake Garda up to the mountains toward Brenner Pass and the center of Europe. However, for many years now, the city has become well known among Italian wine lovers. Avio is home to one of the most beautiful wine estates in all of Italy, Tenuta San Leonardo. Made in the blending tradition of great Bordeaux, San Leonardo, the winery's flagship wine, is a beacon of classic winemaking and style in the Italian landscape.

The estate is rich in history and inspiration. A monastery was constructed shortly after A.D. 1000, precisely where the heart of the wine cellar now stands. Queen Theodelinda and Authari, king of the Lombards, were married here, and Prince Philip, son of Emperor Charles V, stayed at the monastery in 1549 on his way from Ratisbon to a political meeting regarding the fate of Europe. In more recent years, Austria asked for an armistice at the estate during World War I, and during World War II, the Germans set up their counterspy headquarters at the Tenuta.

However, the name most closely linked to Tenuta San Leonardo is without a doubt Guerrieri Gonzaga. This noble family has owned the estate since 1784 and has transformed it into what it is today: a spectacular villa surrounded by a park of age-old trees and 740 acres of land, 50 acres of which are planted with grapes, and an entire medieval hamlet. The estate is open to the public and is a truly peaceful place to escape for the day. In fact, few other places in Italy highlight the beauty of the winemaking process more than Tenuta San Leonardo. The winery helped to revive the entire Trentino region enologically, which historically was overlooked by much of the wine world. In this area, even more so than in others, the phylloxera plague devastated local wine production, causing most of the farmers who resisted emigration to change profession. Those who remained faithful to winemaking were forced to undertake new roads and techniques.

Carlo Guerrieri Gonzaga, the current owner of the estate, was forced to reinvent a tradition and did so with great courage and foresight. Thirty years ago, he decided to focus on growing international grape varieties. His idea was not to dishonor the native varieties like marzemino, teroldego, and lambrusco, but to produce top-quality wines. To rebuild his family's devastated vines he needed to introduce grapes imported from France at the beginning of the twentieth century. Carlo Guerrieri Gonzaga's project was clear, yet rash at the same time: He wanted to re-create Haut Médoc in the middle of Trentino, using the same grapes (cabernet sauvignon, cabernet franc, and merlot) and the same winemaking methods while seeking to make the same wines in terms of quality. In just a few years, his project was complete: San Leonardo, the signature wine of the estate, is clearly a Bordeaux-style wine. Yet the goal was never to make a classically French wine in Italy, but to give the French grapes the stamp of Trentino. Drinking San Leonardo is not like a trip to Bordeaux. It is like visiting Trentino, a place that has been carefully cared for by people who have given it new traditions and where the words "new" and "old" exist in perfect harmony. We can say that Tenuta San Leonardo is the most Italian château and that San Leonardo is the most French of the authentically Italian wines.

Tenuta San Leonardo is an old hamlet located on the left bank on the Adige River, the second-longest river in Italy, running from Trentino down through Verona and continuing out into the Adriatic Sea. The province of Verona and the Lagarina Valley, which borders Lake Garda and the Lessini Mountains, is rich with vitcultural history, not all of which has been pleasant. The phylloxera plague irreversibly changed the land and the winemaking traditions of the region. Beginning in the twentieth century, farmers began to plant cabernet (both sauvignon and franc) and merlot, as well as chardonnay and pinot noir. Here in this area, the cabernet and merlot grapes, classically associated with Bordeaux, outperformed the Burgundy varietals because of the clayey, occasionally sandy soil. A good number of the wines produced here are particularly rich in anthocyanins, which contribute to the polymerization, or stability, of the wine. After one year of aging, these wines reach anthocyanin levels of 50 percent, versus 35 to 40 percent in Bordeaux, or versus the Italian average of 30 percent. The Guerrieri Gonzaga family has promoted the characteristics of the wines produced in Avio throughout Italian institutions and beyond. The denomination "Campi Sarni" is an additional label used to distinguish between these wines.

Few wineries represent their wine the way Tenuta San Leonardo does San Leonardo. The wine was first produced in the early 1980s by the celebrated Italian enologist Giacomo Tachis. Together with Carlo Guerrieri Gonzaga, Tachis employed the "60-30-10" approach used in the old wineries of Avio: The numbers are the respective percentages of cabernet sauvignon, cabernet franc, and merlot, which went into the first vintages of the wine and became the calling card of San Leonardo. If the vintage is less than par, the wine is not released, as was the case in 1984, 1989, 1992, 1998, and 2002.

The average age of the vines is now around thirty years, with the oldest plants growing next to the newer, experimental vines. The grapes are trained using both the Guyot and *cordone speronato* systems at 2,000 to 2,500 plants per acre, with an annual yield of 11,000 to 13,200 pounds. Harvested between September and October, the grapes are then destemmed and softly crushed. The three types of grape are fermented separately and left to macerate on the lees and are punched down daily. After aging in large vats, the three types of grapes are moved to separate, previously used French barriques, where they remain for twenty-four months. Immediately before bottling, the three cultivars undergo a careful examination, barrique by barrique, and are then blended together. Carlo Ferrini, another recognized enologist, oversees the entire process, including the eighteen-month aging of the bottles before release.

San Leonardo has a dark, deep ruby red color with hints of garnet. Its perfumes are intense, crisp, and distinctive, comprising spices, berries, and the classic "green" notes of the French varietals. In the mouth, the wine is full, round, warm, and extremely elegant. Its structure is never overbearing; rather it is mild, elegant, and noble. San Leonardo has a long finish and can be described as a rare jewel, destined to sparkle for years to come.

~VENETO~

Amarone della Valpolicella Vigneto di Monte Lodoletta—ROMANO DAL FORNO

MORE THAN ANY other winemaker, Romano Dal Forno is the incarnation of the will and talent needed to build an enological territory. Recognized by critics across the globe and idolized by wine enthusiasts, Dal Forno built his own legend around the wines of Valpolicella, evolving together with the land. His wines are singular, the very essence of how fruit and earth can merge in a glass. Exaggerated, emotional, and demonstrative—love or hate them—these wines leave an impression.

The region of Valpolicella is located just north of Verona, and the name of the territory derives from the Latin phrase *vallis polis cellae* ("valley with many cellars"), which serves as a testimony to the duration of the local winemaking tradition. As far back as history books go, Valpolicella has been known for Recioto, its sweet wine made from dried red grapes. Since the beginning of the twentieth century, Recioto has had to compete with the region's other more interesting and complex wine, Amarone—also made from dried grapes, but vinified in such a way to make it dry, not sweet.

Amarone is in a class of its own. It is not a sweet wine, even though it is made from grapes that are naturally dried after the harvest, and it is not a classically dry wine, because it has the alcohol content of a passito and the structure and complexity of a great red, made for aging. Amarone is simply beyond comparison, even if the wine's recent success has resulted in imitation, even outside of Europe. Valpolicella is traditionally made with corvina, molinara, and rondinella grapes, with a portion of the grapes being dried.

Until the arrival of Romano Dal Forno, no one produced wine exclusively from dried grapes. His winemaking technique set the standard for today's Amarone—all this from a man just over fifty years old who has been making wine for less than a quarter century. Thanks to Romano, the concept of winemaking in Valpolicella has been irrevocably changed. Product of a family of farmers in Illasi, a small town northeast of Verona, Romano was influenced at a young age by another prince of winemaking in the Veneto: Giueseppe Quintarelli. This "old master" of Valpolicella suggested that Dal Forno adopt certain innovative practices. As a result, Romano changed the blend for his Amarone, replacing molinara with an older grape variety, oseleta; he increased the density of his vineyards to 5,200 plants per acre; shifted his yield to 11 ounces of grapes per plant; and made *appassimento* (a natural grape-drying process) his focus. While Dal Forno clung to centuries of tradition in the vineyard, in the cellar, he decided to radically change his approach, employing the most up-to-date technologies. Romano Dal Forno built his identity around this incredible, and in some ways crazy, mix of ancient and ultramodern winemaking techniques.

Dal Forno's wines and philosophy, however, do not represent all that is Valpolicella. Romano decided to remain a small producer while everyone around him rushed to increase their volumes: In 1997, he produced the same number of bottles of Amarone (15,000) that he does today, while in the same amount of time, the rest of Amarone's annual production went from two to three million bottles to more than ten million. This giant leap in production stirred leading questions about the overall quality of these wines, which had become very popular, and therefore in high demand, almost overnight. The same goes for the price: Dal Forno continued to increase the price of his wine, while his fellow Amarone makers reacted to the fierce competition and the production of lesser-quality wine by reducing their prices. The point is, Amarone costs more to produce than any other wine in Italy (in terms of commercially comparable wines and not niche products). Primarily, 85 percent of the volume of the grapes is lost during the *appassimento* process. In addition, by law, the maximum grape yield is restricted to 18,500 pounds per acre (however, in the case of the best producers, we are looking at half of that). Also, the *appassimento* of the grapes requires spacious drying rooms, or *fruttai*, and because of the long aging times, wineries must hold on to their inventories for years. Although $500 may seem like a lot to spend on a bottle of Dal Forno, it's defensible, since demand is high, production is low, and the quality is unquestionable.

Located northeast of Verona and bordered on the east by the Adige River and to the north by the mountainous area of Lessinia, Valpolicella is undoubtedly one of the top Italian winemaking regions. Compared with other areas, the topology is varied and fairly complex. It is important, however, to distinguish between the so-called classic Valpolicella, a complex of vineyards at the production zone, and the "enlarged" Valpolicella. The first stretches west of Verona and is subdivided into three distinct strips of land: a flat plain along the river, a hilly zone (the most famous), and an area at the base of the mountains at 2,000 feet above sea level. The second is located east of the city and is considered less esteemed, even if this is where the Romano Dal Forno cellar and vineyards are located. The nearby valleys and steeply sloping hills lead down to Lake Garda, which, at 117 square miles, is the largest body of freshwater in Italy. The warm lake breezes interlace with the cool winds of the Lessini Mountains, creating microclimates ideal for growing grapes, olives (Lake Garda olive oil is some of the best), and cherries. In the autumn and winter, the weather facilitates the miracle of the natural *appassimento* of the Amarone grapes. From a morphological point of view, each valley has a unique structure, but they all have a good amount of clay in the topsoil and a rocky layer five feet below the surface. There are around 1,600 companies that make Amarone and 395 official *fruttai* for the *appassimento* process.

Amarone della Valpolicella Vigneto di Monte Lodoletta comes from the cru of the same name, cultivated with extreme care and attention. The grapes are harvested between the third week of September and the first week of October and are then placed in wooden trays or bamboo racks inside the airy drying rooms. These rooms are often located on the top floors of the wineries to make better use of the natural ventilation. The bunches are left in the *fruttai* for three to four months, under constant watch and rotation. Once they have reached the right level of dryness, or *asciugatura*, and concentration of sugars, the grapes are pressed. The must is left in contact with the skins for a long time. The fermentation process occurs in wooden barrels, where the must is left to mature for twenty-five months before bottling and the final aging process.

There is no pleasure so fine—at the same time, no challenge so great—as to describe an Amarone of Romano Dal Forno. A pleasure because it is a privilege and joy to describe such an important, almost legendary wine; a challenge because words often do not do justice to the sensations and emotions that tasting a bottle of this wine can ignite. The result of Dal Forno's exquisite care is "absolute," statuesque, extreme wine. Dal Forno's Amarone has a unique personality. It is so highly extracted and high in alcohol (over 17 percent) that one might expect to have to chew, rather than drink, the wine. Although the wine may seem destined to be too big and heavy, it has an incredible grace and an almost silky elegance. Before one can truly enjoy the wine's nose—composed of dried fruit, sweet spices, herbs, and graphite, just to name a few—the bottle should be uncorked a couple of hours prior to tasting so that the wine can open. In the mouth, the wine is opulent and balanced with a long finish. Monte Lodoletta can be enjoyed young, but is better after a decade of additional aging. The question is, after having made the investment to acquire a bottle, are you really willing to wait to drink it?

Amarone della Valpolicella Classico—GIUSEPPE QUINTARELLI

IT IS SAID that Valpolicella, the most famous winemaking area of the Veneto and one of the most prestigious in Italy, has both a myth and a legend. If the myth is young Romano Dal Forno, a name fixed in the minds of all Amarone lovers for the extraordinary wine he produces, then the legend would be Giuseppe "Bepi" Quintarelli, the patriach of Valpolicella and a winemaker who for the last half century has made immortal wines. His wines are ultrapersonal expressions that defy any preprescribed discipline or typicity. They are unique and all his own.

More than a winemaker, Bepi is a sculptor: He believes that great wines already exist within great grapes and that the farmer's only job is to bring them out, or to shape what nature has already created. Like Michelangelo's approach to marble, Quintarelli molds his grapes into a wine that already exists within. Although this explanation may seem simplistic, or perhaps overly poetic, in reality, there are decades of experience, tests, successes, and failures that support the concept.

Giuseppe Quintarelli was born into a family of generations-old farmers. His father exported wine to the United States beginning early in the twentieth century, and the company recently celebrated its one-hundred-year anniversary of selling wine across the Atlantic (originally, the red wines of Valpolicella traveled across the ocean on ships in 50-liter barrels). In 1924, the Quintarelli family moved to Negrar, a sort of grand cru of Valpolicella, with the highest concentration of great vineyards in the region and, therefore, the highest number of famous wineries. After World War II, Bepi took over control of the company and has since shaped it into what it is today. Shy, humble, patient Giuseppe Quintarelli's focus is on the important, traditional red wines of Valpolicella, namely, Amarone and Recioto. His wines have become the canon by which all other Amarone and Recioto are judged.

Quintarelli wines are complex, multifaceted, cerebral, enthralling, and much more. There is no better way to get to know Quintarelli than to go and visit the winery in person. But do not expect an avant-garde cellar: There isn't even a street sign indicating that you have arrived. And don't think that Giuseppe will be free to explain every detail of the production process or the organoleptic properties of his wines. It is quite possible that he will be busy harvesting cherries and not even give you a nod. (However, shortly afterward, he is likely to guide you through the best wine tasting of your life.) With his wines, don't pretend to know something about the various vintages: Every wine has its own story. In fact, more often than not, crazy old Bepi only releases his Amarone in exceptional vintages, using the grapes from lesser vintages to make a new wine or blending them with other wines. The prophet of tradition, the master of the Veneto, Quintarelli is not opposed to innovation and experimentation: In his vineyards, you will find cabernet, nebbiolo, and other grapes not native to the region. Grown in the soil of Negrar and touched by the hands of Bepi, these grapes have become extremely *veneti,* or rather *quintarelliani.*

Valpolicella is a vast area of land located north of Verona. Traditionally, the local economy was based on agriculture, but in recent years, construction and the growth of light industry are threatening the landscape and the natural biodiversity. Valpolicella is considered one of the nerve centers of Italian economic growth and is being referred to by the economists as "the miracle of the northeast." Thankfully, there is still room for agriculture, and for winemaking in particular. The recent Amarone boom on international markets has helped producers attract new financial investments. Valpolicella has two hearts: one in the hills of the northernmost part of the region that borders the Lessini Mountains, and the other in the flatlands of the south that extend to the gates of Verona. From an enological point of view, the division exists between the so-called classic Valpolicella and the "larger," or extended, denomination. The former is located northwest of Verona and, as the name suggests, is the historical center of winemaking in the Veneto. The latter, located to the northeast of the city, is a more recent production zone and is generally considered of lesser regard. Quintarelli is located in the classic area of Valpolicella, Dal Forno in the extended area. Negrar, among the many winemaking zones, is the most appealing and is surrounded by small towns with long-standing winemaking traditions. The Quintarelli cellar is tucked away on the hills of Cerè, a beautiful area of vineyards and olive and cherry trees. In place of street signs, once you have found the road leading to the cellar, you will find a handwritten plaque saying *"Prego suonare il clacson"* (Please honk). This is the stuff of legends.

Giuseppe Quintarelli's Amarone della Valpolicella Classico is made from the careful selection of grapes from the vineyards surrounding the cellar, in the part of Negrar known as Cerè. The soil is karstic and without much water, adding to the peculiarity of Quintarelli's wines and those of Negrar in general. The density of Giuseppe's plants per acre almost never reaches that of the other great modern winemakers. The grapes he uses to make Amarone are the usual suspects: corvina, molinara, and rondinella. Harvest takes place between the last ten days of September and the first ten days of October, even if the recent changes in microclimate (increased dryness and higher temperatures) have led to earlier harvests. Once harvested, the grapes are placed on mats and left to dry, taking advantage of the natural ventilation of the area in which they are located. The grapes are then pressed and macerated for two to three weeks. The must is fermented until it has just the right amount of sugars and alcohol. The wine is aged in wood for a very long time: To make Amarone—but also to make Recioto—Bepi is willing to wait a lifetime.

All this results in a memorable wine: ruby red with granite tones, which open slowly. Quintarelli Amarone is rich in ripe fruit, spices, herbs, blackberries, and jam. The wine then takes on notes of cognac, rum, and even whiskey. In the mouth, it is huge, chewable, yet enjoyable. It is both sweet and dry, creating a balanced contrast. There is enough acid to guarantee a long, long life. This Amarone is inimitable and unmatchable, one of the greatest wines in the world!

Amarone della Valpolicella Classico Vigneto Monte Ca' Bianca—LORENZO BEGALI

AMARONE, more than any other wine in the world, is directly affected by human hands. The agricultural vintage and then the drying period are a double jeopardy that every bottle of Amarone must conquer to achieve greatness. When the great producers of the Veneto, like Lorenzo Begali, can master both disiplines, the result is great Amarone.

The history of Lorenzo Begali best represents the evolution of a territory as complex as Valpolicella, the enological heart of the Veneto. The company is relatively new (everything started with Lorenzo's father around World War II), and until twenty years ago, when Lorenzo took over, the winery was producing decent, but not particularly significant, wines that were often sold in bulk. Following the regional trend of improving winemaking technique, studying the land, and focusing on the needs of the market, Begali released wines that were increasingly more interesting from one year to the next. Today, Begali is one of the most important names in Valpolicella, and his reds, especially Amarone and Recioto, have ranked at the top of their respective categories. Today, Lorenzo's children, Giordano and Tiliana, are following in their father's footsteps. Here, the success of the territory was not determined by a grape variety or the combination of variety and *terroir,* but by human beings and their ability to make the best of what nature gave them.

In Valpolicella, the landscape is a mix of flatlands and hills that are not particularly blessed for quality winemaking. In fact, the territory was at risk of becoming one big cement parking lot, given its vicinity to Verona and the industrial hubs of northeastern Italy. There are no legendary vineyards, and the traditional grapes (corvina, rondinella, and oseleta) are certainly not fantastic varieties. These grapes are hardly known outside the Veneto and are most often blended with other wines. It therefore took research, determination, and time to create a winemaking tradition in Valpolicella. Amarone is the product of technique rather than technology or nature. Although some people may turn up their nose at a "forced" product, Amarone has an extremely clear and well-defined character. It is made from fermenting dried grapes, resulting in a wine that is neither sweet nor dry. However, it is not a "midway" wine, and this is the real miracle: Amarone is an excellent red wine in terms of character, harmony, and elegance. There is nothing like it in the world. Although winemakers are trying to imitate the process in other countries and continents, the original has yet to be beat. Valpolicella has discovered its jewel and has had to learn how to maintain it. It will be important that the quality of the wine remains high and that it keeps close ties to the area in which it is produced. With wineries like Begali, producing only a few thousand bottles from only 20 acres of land, it seems that the level will be kept high.

The cellar of Lorenzo Begali and his family is located in San Pietro, in Cariano, a small town north of Verona, halfway up the road to Lake Garda. The location is in Valpolicella Classica, the heart of the region's quality wine culture. Like all of the other areas surrounding Verona, San Pietro has both plains and hills. The Begali vineyards are located in both areas, but the best grapes—those used to produce Recioto and Amarone—come from the hills. The family has the good fortune of owning some of the best plots on the hillside of Castelrotto, one of the most promising areas. Monte Ca' Bianca is another hillside vineyard that is proving to be well suited to native grape varieties. The soil is primarily clay, with a presence of rocks: The area of San Pietro where the Begali cellar is located is called Cengia ("protrusion"), like the rocks found on the hillside.

Amarone della Valpolicella Classico Vigneto Monte Ca' Bianca by Lorenzo Begali is the modern evolution of tradition. Of course, this is all relative. In Valpolicella, when we refer to "tradition," we are referring to the region's recent history. Unlike Amarone, Recioto (a sweeter version of the wine) has been made here for centuries. Amarone as we know it today is a newer wine; however, production can already be classified into traditional and more modern styles (as with any great red wine, depending whether the wine is aged in small or large wooden barrels). Begali is a modernist, and his vision of Amarone is supported by his work in the cellar and the vineyard. In Monte Ca' Bianca, he blends corvina (40 percent), corvinone (35 percent), rondinella (20 percent), and oseleta (5 percent), all of which are included in his Amarone. After careful selection in the vineyard, the grapes are harvested from the end of September until the beginning of November and are placed in a *fruttaio,* or storage house, where they are kept to dry until January or February. The grapes are then pressed, fermented, and aged in small barrels.

The wine is kept in wood for four years, then aged in bottles for an additional eight months. The result is a deep and multifaceted wine: On the nose, the wine expresses notes of ripe fruit, no doubt a result of the *appassimento* (natural drying process). In the mouth, the wine is big, but not excessive, and has both silky and acidic veins running through it. The wine has a really long finish, which is perfectly balanced with the fruit. This classic Amarone will serve as a guiding light for future generations of Valpolicella winemakers.

Recioto della Valpolicella Classico TB—TOMMASO BUSSOLA

TOMMASO BUSSOLA WILL tell you that his Recioto is one of the most intriguing Italian sweet wines. Rare and with indefinable elegance and power, his style of wine is born from tradition and necessity, not innovation and fancy.

By 1986, wine was being made in every region in Italy. Practically anyplace that would produce good-quality grapes was covered with grapevines. But if we were to choose a true enological phenomenon of the past ten years, it would have to be Amarone. Until 1996, barely 4 million bottles of Amarone were produced per year. By 2004, production had already risen to 12 million, and in 2006, it reached an all-time high of 16 million bottles. Making Amarone is not a simple task, nor is

Amarone easy to drink. Amarone is made from dried fruit and can reach alcohol levels of 16 percent or more. The huge increase in consumption is primarily due to the marketing of the wine and the region. Few people know that Amarone is actually a by-product of another wine called Recioto, which is made in the same part of the Veneto using the same grapes: corvina and rondinella. Recioto is a sweet dessert wine with residual sugar levels easily reaching 100 grams per liter. Before modern technology came along, sweeter wines could age for longer periods of time than wine with less sugar. Compared with the dry red wines of the area, which had to be much more stable if they were to last through the years, the high levels of residual sugar in Valpolicella wines preserved quality longer. Before the advent of sulfites and many of the other physical and chemical techniques that are now available to make winemaking much more simple, Recioto was really the main wine of this area. Now the production is in the hands of some of the great masters of our time who have contributed enormously to the increasing quality of the wine. The production of Recioto didn't increase exponentially like that of its "younger brother," Amarone. It is very complicated and expensive to make Recioto. Additionally, it is equally as complicated to reach a large market and ultimately too expensive to compete on a global level. What we have, therefore, is a rare wine, reserved for special occasions.

Tommaso Bussola is the son of peasants who had very little property to their name. He began working in 1977, at a very young age, at his uncle Giuseppe's winery. The first years of his apprenticeship were dedicated to unraveling the secrets of the land and, above all, mastering winemaking in the *appassimento* (natural grape-drying) style. Only in 1983 did he decide to take the big step of beginning to grow grapes on his own property. He began to apply the same philosophy that he learned from his uncle, but at the same time he began to experiment with some new techniques. Around ten years passed before Tommaso decided to create his own cellar and began barrique-aging his wines for the first time. Tommaso's more modern wines are labeled with his initials, TB, while the wines produced in the traditional manner bear the initials of Tommaso's uncle, BG. Bussola's wines captured the attention of international wine critics, starting a new chapter in the life of the winery.

Valpolicella is one of the most celebrated *terroirs* in all of Italy. It is located to the northwest of Verona and is flanked by the Adige River on the west and the Lessini Mountains on the north. The heart of Recioto production is centered in the zone of Valpolicella Classica and comprises the *comuni* of Marano, Fumane, Negrar, Sant'Ambrogio, and San Pietro in Cariano. Some of these give rise to the three main valleys of Fumane, Marano, and Negrar.

As mentioned previously, Recioto is a rarity in the Italian wine world. It is certainly a wine that is born in the vineyards, but the more delicate phase of its inception occurs during the drying process. This step takes place on mats, which are placed in the area where the best grapes are grown and specifically selected for the production of this wine. The fruit needs to be selected with extreme care because during the production of Recioto, the grapes need to dry for a long period, usually around seven months. During this time, the grapes must not get moldy. The area is very humid, so to help dry the grapes, winemakers use fans and dehumidifiers to prevent the risk of losing an entire harvest. After these seven months, the grapes can finally be pressed and made into wine. Fermentation often lasts more than fifty-six days and occurs at 57 degrees Fahrenheit. The complexity and cost of the production of Recioto are best expressed by one fact: 40 pounds of grapes are needed to produce 1 liter of this wine! By the end of fermentation, the wine has an average of 260 grams of sugar or more per liter. The wine finishes its time in the cellar in French barriques for an additional thirty months. The resulting wine is not easy to describe because of its complexity. On the nose, there are clearly notes of chocolate, fruit preserved in alcohol, and cherry jam. In the mouth, there is an explosion of taste and sweetness, balanced by firm tannins and sugar that cleans the palate and leaves an impression of great complexity.

Soave Classico Calvarino—LEONILDO PIEROPAN

SOAVE IS a noble wine made from what many consider to be a slacker grape varietal, garganega. At its best, Calvarino can become a honeyed nectar, with a firm mineral grip and a classic peachy sweetness that is typical of Soave.

When talking about the great wine Soave, the conversation inevitably turns to the Pieropan family: Leonildo and his wife Teresità. Their commitment to quality wine production helped save and reestablish the reputation of a wine zone that was awash with supermarket-quality products.

The Cantina Sociale di Soave cooperative dominates at 80 percent of the local annual production, and produces inexpensive wines by working with economies of scale. In the co-op system, farmers are paid by yield. Overcropping results in diluted wines that are devoid of any sense of *terroir* and lack individuality and regional character. The Pieropan family has countered these trends by producing single-vineyard Soaves that can sit on the tables of great restaurants and age in cellars along with the greatest white wines from around the world. Top Soaves join a limited crew of new Italian white wines that evolve in complexity and become better with age.

However, Soave's reputation as a cheap white wine can be traced back to the Italian economic boom of the 1950s and '60s, following World War II. Pieropan was up against strong consumer prejudice when he set out on his mission to create a great Soave, as most people thought of Soave as a simple, characterless yellow water. Leonildo Pieropan and Teresità decided to focus their attention on improving the quality of their wine by lowering yields to one-third that of industrial winemakers. The price of their wines ended up being significantly higher than that of their competitors, but in the end, the winery's positioning proved successful, and wine-loving Italians started to have a renewed interest in Soave.

Leonildo, "Nino" to his friends, is generally quiet and reserved.

However, when Nino senses that there is someone passionate about wine in his presence, he will easily open up to talk about his two favorite subjects: the *terroir* of Soave and his wines. And if you are very lucky, he will invite you to one of his famous vertical Soave tastings: Even his ten-year-old vintages have remarkable minerality, freshness, and perfume. In recent years, Nino and Teresità's two sons, Andrea and Dario, have joined them in the winery. With the increase in employees, Nino decided it was time to grow the company, and in 2003 he purchased 25 acres of land in Illasi, part of the Valpolicella area. His new vineyard was planted with native grape varietals: corvina, rondinella, and croatina. In the future, the Pieropan name will also stand for a great red wine, which, at least in the beginning, will not be an Amarone because the vines are too young. Over the years, the winery has grown to produce 400,000 bottles annually. Compared with their magnificent Calvarino, the Pieropan Soave Classico La Rocca, which is aged in different-sized wooden barrels for twelve months, is a little less fresh, but richer and fuller bodied. Their bestseller is their basic Soave, which in terms of the price-to-quality ratio can't be beat.

The Pieropan winery is located in the center of downtown Soave, in the fifteenth-century Palazzo Pulici. By climbing the two sets of stairs inside the palazzo, you arrive at a terrace that looks out onto the Soave hills. From here you can see the historic Pieropan vineyards: La Rocca is located behind the walls of the castle of the medieval city, and Calvarino is to its left. Calvarino is one of the most famous crus in Soave, thanks, for the most part, to Leonildo Pieropan. The Pieropan winery owns 18 of the 74 acres that make up the cru, and their property is divided among separate parcels, all of which get excellent exposure to the sun. Calvarino is located at the base of Mount Foscarino, at 330 to 500 feet in elevation. The soil is rich in clay and silt, in addition to a good amount of calcareous sediment. The name Calvarino comes from Mount Calvary, where Christ was crucified, and is a testimony to how difficult it must have been for farmers to work on its steep slopes. The land was purchased in 1901 by Leonildo's grandfather, who was also named Leonildo. Until the 1970s, Calvarino was not planted exclusively with grapes, as it is now; there were also fruit trees that provided sustenance to the local farmers. The hillside has been terraced to deal with the steepness, and the grapes are grown using a unique training system known as *pergola veronese*. Leonildo was the first person to prune his plants to have branches, or shoots, on both the left and right sides. He also trims his vines back quite heavily. At the beginning, Pieropan was considered totally crazy for letting bunches of grapes fall to the ground before harvest, but his training and pruning system have paid off.

I decided to focus on Calvarino, rather than on Soave La Rocca, for one very simple reason: Calvarino is a clearer, more pure expression of Soave because it is not aged in wood. The aromas and flavor of the wine reflect the spirit of the *terroir*. This wine is aged in stainless steel and cement and has impressive aging potential: A bottle of 1986 Calvarino can easily be enjoyed today. The wine is known for its minerality and perfumes of warm, wet earth and mountain musk. The wine also has an acidic, fresh vein. Over time, the wine develops salty, marinelike notes, as well as those of citrus and hazelnut. In the mouth, Calvarino is fresh, but never heavy, even in the hottest vintages like 2003. After a decade, Calvarino ages with grace and can be enjoyed after years in the cellar. Some of the top vintages to look for are 1996, 1986, 1985, and 1978.

Soave Classico Monte Fiorentine—CA' RUGATE

A MODEL SOAVE and truly *terroir*-driven wine, Soave Classico Monte Fiorentine is a wine that recalls with startling clarity the characteristics of the place where it was produced. Elegance and clarity prevail in this wine, a Soave made for modern times.

The charming town of Soave is a lovely little hamlet dominated by a medieval walled fortress. Tucked behind the city is the hilly region where the best vineyards are located, most of the Ca' Rugate vineyards among them. Perched atop the Rugate hills, the grapes are cultivated traditionally, using both the *pergola veronese* and the Guyot training systems. The land is basaltic, rich in clay and silt. The main grape grown here is garganega, and though its origin isn't clear, it grows as well as any indigenous varietal in this part of the Veneto. Garganega is a very productive and fairly disease-resistant grape that, for a long time, was planted by farmers looking to produce large quantities of wine. Only recently have winemakers focused on the quality of the grape in the vineyard, which they do by increasing density, pruning the vines, and using more modern training and trimming systems. Garganega also produces good results when dried: Recioto di Soave (an excellent version of which is produced by Ca' Rugate) is an emergent sweet Italian wine. Made for generations, the sweet Soave, like the dry version, has improved in quality only in recent years.

The increase in quality is due in part to the dynamic entrepreneurs and capable communicators of the Tessari family, fathers of Ca' Rugate. The name of this Veneto-based company has circulated widely in various countries and continents for the past twenty years. Yet in spite of its far-flung fame, the winery remains firmly entrenched in the traditions of its home in the Soave *terroir* and in the history of the Tessari family, who made it what it is today. It all began in the early twentieth century with Amedeo Tessari, who owned a small *osteria* (inn) that retailed wines, including his own. In the 1980s, Amedeo's son, Fulvio, expanded the operation and increased productivity, giving birth to the commercial family winery Ca' Rugate, which they named after a cottage in the hills out of which the winery first operated. Fulvio's sons, Amedeo and Giovanni, later joined the team at Ca' Rugate. Today, though the cellar has been relocated into a new and more functional building, the winery is still very much a family-owned and -operated business: Young Michele Tessari, who recently started working for the family, is the fourth generation of Tessaris in the wine profession. In four generations—a mere century of activity—the Tessari family business has grown from a provincial *osteria* to a supermodern winery with 124 acres of land able to produce almost half a million bottles per year.

Along with the growth of the winery came the growth of the entire region of Soave; unfortunately, the latter's growth was not as consistent, nor as well managed. To some degree, Soave fell prey to nearsighted winemaking politics that, in the past decades, caused production to balloon without any attention paid to quality. For a while, Soave was popular plonk, inexpensive and easy to drink. The vineyards, often located in the best parts of the plain near the Milano-Venezia autostrada, did not impart any special qualities to the garganega grapes, long considered a second-tier variety. Ca' Rugate, however—along with a few other ambitious wineries in the region—reversed the trend of quantity over quality, working with academic institutions to study the land and exploit particular aspects of the *terroir* while controlling others. They also acquired new techniques and technology—a necessity for white wine production. In just a few years, they were able to achieve what hadn't been done for decades. They discovered that garganega could be considered one of the noble native Italian grape varieties, able to rival friuliano (formerly tocai) in Friuli, verdicchio in Marche, and greco or fiano from Campania. Soave turned out to have great potential in terms of *terroir*. The rest of the progress came as a result of investments and courageous winemakers, who were willing to create a brand that continues to be popular in Italy and abroad, but that has shed its negative image for one of quality and excellence.

Having now found its home at the top of wine rankings for years, Soave Classico Monte Fiorentine is one of Italy's great white wines. (Ca' Rugate also produces an admirable Soave called Monte Alto, which is aged in wood.) Monte Fiorentine has uncommon grace, lightness, freshness, and unbeatable harmony. The wine is made solely from garganega grapes harvested from vineyards with a small percentage of volcanic rock in the soil, which is able to give the grapes and the wine an additional touch of minerality. The grapes are harvested late in the season, around mid-October. The yield does not exceed 8,000 pounds per acre—a surprising figure compared with the 13,000 to 18,000 pounds per acre typically obtained by larger wineries. Fermentation occurs in stainless steel tanks at 60 to 64 degrees Fahrenheit and continues for ten to fifteen days.

Soave Monte Fiorentine is dark straw-yellow in color. On the nose, the wine has an extraordinary freshness, intensity, and harmony: There are notes of minerals, exotic fruit, citrus, and sage. In the mouth, the wine is round, juicy, and fragrant. Despite never having seen wood, this wine has body, well-balanced acidity, and structure. The long finish reveals aromas of fruit and the wine's great complexity.

NORTHWEST ITALY

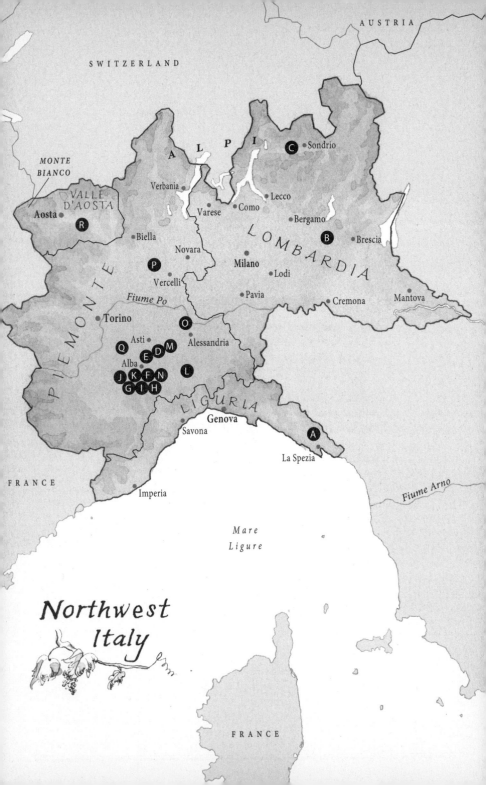

AUSTRIA

SWITZERLAND

*MONTE
BIANCO*

MONTE
BIANCO

*VALLE
D'AOSTA*

Aosta

R

A **L** **P** **I**

Verbania

Varese

Como

Lecco

Bergamo

C Sondrio

Brescia

B

L O M B A R D I A

Biella

Novara

P

Vercelli

Milano

Lodi

Pavia

Cremona

Mantova

Fiume Po

P I E M O N T E

Torino

Asti

O

Q

Alessandria

E **D** **M**

Alba

L

J **K** **F** **N**

G **I** **H**

L I G U R I A

Genova

Savona

A

La Spezia

Fiume Arno

FRANCE

Imperia

*Mare
Ligure*

Northwest
Italy

FRANCE

LIGURIA

A *Cinque Terre Sciacchetrà* Walter De Batté

LOMBARDIA

B *Franciacorta Cuvée Annamaria Clementi* Ca' del Bosco

C *Valtellina Sfursat 5 Stelle* Nino Negri

PIEMONTE

D *Barbaresco Vigneto Brich Ronchi* Albino Rocca

E *Barbaresco Santo Stefano Riserva* Bruno Giacosa

F *Barolo* Bartolo Mascarello

G *Barolo Brunate* Roberto Voerzio

F *Barolo Brunate–Le Coste* Giuseppe Rinaldi

F *Barolo Cannubi Boschis* Luciano Sandrone

H *Barolo Ginestra Vigna Casa Maté* Elio Grasso

H *Barolo Gran Bussia Riserva* Aldo Conterno

I *Barolo Lazzarito Vigna La Delizia* Fontanafredda

J *Barolo Monprivato* Giuseppe Mascarello e Figlio

H *Barolo Ciabot Mentin Ginestra* Domenico Clerico

K *Barolo Rocche dell'Annunziata Riserva* Paolo Scavino

I *Barolo Vigna Rionda Riserva* Massolino

G *Barolo Vigneto Arborina* Elio Altare–Cascina Nuova

L *Colli Tortonesi Bianco Costa del Vento* Vigneti Massa

D *Langhe Nebbiolo Sorì San Lorenzo* Gaja

D *Barbaresco Vigneti in Montestefano Riserva* Cantina Produttori del Barbaresco

M *Barbaresco Rombone* Fiorenzo Nada

N *Barbaresco Vigneto Starderi* La Spinetta

O *Barbera d'Asti Bricco dell'Uccellone* Braida

P *Gattinara Vigneto Osso San Grato* Antoniolo

Q *Roero Mombeltramo Riserva* Malvirà

VALLE D'AOSTA

R *Valle d'Aosta Chardonnay Cuvée Bois* Les Crêtes

~LIGURIA~

Cinque Terre Sciacchetrà—WALTER DE BATTÉ

THIS LITTLE-KNOWN DENOMINATION and wine so clearly bring to light the very essence of Italy's regionality in wine production. The nose of this sweet wine starts off with Mediterranean brush and green sage, then evolves to show dried dates, golden rasins, and vanilla notes. This wine is the real nectar of the Mediterranean coastline.

Walter De Batté is a man of impossible undertakings. In a world that seeks comfort and ease, Walter has chosen one of the most difficult jobs out there: winemaking in the Cinque Terre. Although he could have easily become a factory worker or naval officer in La Spezia, he decided to throw himself into the precarious world of wine. Walter, however, is steadfast, firm in his beliefs, and even a little crazy, like the rest of the people who have chosen to live in the Cinque Terre, an area made up of five small towns, all clinging to the rocky Ligurian coastline. Here, the mountains—and we are talking about the real mountains—meet the sea, without any interruption.

In the past, the inhabitants of this area were not fishermen, but farmers. Afraid of the mighty Mediterranean, many people feared being swept out to sea. Therefore, most decided to work the land: an extremely difficult task because the hills sloped at more than 45 degrees. Farmers had to build large, strong terraces to define the local landscape. Today, there are almost 4,000 miles of dry-stone walls, from the sea to 3,200 feet above. And to top it all off, the soil itself was rocky and of poor quality. These crazy farmers were forced to retrieve sand from the beaches and carry it on their backs in large baskets up to their fields to enrich the soil. It is for good reason that the sister monument of the UNESCO-protected Cinque Terre National Park is the Great Wall of China. Until the end of the seventeenth century, around 4,000 acres of the area were covered with vineyards. The number has since dropped to 200 acres. The only cultivated areas are those near roads, because the rest of the land is too expensive and too physically demanding to harvest.

Walter is fighting a battle to keep agriculture alive in the Cinque Terre. The abandonment of the terraced fields, or *fasce* as they are called locally, has led to the erosion of the soil and landslides. But thanks in large part to the hard work and tenacity of Walter, critics across the globe have started paying attention to the wines of the area. Walter has made a name for himself for his revival of the bosco grape variety, the use of barriques, and the length of time his must spends on the lees. At first, Walter's fellow winemakers turned their nose up at his "inventions," but within fifteen short years, he has proved himself right. Walter's wines are rich in minerality and salty notes, followed by floral and fruity aromas. The price of one of his bottles is definitely higher than white wines produced from vineyards that are easier to cultivate. And justly so. To harvest his grapes, Walter and his staff have to climb up and down seven hundred to eight hundred stairs carrying 25-liter containers full of hand-harvested grapes on their backs—quite a time-consuming and exhausting feat.

Walter Batté's winery is located in downtown Riomaggiore—the fifth and farthest south of the Cinque Terre—on one of the town's picturesque narrow roads, called *carrugi* in Liguria. It can be reached only by foot and only by climbing a good number of stairs. A bunch of grapes painted on the winery's small wooden door and the aroma of wine perceptible from the street tips off the attentive wine lover that there is another world behind that door and that it is not someone's home. The barriques and fermentation vats are located on the ground floor of this unassuming building. Inside his cellar, Walter produces no more than 3,000 bottles annually, with grapes from his 5 acres of land divided among eighteen different parcels of Riomaggiore. These parcels vary in size from microscopic (a row or two of vines) to 5,400 square feet. In addition to the already difficult agricultural conditions, in recent years the vineyards have also been under the attack of wild boars. The boars present a real threat, especially because they multiply like rabbits and are protected by the Italian national park service. On multiple occasions, Walter was unable to produce his wine because of the hungry beasts. What may have seemed like a dream at the beginning— that of reviving the agricultural traditions of the Cinque Terre—has proved to be a real challenge.

One of the first difficulties Walter encountered when he set out to make wine in the Cinque Terre had to do with the grape variety he selected to grow: bosco, which means "forest" in Italian. Bosco is a wild variety, native to Italy, that had practically disappeared over the years. The local farmers were reluctant to plant bosco because of its low productivity and acidity, tending to prefer simpler grapes like vermentino and trebbiano. But Walter and a few other pioneering winemakers understood the value of this variety and its strong bond to the territory. Most of the soil in the Cinque Terre is composed of rock; there is very little fertile earth. Bosco grapes, however, are accustomed to the rocky soil and have a wild, yet very resistant, character. They need just a little water to survive and do not suffer from the sea air that leaves salty deposits on the leaves of the plants. Bosco was born to live and thrive here.

Sciacchetrà, Walter's wine made from bosco grapes, is an anthem to the land: sapid, minerally, and containing strong perfumes of rosemary and Mediterranean flora. In the mouth, the wine's sweetness is never cloying, but evocative and refreshed by fierce and juicy acidity. With annual production limited to 1,000 bottles a year, Sciacchetrà is a rare gem for lovers of sweet wines.

~LOMBARDIA~

Franciacorta Cuvée Annamaria Clementi—CA' DEL BOSCO

BOLLICINE ("little bubbles," or sparkling wine in Italian) are the way that Italians celebrate life. Annamaria Clementi is stylistically and quantitatively the pinnacle of sparkling wine enology in Italy. To offer a *brindisi* ("toast") with this captivating and rare wine is a celebration of the highest order.

Not only is Ca' del Bosco one of the most exciting agricultural-based companies in Italy today, the winery is at the heart of an enological phenomenon. As is often the case, the founder of this winery, Maurizio Zanella, is a dreamer. Despite his young age, Maurizio is responsible for the incredible success of a cellar, a denomination, and a style. Located in the middle of what once was a chestnut forest (*bosco* means "forest" in Italian), Ca' del Bosco produces 1 million bottles of wine a year from 370 acres of vineyards that are cared for like noble gardens. Today this area, known as Franciacorta, is one of the most prestigious winemaking regions in Europe.

In this corner of northern Italy near Lake Iseo and only 30 miles from Italy's industrial and financial capital, Milano, you feel as if you could be on the other side of the world. Maurizio's mother, Annamaria Clementi, had purchased a small farmhouse in Erbusco during the mid-1970s. Little did she know that in just a few years, her son would transform the property into a forward-thinking winery known throughout the world. While he was still very young, Maurizio traveled to France and returned home with a plan: Franciacorta had the morphologic, climatic, and historical characteristics needed to make a new wine region. Beginning in the 1970s, Maurizio Zanella and a group of fellow producers/followers sought to reproduce France's Champagne region on a much smaller scale. Since Maurizio first planted his vineyards with chardonnay and pinot noir at 4,000 plants per acres, and now with his recent improvements in the cellar, the Ca' del Bosco has always produced top-quality Italian *champenoise*-style sparkling wine.

Locally, Franciacorta has come into its own, known, together with Trentino, as the most famous region in Italy for the production of Spumante, or *bollicine* (because of those "little bubbles"). In contrast to 300 million bottles of Champagne produced in France each year, Franciacorta releases only 10 million botles of Spumante a year. This is still an impressive number, considering how recently Italians started making wine in Franciacorta, the much smaller size of the area, and the constant growth in production. (Production in the region has gone from 2 million to 10 million bottles in just fifteen years.) On the national scale, Franciacorta has become a key player in the vast world of Italian sparkling wine and is even competing with the top white and red still wines. Trentino, the small mountainous region to the northeast of Franciacorta, produces 8 million bottles of Brut a year and has become synonymous with great sparklers like those of Ferrari, perhaps the most famous sparkling wine producer in Italy along with Ca' del Bosco. In addition, sparkling wines are made in Piemonte (Asti Spumante) and in the Veneto (Prosecco). The former is made with sweet, aromatic moscato grapes and is without a doubt the most famous Italian Spumante in the world. Asti is strong in numbers (over 70 million bottles produced per year), but less so in quality, but still enjoyable. Prosecco, on the other hand, is produced in lesser quantities (40 million bottles per year) and is experiencing great success in recent years, thanks to its price (which is lower on average than other Italian *bollicine*), to its novelty, and to the seriousness of some Prosecco producers.

In just forty years, Franciacorta has become synonymous with the highest levels of sparkling wine. Although this miracle may seem haphazard at first glance, the revolution was based on the work of a few good men. Maurizio Zanella is credited with having the foresight of what the region would ultimately become. He grew up on the land—following the footsteps of his mother, Annamaria Clementi, to whom he dedicated the company's top wine—and knows it well. Maurizio also benefited from his admiration for the world's top sparkling wine producers, especially those of France. In addition, Maurizio arrived at a time when the Italian wine scene was changing, allowing him to experiment with high-quality production techniques.

Franciacorta is an area of soft, rolling hills and is a break from the monotony of the Pianura Padana, a plain divided down the middle by the Milano-Venezia autostrada, a passage of important economic value to northern Italy. Although grapes have been grown in the region for centuries, the vineyards were completely reinvented in the 1960s and '70s specifically for sparkling wine production. Zanella experimented freely and was able to create a new "bubbly" phenomenon. He decided to focus both on top vineyard management and on employing technology in the cellar, allowing for the birth of a true sparkling wine culture. Despite the name of the territory (and the wines produced there), France (Francia in Italian) has nothing to do with it. The name comes from the Latin term *curtes francae,* which is the name of the small communities of Benedictine monks established in the High Middle Ages in the hilly area near Lake Iseo. The monks were excused from paying taxes to the lords and the bishop for the transport and sales of their products because they taught farmers how to cultivate the fields.

Annamaria Clementi is the most famous Cuvée made by Maurizio Zanella's winery. Only the best of his chardonnay (about 50 percent), pinot bianco (25 percent), and pinot nero (25 percent) grapes, harvested from the various crus and only in the best vintages, end up in this symbolic wine. The yield of his vines is 4,900 pounds per acre, and their average age is thirty-eight years. The harvest occurs early in the season, around mid-August. The base wines are made from the alcoholic fermentation of must from a portion of the top grapes (about 40 percent in terms of weight), and this fermentation takes place inside small oak barrels, where the wine rests for about seven months. The best bases, coming from at least ten different selections of must, are blended to make the Cuvée. The wine then spends a long time in the bottle (sometimes many years), in direct contact with the yeasts, in the Zanellas' spectacular cellar, regulated to be a constant 54 degrees Fahrenheit. At the time of disgorging, 7.5 milliliters of *liqueur de tirage* is added, giving the wine its almost mystical character.

When opened, a bottle of Annamaria Clementi has an extremely fine, persistent, and continuous *perlage*. The aromas vary from just-ripe white fruit to white flowers and vanilla, with woody notes that develop into mineral tones. In the mouth, the wine is luxurious, rich in fruit, with good acidity that balances out the wine perfectly. The finish seems endless and irresistibly seductive.

Valtellina Sfursat 5 Stelle—NINO NEGRI

DESCRIPTIONS OF the unusual wines of Valtellina always draw a direct parallel to the subtlety and power of red Burgundy. Like their French counterparts, these wines can be elusive and shy, but when they sing, few others can hold a note in comparison.

Valtellina is a lesser-known wine-producing zone of Italy that is definitely an area worth exploring because it is an extreme viticultural enclave. This mountainous region, located at the northern end of Lake Como, is a captivating place, and it has recently been discovered by international celebrities, including George Clooney, who owns a house there.

As unlikely as it may seem, Valtellina is gaining growing attention not only for its celebrity guests, but for its wine. This region is one of the most difficult places to cultivate grapes because the altitude of the region reaches 2,600 feet; it is covered with steep, sloping hills; and the soil is poor for general agriculture. The winter temperatures are harsh, and the summers are extremely hot. Despite all this, farmers—preceded by a community of monks—have grown grapes at the foothills of the Alps for centuries. They literally built "flying vineyards" on the sides of the mountains, shored up by miles of dry-stone walls. They were able to win a battle against nature, giving life to an important winemaking tradition.

Nino Negri is one of the pioneers of modern viniculture in Valtellina. In 1897, he created a company, based in the small town of Chiuro, that specialized in the sale of locally produced wines. He attributes much of his initial success to his proximity to the wine-friendly Swiss market. A couple of decades later, his son Carlo expanded the company, giving it a more market-driven structure. In the 1960s, the company was sold to Winefood, a Swiss enterprise, which slowed the growth of the brand. Then in 1986, GIV (Gruppo Italiano Vini), the highest-grossing Italian wine company, made up of fifteen Italian wine producers, came to the rescue, buying the estate from the Swiss. Thanks to the financial means and interest of the group, the Nino Negri estate became the pride of Valtellina, and it introduced the world to the two enological strengths of the area: the nebbiolo variety of grapes and the *appassimento* technique. The first may surprise most Italian wine lovers because the grape is usually associated with the Barolos and Barbarescos produced in Piemonte. However, in Valtellina, nebbiolo grows as well as it does in the Langa. In fact, some people say that the variety originated in Valtellina and was then "lent" to the Piemontese. It is hard to believe that this variety, which has often proved unfruitful outside of northwest Italy, thrives in the harsh habitat of Valtellina, where it is known by the name chiavennasca. In terms of the *appassimento* technique—an ancient practice of the drying out of the grapes before vinification—Nino Negri was the local winery that officially began this process in modern times. The farmers would commonly leave the grapes on the plant until they were overripe or, better yet, place them into special drying rooms called *fruttai,* where they would remain until December—sometimes until after Christmas—before being pressed. It is a risky and expensive technique because of the high percentage of loss in the product due to drying out the grapes, but it has made the wines of Valtellina special, giving them a territorial identity and complexity.

Valtellina is a part of the region of Lombardia and is bordered on the north by the Alps. On a clear day, you can see the snow on the Adamello Mountains in the distance. The land is tough, bitter, and at times outright harsh: Italians recall the tragic images of the 1987 avalanche, when a month of torrential downpours turned the valley into a huge lake and led to the death of more than fifty people. Yet the area is beautiful and good to those who treat it with respect, as have the generations of farmers who have lived off the land. The valley spreads from the east to the west and almost seems to follow the sun: The vineyards, all south facing and well protected from the cold winds from northern Europe, get sun and heat for a good part of the day. The results are generally good, but Valtellina has its fair share of problems: A part of the valley is referred to as the Inferno because of the total isolation of the vineyards during certain times of the year. People are hesitant to manage cellars here and in some of the other remote areas of the valley. In addition, water is scarce; it is not uncommon to see the roots of the grapevines sprouting out of the soil and nestling in stone walls and rocks. Despite these conditions, the grapes have flourished, and viticulture has become an integral part of the landscape and economy. The indissoluble bond between humans and nature is based on the winning combination of adaptation, persistence, experience, and the land. The rest is nebbiolo.

Valtellina Sfursat 5 Stelle had the difficult job of being the flagship wine of not only Nino Negri, but of the entire winemaking region, which turns out volume, quality, and communication efforts like few other places in Europe. The wine, however, has certain attributes that support its position. To begin with, 5 Stelle is made from a well-known grape variety, nebbiolo. Second, Casimiro Maule is the enologist, director, and soul of Nino Negri. Born in Trentino, but from Valtellina by adoption, Maule was able to bring out the best expression of the grapes in terms of quality. Only the top grapes of the top harvests end up in

5 Stelle: Here we are talking about a rigorous selection from vineyards in the "Inferno," Grumello, and Fracia, all of which are sort of "grand crus" all owned exclusively by Negri. Harvested between the end of September and early October, the grapes are left to dry until mid-December then vinified with a twelve-day maceration. After sixteen months in new Allier and Nervers barriques and a careful blend of the base wines in the bottle, we have before our eyes—or better, under our noses—a deeply granite-colored wine with incredibly fresh aromas, as well as notes of balsamic vinegar and a delicious blending of crusty bread, licorice, chocolate, pepper, and dried fruit. In the mouth, the wine is concentrated and strong with notes of vanilla and soft tannins. The name Sfursat stands for *sforzato* (forced), referring to the drying of the grapes, a well-calculated, forced maturation of the bunches. In Valtellina, this wine became a typology, and the typology became a DOCG, the top classification in terms of quality according to Italian legislation. A well-deserved title for a wine of great merit.

~PIEMONTE~

Barbaresco Vigneto Brich Ronchi—ALBINO ROCCA

THE BARBARESCOS OF today are expressed in extremes. Some offer a more modern style of superextracted fruit and sweet toasty oak, while others are more traditional, offering accentuated tannins and more earthly olfactory sensations. Albino Rocca's Barbaresco Vigneto Brich Ronchi is the perfect marriage and balance of these expressions.

The history of the Rocca family is similar to that of many other winemaking families in Piemonte. They started off as *contadini* (farmers who sold their grapes to bottlers or cooperatives) and over the course of a few decades came to be known as some of the world's greatest winemakers. Albino Rocca is the head of the operation as we know it today. Before him, however, came both his father and his grandfather, who cultivated grapes and other fruit that was sold at the local market or kept for self-consumption. Albino deserves the credit for expanding the farm and for allowing his son, Angelo, to continue growing and evolving the winery through the 1990s. It was during this period that the major change occurred. Riding in the wake of the other great *nebbiolisti* (nebbiolo grape growers) of the Langa, Angelo started down a path of conceptual and material renovation, beginning with the vineyard, then moving to the cellar, and eventually arriving at a new vision of the market and the company's image. Angelo remembers the first prunings of the vines well, and he still talks about it today as a both a physical and psychological "cut" (green harvest) with the past. His decision to restrict production resulted in healthier, fuller, richer grapes.

In the cellar, however, Angelo was not overtaken by the mania of modernity. Although he did decide to use barriques, which round out and soften the rigid tannins of the nebbiolo grapes destined to become Barbaresco, he never denounced tradition or the tie with the noble values of yesteryear. Angelo, for example, never stopped using *botti grandi* (large oak casks), the quintessential element of old-school red wines, which bring out the essence of nebbiolo: tobacco, tar, and notes of the forest bed. His decision not to take either road exclusively ultimately led to wines of great balance. He himself is an emblem of this balance between tradition and modernity, customs and experimentation, a sense of limits and the continuous growth into new markets and outlets. Another word describing Angelo is "elegance." His two very well-known Barbarescos—Vigneto Brich Ronchi and Vigneto Loreto—are a perfect equilibrium of power, coming from the nebbiolo grape and style and from Angelo's hand in every phase of the winemaking process. Then nature adds her part, giving the wines from this property very robust and decisive, yet refined and almost silky, notes. Today the Albino Rocca winery produces a little over 100,000 bottles a year, most of which are red. In addition to the nebbiolo-based wines, Rocca makes a distinctive Barbera and Dolcetto. The winery has also experimented in white wines, including chardonnay and moscato, a symbolic variety of the Monferrato hills that begin just a few miles above Barbaresco.

The Albino Rocca winery is located in the *comune* of Barbaresco, not far from the ancient tower that looks down on the Tanaro River and is the sentinel of perhaps the most famous and most beautiful vineyards in Italy. The landscape is unique: The land is literally covered in vineyards that follow the wavy line of the hills that open up onto numerous natural amphitheaters, basins, and valleys. The undulation allows for cold air to pass across the land, creating many diverse microclimates. Barbaresco is one of three *comuni* in the Barbaresco denomination. Barbaresco alone covers almost half the entire wine production area. The *comune* is known for having "created" the wine to which it has lent its name, thanks to the Produttori del Barbaresco cooperative. For historical, cultural, and environmental reasons, this area of the Langa is one of the most prestigious outposts of regional and national viticulture. The presence of many noble wineries and the dynamic promotion of the Barbaresco brand has made the area a true sanctuary for serious wine lovers.

Barbaresco Vigneto Brich Ronchi—together with the other Angelo Rocca Barbaresco cru, Vigneto Loreto—is the shining star and most award-winning wine of the cellar. The grapes for this wine come from a swatch of land located directly under the Rocca family farmhouse, on the eastern side of the main hill that cuts across the *comune* of Barbaresco from east to west. The sun exposure, like the soil, is fairly homogenous, facing east to slightly southeast. Traditionally, this vineyard has produced very interesting wines, characterized by their profound aromas, good structure, and elegance. In the case of Brich Ronchi, the grapes, which come from a forty-year-old vineyard, never yield more than 5,300 pounds per acre and are regularly harvested at the end of September. The fermentation and maceration occur in stainless steel and normally last four to five days in a temperature-controlled environment. The wine is aged for eighteen months, half in barriques (50 percent new, 50 percent used) and half in 2,000-liter barrels. The result is wine with a deep and alive ruby/granite red color and notes of spices, tobacco, black fruit, and leather on the nose. In the mouth, it seduces with its soft tannins, balances with strong structure and, at the end, the sensation of length and harmony.

Barbaresco Santo Stefano Riserva—BRUNO GIACOSA

ALONG WITH being one of the greatest wines of Italy, Barbaresco Santo Stefano Riserva is also one of the most important because it captures the evolution of the process and business of winemaking in the region of Piemonte, and in the specific area of Alba.

Bruno Giacosa, with his reserved character and perfect manners, is truly adored by his fans. They love him for his style, his history, and the place he carved out for himself in the wine world. Son of a grape broker from Neive, young Bruno spent his childhood on long walks with his father through the vineyards of Barolo and Barbaresco, acquiring with time an unparalleled knowledge of the Langa territory. When he took over the family business in 1960, Bruno found himself in possession of a well-established and diffused wine brand. The Giacosa family was known for being able to purchase the best grape lots on the market. During the 1950s and 1960s, in a time when winemaking was a very different business, the financial and personal relationships between farmers and brokers was paramount in the quest to make great wine. This was the real balancing point of the entire economic system of the Langa region.

For decades, high in the sunny slopes of the hills between Barolo and La Morra, Serralunga and Monforte, Barbaresco and Neive, the wine industry was polarized between an army of owners of small vine-yards who did not have the means and skills necessary to turn grapes into wine, and a few bottlers who were usually expert, shrewd men who knew the territory and would comb the farms looking for the best grapes to take back to their cellars, turn into wine, and sell. On the market, the grapes of Alba, the capital of the Langa, became legendary. The area was considered to be overflowing with precious bunches of nebbiolo, barbera, and dolcetto grapes just waiting to be bought. How-ever, the farmers often had to wait and pray that their grapes would sell for a good price. Sometimes they were disappointed, especially when they had to return home with unsold grapes that risked going bad and becoming unusable.

In this environment, Bruno Giacosa was able to carve out a position for himself as the go-to man: His respect for the work of others, com-bined with his determination to produce memorable wines, allowed him to gain the trust of the owners of the top crus in Barbaresco and Barolo. His unique position shielded him—at least in part—from the great changes of the 1970s. In that decade, and even more so in the following one, a large number of farmers began to vinify their own grapes, opening tiny cellars, first producing demijohns and then moving on to bottle their own wines. The immediate consequence was an unanticipated shortage of quality grapes for the brokers, who were therefore forced to take a different approach, often purchasing land rather than grapes. Giacosa did not miss a beat and bought vineyards in areas like Asili, Rabajà (Barbaresco), and Falletto (part of Barolo), which were already considered famous, but were made legendary under Giacosa. However, Bruno Giacosa has remained almost the only winemaker in Piemonte who is still able to make great wines with other people's grapes. The faith and respect that small, longtime growers have for Bruno has allowed him to continue to acquire grapes from fantastic vineyards, like the cru of Santo Stefano di Neive. In fact, his Barbaresco Santo Stefano is certainly one of the most admired wines in the entire Italian landscape. The attributes of this wine are a mirror reflection of the genius this man embodied. The wine is a perfect, unmatched blend of knowledge of the land, experience, and technical ability. As an example of his gentle and generous disposition, when Giacosa was asked why he decided to stop purchasing the top vineyards in the Langa, he said, "Because they didn't want to sell!"

Another striking characteristic of Bruno Giacosa and his company is the extraordinary, and to some degree incomprehensible, ease with which he is able to make excellent wines in both Barbaresco and Barolo. The best explanation for Giacosa's success in both regions is an understanding of the *terroir*—or rather *terroirs*—that is timeless and trendless. Although wine lovers and producers alike often debate whether Giacosa is more of a *barbareschista* or more *barolista,* he is better described as a poet, an entrepreneur, and a leader who never ran after the quick buck or chased easy money. Among his many achievements, he has discovered the elegance of the Asili cru, exalted the harmony of Rabajà, given a name to Falletto, captured the greatness of the vines of Serralunga, vinified (until 1993) the grapes of the Rionda vineyard, and become a legend. In fact, Santo Stefano is known more for the forty harvests with which Giacosa defined his character and personal style than for the vineyard's ideal combination of altitude, exposure, and morphology. It is a rare example of how humans can in no way take the place of nature but can be its best ally when human talent matches the excellence of the land.

The production of Santo Stefano is heavily informed by traditional winemaking in the Langa: Giacosa subscribes to long aging in large Slavonian oak casks, harvests as late as the end of November, and very long maceration times. Despite all this, he is rarely drawn into the debate between the so-called traditionalists and modernists: It is as if his wines are almost beyond categorization, unclassifiable jewels of the earth and human know-how. Barbaresco Santo Stefano—which is part of the "Bruno Giacosa" line along with his other wines that are made from grapes he buys (while Barbaresco Asili and Barolo Falletto are part of his "Azienda Agricola Falletto")—is an expression of elegance and power, refinement and muscle. The wine is complex and original, year after year. In the top vintages, and only then, is the wine aged further and given the Riserva status. These are bottles known for their extraordinary propensity for longevity. Few wines in Italy age as long—and as well—as Bruno Giacosa's, his Barbaresco Santo Stefano Riserva in particular. It is a characteristic of a true gift of nature and of this man who has made history with the land.

This is a sweet and balanced Barbaresco of great harmony and powerful extraction. Notes of tar, cherries, and damp forest give way to elegant velvet tannins that persist and resonate on the palate. Earthy minerality and firm structure will give this wine a long life to live.

Barolo—BARTOLO MASCARELLO

THE UNCOMPROMISED PURITY of Mascarello's Barolo reflects the life he lived. As in life, truth in wine is to be lauded and savored. There are few wines that speak so truthfully as this Barolo.

Born in Barolo in 1926, Bartolo grew up in the shadow of his charismatic and highly esteemed father, Giulio Mascarello. Giulio's life could have been taken right out of an early twentieth-century novel. He spent his youth working in a *bottega* in Genova. He supported the socialist movement and labor unions *(leghe operaie)*. He left his homeland during World War I but returned to the Langa, ultimately making a revolutionary decision in 1920 to open a small winery that would later produce wine only from his own grapes.

Blessed with a strong personality and a deep curiosity for life, young Bartolo quickly learned to carve out a place for himself within the family and his hometown, taking after his father. Bartolo developed a deep sense of civil duty, thanks to his encounters with some of the most famous intellectual thinkers of the time. (His father was a personal friend of philosophers like Norberto Bobbio; publishers and politicians like Luigi Einaudi, who later became president of the Italian Republic; working writers; and internationally renowned painters, partisans, and dissidents.)

Within this complex network of friends, interests, and relationships, Bartolo never lost sight of his life's goal: to make an excellent Barolo, following the most strict traditions of the Langa while respecting the rhythms of the earth and never tampering with seasonality or nature. Bartolo was able to accomplish his goal at a time when Barolo was not yet considered the "King of Wines." His greatest achievement, however, was to maintain a standard and an unchanging style, even in the years when Barolo became the cult wine of wine lovers throughout the world. It would have been all too easy for him to succumb to the market preferences and increased revenues, but he would have had to alter the soul of his product, which he was never willing to do.

Bartolo aged his wine only in large casks, rejecting the "trend" of using the smaller barriques. He began doing so in the 1960s, when he first started working with his father in the cellar, and he continued to do so until the end of his days. He started blending grapes from different vineyards from the very beginning of his career and continued to do so until his very last harvest (when everyone else was marching to the beat of the "cru"). Uncompromising, above all to himself, Bartolo was dedicated to protecting the identity of his wine and of his land. He was a proud opponent of Hollywood-style wines and the colossal wineries that were sprouting up in Piemonte, riding the wave of success and new-found wealth. Bartolo remained faithful to his history and his ethics. Even his bottles are, as they are adorned with cunning and brilliant labels designed by Bartolo as an older man, and on which he enjoyed making fun of the vices and hypocrisies of our time: His famous label/manifesto "No barrique, no Berlusconi," intended to amuse his friends and fellow wine drinkers, became a resistance cry for everything that, according to Bartolo, was insubstantial, fashionable, and trite. This was Bartolo Mascarello. He was met with great opponents during his lifetime, people bothered by his extreme positions, which were, more important, consistent with his lifestyle. Today, years after his passing in 2005, the entire wine world recognizes that he was an example of virtue and of rare, farsighted intelligence.

There is a whole lot of Langa in the wines of Bartolo Mascarello. He always refused to give up the custom of blending grapes and never changed his formula for "sewing" together in a single bottle (or under a single label) grapes coming from all his vineyards. According to his parents and grandparents, this system allowed for more consistent results, especially when a specific vineyard was weakened by drought, hail, or disease. His father, Giulio, founded the winery in the 1930s, and it remained unchanged: He purchased a few acres in Barolo in the areas of Cannubi, San Lorenzo, and Ruè, adding to them a small estate in La Morra, in the area called Torriglione. Of these four vineyards, all with excellent exposure, the first, Cannubi, is possibly the most famous vineyard in Italy (and certainly the one able to fetch the highest prices for its grapes and the wine produced with them). Located on a gentle hill at the entrance to Barolo, the Cannubi vineyard precedes the birth of the Barolo wine, having been listed on a bottle made in 1752. About 37 acres, the vineyard was traditionally subdivided among various wineries that occupied small or very small areas and used the precious grapes to cut or blend with grapes from lesser vineyards.

Tradition, austerity, and consistency are the three keys to understanding the mysterious product that is Barolo by Bartolo Mascarello. It is a wine that has remained unchanged since its birth. It is a wine made from grapes harvested at their perfect ripeness on each plot of land (despite being mere miles apart, Bartolo's vineyards have different characteristics and vegetative cycles); long maceration; aging exclusively in large casks; skillful and calibrated blending and co-fermenting. Wines that are labeled Bartolo Mascarello are not only good or extraordinary, they have a timeless draw that comes from the exact replication of the wine of the nature of the land from which it originates. These wines are strongly linked to the territory and are therefore "imperfect." By that, I mean that they are not easy or immediate like so many modern wines, but eventually they mature and develop like thoroughbreds, able to astonish you because they are different from everything else—they are unique and unrepeatable. There was a time when Bartolo Mascarello's wines were singled out as the leader of the traditionalist movement, contrary to the modernist winemaking style with short macerations and a short time in barriques. Having fortunately surpassed this period—which served more for writing newspaper articles and generating fierce competition among Italian wines—today his wines are made with a serene spirit. Thanks to his wife, Franca, and daughter, Maria Teresa, Bartolo's work and mission live on passionately.

Mascarello's Barolo is simultaneously expressive and elusive. It is a wine that gives earth, tar, and leather on the nose, with an explosion of tart cherries and stone fruit on the palate. The wine echoes and resonates in the mouth with a profound, vibrating finish.

Barolo Brunate—ROBERTO VOERZIO

LIKE A power slugger for the New York Yankees, Voerzio's Barolos command some of the highest prices because they are consistently hit out of the park. We are talking about full-throttle, loaded wines that carry oak and fruit with structure and power to spare.

Roberto Voerzio is one of the most powerful names in the Italian wine world. His name has grown stronger over time; he has progressively become a so-called international icon of the modern style of Piemontese winemaking. Born into a family of generations-old farmers, Roberto began making wine in 1986 together with his brother Gianni, who is now the owner of his own winery. The brothers had a difficult start: That year in Italy, the methanol scandal broke out, and some bottlers in Piemonte were accused of adulterating their wine with excessive amounts of methanol to increase the alcohol content, resulting in methanol poisonings and twenty-six deaths. The brothers were never accused of practicing this method, but it proved to be a difficult time to start their enterprise.

Roberto Voerzio, along with his many colleagues, set off on a decade-long journey that would propel them to the stage of Europe's greatest winemakers. These young pioneers of new Piemontese winemaking set their sights on Europe, in particular France, which they watched with extreme interest. They began to visit winemakers in Burgundy who had built their fame on the "evolution of tradition," creating new farming and vinification techniques that were able to bring out the most from the land and its original characteristics. By the end of the 1980s and the beginning of the 1990s, Roberto Voerzio—who dreamt of creating great red wines like Vosne-Romanée, Nuits-Saint-Georges, and Beaune in the Langa—began applying what he'd learned abroad on the vineyards of his own hometown, La Morra.

I would not be writing about Roberto Voerzio if it were not for the fortunate fact that he was born and raised in the Langa, more specifically in La Morra, a mosaic of unrivaled grand crus unlike any other in Italy. Since the dawn of winemaking in this region, La Morra has been synonymous with Barolo wine. The town is located on top of a 1,606-foot hill. Bricco del Dente is the highest hill in the area, and it protects the vineyards below from the cold alpine winds. The cru itself is astonishing and is, without a doubt, one of the most dramatic landscapes in the world. In this context—and only in this context—have Voerzio and his fellow winemakers been able to raise the bar in terms of quality

winemaking. Two of Roberto Voerzio's "super vineyards" are Cerequio and Brunate. Cerequio is an incredible 47-acre plot divided among numerous producers and able to make very structured and tannin-rich wine. Brunate is a 62-acre vineyard with various exposures, cut off from Cerequio by a little river; the grapes of this vineyard produce some of the most well-balanced and most complex red wines in Piemonte.

Yet, to produce truly great wine from this land, Voerzio had to modify tradition and introduce foreign, yet proven, winemaking practices that he had observed in the cellars of Burgundy and that contributed to the legendary reputation of Burgundian wines. Roberto Voerzio worked with small parcels of collective nebbiolo vineyards in some of the most famous Barolo crus (Brunate, Cerequio, and La Serra, followed by Rocche dell'Annunziatal Torriglione Capalot, and Sarmassa di Barolo). He planted these areas very densely, 4,000 plants per acre, and began pruning the bunches when the grapes were nearly ripe, reducing the yield from 4,500 pounds to 3,600, to even 2,700 pounds per acre. His actions in the vineyards had a multitude of strong effects: The density of the vines caused the plants to root deeper into the earth to compete with other nearby vines for water and nutrients; the pruning caused the grapes left on the vine to plump up and become concentrated with aromatic and flavor substances that would otherwise have been distributed among a larger amount of fruit. Lower yields, and therefore lower production, led to bottles of higher quality and rarity, fetching significantly higher prices.

Roberto Voerzio has become the undisputed standard bearer because of his uncompromisingly focused approach to winemaking, making cru Barolos with his unmistakable style of richness, concentration, and balance. In recent years, he has brought the same passion and technique to Langa's more accessible wines, including Dolcetto. Yet even with an everyday wine, the impact of Roberto's style and his vision for the product are unmistakable in the glass. His ability to reinterpret the great traditions and techniques of French winemaking at the highest level and to efficiently apply them to contemporary Piemontese winemaking illustrates his capacity to look into the future by studying the past. Even as a devout Barolo traditionalist, I have nothing but the greatest respect and admiration for the power and impact of Roberto's wines.

In the cellar, Voerzio works quite simply to bring out what is already captured inside the grapes. The maceration times are very short; the time spent in the barriques, on the other hand, can be very long. But as Voerzio loves to say, the use of small casks is simply the answer to a logistical and organizational need created by the small spaces for moving around in the cellar and, especially, to the need to manage and manipulate the quality and style presented by each individual microvineyard. For these reasons, toasty notes never dominate Voerzio's wines: What stands out is the extraordinary richness of the grapes themselves, a concentration of fruit that can be found in few wines and a sturdy structure that Roberto is able to keep at bay with the elegance of the wine. The wine is not always miraculous, but when it is, its elegance and body carry its magnificence. However, with Voerzio, the outcome is always impressive.

Barolo Brunate stands out because of its rich extract and concentration. Its powerful nose is dominated by dry flowers, black licorice, leather, box spices, and a stand-out vanilla tone. Toasty sensations are apparent, but never dominate because of the constantly surging fruit. On the palate the wine is a powerhouse, yet it is also round and soft. Though in an "off" vintage this wine can lack some finesse, a wine from a good year delivers on all levels.

Barolo Brunate–Le Coste—GIUSEPPE RINALDI

BAROLO LE COSTE is a trip through history in a bottle. Giuseppe Rinaldi brings his family tradition and the history of Barolo to every bottle of this rare cru. Traditional farming and vinification create a wine with notes of cherry brandy, licorice, and tar. Barolo Brunate–Le Coste is a wine that brings us to another time.

Giuseppe Rinaldi is essential to the image and essence of classical Barolo. If you are lucky enough to visit his house/cellar, located on the old road leading from Barolo to Monforte, you will encounter one of the authentic, lively spirits of the Langa. Veterinarian turned enologist, Giuseppe is reknowned for his classic storytelling and his categorical knowledge of every cru in Barolo. He animates the legend and history of these fabled hills in the way he lives his life and makes his wines. With his cousin Maria Teresa Mascarello, daughter of the legendary Bartolo (see page 170), and with the late Teobaldo Cappellano, a similarly spirited producer, he embodies, protects, and continues to proliferate what is traditional, classical, and old-world in making Italy's, and perhaps the world's, greatest red wine.

Giuseppe Rinaldi is a champion of traditional winemaking, thanks to the tutelage of his father, Battista, one of the most historically significant people in the Langa. In 1947, at the age of twenty-nine, Battista took over the reins of the winery from his father, who was one of the most respected people in Barolo for his high moral standards, serving as mayor of the town from 1970 to 1975. Under the leadership of Battista's father, the picturesque castle that dominates the town center was purchased by the city and converted into the first Regional Enoteca (wine-tasting store sponsored by the denomination) of the denomination, with Battista as its first president. Battista's father was also lucky to have in his property some of the best vineyards planted with nebbiolo. The names of these legendary areas include Brunate, Le Coste, Ravera, Cannubi, and San Lorenzo.

In the tradition of his father, Battista vinified the crus separately and with different techniques. The Brunate, considered the best cru, was made into a Riserva and left to rest for ten years before being released. The others contributed to the base Barolo of the cantina. When Giuseppe started to work side by side with his father, Battista, he embraced the successful tradition of Barolo, though he did propose a change that was made in 1993: The categories of Riserva and base Barolo were eliminated, and two wines were made based on their respective crus. Brunate and Le Coste created one Barolo (10,000 bottles), and the other, no less important, came from grapes grown in the Cannubi San Lorenzo and Ravera (3,500 bottles). Giuseppe's one change turned out to be a recalibration that brought success and notoriety to the winery. Since this major change, production has stayed the same; trends and fashions in the cellar and in the world have little influence on Giuseppe's philosophy. Often found with an unlit Toscano cigar dangling from his lips, Giuseppe is a classicist and collector of sixties-era mopeds. His wine and his life are strongly linked to Italian tradition.

Giuseppe lives in Le Coste, one of the two crus that make up Brunate–Le Coste Barolo. The rows of vines are planted directly below his house, which was built in the early 1900s. Le Coste is a highly regarded cru in Barolo and benefits from a climate similar to that of Cannubi, the other legendary Barolo cru. Covering 10 acres of land—only a part of which is owned by Giuseppe—Le Coste has an average altitude of 1,000 feet. Brunate, on the other hand, has few equals and is one of the most celebrated vineyards in the Langa and perhaps in all of Italy. At the border of the *comuni* of La Morra and Barolo, this land has a history that dates back to the fifteenth century. Documents held in the La Morra city archives refer to the denomination as Brinatum, and in nineteenth-century texts, the area is called Brinate. Only in the last century did it become known as Brunate, a grand cru coveted by many Piemontese winemakers. The vines get excellent south-southeastern exposure and the altitude of the land varies from 780 to 1,200 feet, covering a total of 62 acres. The wines that are produced from this vineyard are particularly well balanced between the aroma and structure. Giuseppe Rinaldi is able to pay great attention to his small properties, using chemicals sparingly and truly caring for the soil—facts that clearly contribute to the greatness of his wines. The combination of grapes from these two areas makes for a fiercely territorial wine.

In the Rinaldi household and winery, tradition is like a second religion. Human intervention in the cellar is limited to the bare minimum, allowing for the true essence of the nebbiolo to shine through. After a long period of maceration, the wine is transferred into large Slavonian oak barrels, which are racked after thirty-six months. During this

period, the wine gains roundness and equilibrium of tannins. There are no shortcuts to Giuseppe's objectives with this wine; it is made using a completely natural process that is curated by nature, and no interventions like small barrels and other products interfere whatsoever. Brunate–Le Coste Barolo is a long-lived wine that should be cellared for over a decade, depending on the vintage.

In the decanter and glass, this wine can be shy and needs the coaxing of time and air to present itself. The color of the wine is that of a classic nebbiolo: light red and very inviting. The nose gives classic notes of dry roses, raspberries, and violets to white tobacco. On the palate, the tannins are robust and precise. The wine is juicy and rich of extraction. It has an extremely long and entrancing finish.

Barolo Cannubi Boschis—LUCIANO SANDRONE

IT WAS the summer of 1990. I sat on a box of wine with Luciano Sandrone in his garage as we prepared to taste his Barolo with Castelmagno, the legendary high-pasture cow-milk cheese from the area. Sandrone was a new producer with lofty ambitions who always took the time to share some Barolo and his vision with young wine lovers thirsting for knowledge. At that moment Sandrone's wines were already creating quite a stir in the local scene, but two futures were launched on that fateful day. For Luciano, the 1989 Cannubi Boschis had finished its fermentation and had begun developing in the cellar, and the 1990 vintage was reaching perfection in the vineyards that surrounded the garage. These two wines would go on to become legendary and would propel Luciano Sandrone into the ranks of the great modern *barolisti*. For myself, as I sat in the dark garage listening to the passionate words of Luciano, drinking Barolo and eating this cheese, I was overcome with a sense of clarity and purpose. At that moment I knew that I would spend the rest of my life working in food and wine.

After having worked in a number of cellars in Barolo, in 1978

Sandrone decided to start producing his own wine. He made only 1,500 bottles, which he presented to the market with some hesitancy at Vinitaly in 1981. His wines were immediately well received, and thus he began a career that would lead him to the top of the Italian wine world. Luciano is very timid and would have never imagined the wild success of his 1985 vintage Barolo Cannubi Boschis, which is made from a 5-acre vineyard located in one of the most famous crus of the Langa. Even today, this Barolo is considered one of the "great ones" and a resounding example of Barolo at its greatest.

Cannubi is without a doubt the most celebrated vineyard in Barolo. There is even a bottle from 1752 with the word "Cannubi" written on the label, produced in a time when the name "Barolo" was practically unknown. In recent decades, the fame and prestige of this cru has never waned. As a result, people started buying up parcels of the vineyard, causing real estate prices to skyrocket. In the past, grape farmers used to love the Cannubi hill because the grapes cultivated there would maintain quality, even in difficult years. Cannubi vineyards, located at the center of the *comune* of Barolo, benefit from pebble-rich soil, which produces good results in both rainy and dry years. But now the fame of this cru has become so widespread that nearby vineyards have adopted the Cannubi name as well. For example, Renato Ratti, a winemaker and the first expert to have mapped the cru of the Langa, renamed the area of Monghisolfo "Cannubi Boschis" to play off the success of the cru. It is this historic *terroir* that gives life to Luciano's Cannubi Boschis Barolo.

Much has been written about Luciano Sandrone's Barolo in an attempt to capture the essence of this elusive wine. Luciano's wines are neither modern nor traditional; they are simply the wines of Luciano Sandrone. His personal winemaking and aging techniques are difficult to categorize. His maceration times are fairly long, something typical of traditional winemaking, but he is untraditional in his decision not to use large wooden barrels for aging. Instead, he uses classic 500-liter tonneaux made of slightly toasted wood, giving his Barolo notes of coffee or chocolate.

Sandrone's wines tend to emphasize balance and elegance over tannins and an excessively muscular structure. They are the reflection of grapes from one of the oldest, most classic crus of Barolo. The nose of a young Cannubi Boschis is decidedly fruity, yet delicate and never too sweet. The aromas vary from raspberry to cherry, with notes of red currant and blueberry. With age, this wine develops notes of violet and dry fruit, in addition to leather and tobacco. In the mouth, the tannins are not overwhelming, but add to the wine, giving it a longer finish.

Barolo Ginestra Vigna Casa Maté—ELIO GRASSO

DEEPLY DEDICATED to traditional winemaking practices, Elio Grasso has developed magnificent wines by delicately utilizing touches of modern techniques in his otherwise faithfully old-world production. Beautifully expressive, his wines demonstrate the finesse of this legendary winemaker.

Until the beginning of the 1980s, the Langa hills were known as a very poor area of Italy. Even though Piemonte, compared with other Italian regions, went through one of the strongest phases of industrialization at the beginning of the twentieth century, the Langa hills area did not profit from this growth. The majority of young people left their homes and agricultural lifestyle in the hills for Torino in search of fortune, called by the sirens of megaindustrial plants like Fiat. Few decided to stay in the Langa. One who did was Elio Grasso, whose family owned various acres of land in one of the most beautiful parts of Monforte.

Since 1978, the first year Elio Grasso released his two Barolos, the Langa area has changed completely. A wine boom ensued and caught local inhabitants completely off guard. They were not capable of anticipating the wave of prosperity and wealth that wine would bring to these once sullen and always challenging hills. Over the course of only two decades, the number of acres under vine doubled, imbalancing the ecosystem and destroying most of the forests, which are home to the prized white truffle. The winemakers went from being seen as farmers to being thought of as artisans: artists of the bottle. As soon as the money started rolling in, people began expanding their homes and building larger and more impressive cellars. The local landscape changed radically, with various consequences. There are limitless examples of wineries disproportionate to the number of bottles they actually produce, in contrast to Burgundy, where the vignerons remain proud and true to their old cellars, often very humble and rustic. In Piemonte, however, winemakers started investing in technologies to make great Barolos and expanding their production areas, with the unfortunate result of lesser-quality wines.

Despite such dramatic changes and uncontrolled growth, there are, however, some examples of virtuous winemaking. Elio Grasso, for example, decided not to add on externally to his cellar, but to dig a tunnel deep into the rock behind his house, creating space for the barriques and large oak barrels that he uses for his wine. A huge undertaking, it was an equally important investment. The tunnel is more than 330 feet long and has become a proud addition to the family holdings, guided by the steady hand of Elio, his wife, Marina, and their young son, Gianluca. Elio Grasso is a living statement to the merit of prudence and humility, even in the face of great prosperity. Swimming against the tide, he understood that great architectural monuments don't necessarily make great wine, but that embodying the spirit of old-world tradition and technique will ultimately bring forth the greatest results in the bottle.

In France, and particularly in the top winemaking regions like Bordeaux, Burgundy, and Champagne, the best vineyards are identified and classified by legislation, each as its own cru. This rigorous and precise classification occurred 150 years ago. In Italy, and in particular in Piemonte, there is no official classification system. However, since 2009, the Consorzio di Tutela del Barolo e del Barbaresco has been working to classify the top nebbiolo grape vineyards. Once the research has been completed, the Ginestra and Gavarini vineyards, areas where

Grasso owns some of the best plots, will be known as two of the top crus of the entire Barolo production area.

Ginestra is a vast vineyard spread across about 37 acres positioned at an altitude of between 900 and 1,400 feet. In addition to Elio Grasso, some of the other important winemakers owning property in Ginestra are Domenico Clerico, Paolo Conterno, and Renzo Seghesio. Although the producers have very different styles, the wines from Ginestra all have similar and recognizable characteristics: strong herbal notes, extreme longevity, and great flavor potential.

Elio Grasso has always been faithful to himself and his ideas. He has never been attracted by convenience or ease. His two Barolos, Gavarini and Ginestra, always have been made using traditional methods, with a pinch of the right kind of innovation. His fermentation times are usually fairly long—from sixteen to eighteen days—and go against the new winemaking trends in the Langa. Grasso does not, for example, use rotofermentors that reduce the time the must sits on the skins—in extreme cases down to as few as forty-eight hours.

In the past, Gianluca Grasso, with the complete consent of his father, created a special selection of Barolo called Rüncot that was well received by the public, and especially by the Italian and foreign press. Compared with Grasso's other Barolos that are aged in large, 2,500-liter Slavonian oak barrels, this wine spends twenty-four months in barriques. The last vintage released was 2001; however, the 2004 is now available as a Riserva. This wine is an exception in the otherwise fairly traditional Grasso winery, known for its more classic, *terroir*-driven nebbiolo wines that are powerful and rich in tannins.

Barolo Ginestra Casa Maté has perfumes of violet and cherry, with an elegant and attractive undercurrent of mint. In the mouth, it is rich with a good structure and soft tannins, and worth exploring. A wine of great aging potential, elegance, and complexity, Barolo Ginestra Vigna Casa Maté will continue to deliver for years to come.

Barolo Gran Bussia Riserva—ALDO CONTERNO

AT SLOW FOOD'S Salone del Gusto food and wine event in Torino in 2006, Aldo Conterno received a standing ovation when one thousand vignerons chose Barolo Gran Bussia Riserva 1989 as the best wine ever to be featured in the Slow Food/Gambero Rosso *Italian Wines* guide, then celebrating its twentieth anniversary. The vintage belies the theory that a truly great Barolo can only come from a single vineyard, as in the case of Gran Bussia, grapes from a variety of sites give the wine its unique character, personality, and style.

Piemonte's Langa hills are famous the world over for their great wines, but they have also been the scene of events that have shaped the course of modern Italian history. Recently, an enological revolution has turned this once depressed farming area into the new El Dorado of winemaking. One of the men behind the transformation is Aldo Conterno, whose winery is now one of the brightest stars in the Italian wine firmament. Some of his labels, such as Colonnello, Cicala, and Gran Bussia, are universally acknowledged as synonymous with class and excellence.

Born in 1931, Aldo, as a child, was exposed to the tragedy of war, the hills around his native village of Monforte being the theater of much bloody fighting. In those tough times, land was worth little and wine even less. It was only thanks to the indomitable spirit and far-sightedness of Aldo's father, Giacomo, a formidable grape selector, that the Conterno family managed to scrape through that long period of privation, then reconstruction. In the early 1950s, the young Aldo tried to make a new life for himself in California, a land of promise and prosperity. In tow of an enterprising uncle of his, he set up one of the early wineries in the Napa Valley. The venture would likely have proved a success, but it came to a sudden end when the uncle died. After being called up by the U.S. Army and sent to fight in Korea, Aldo had no one left to go home to in the States, so he decided to return to the country-side of Piemonte. From that moment on, his rise to the top was unstoppable. Back in Monforte, he started from scratch, running his father's winery in partnership with his brother Giovanni. Then, in 1969, Aldo opened a nearby winery of his own. In 1970, he marketed the first version of Barolo Gran Bussia, a selection of the company's finest grapes. In more recent times, true to the old adage that it's best to retire at the top, he has gradually handed the business over to his children. Even behind the scenes, though, Aldo Conterno remains a charismatic figure and a repository of the art of Langa winemaking.

The Barolo DOCG zone area extends over eleven *comuni* in southern Piemonte, just south of the city of Alba. Aldo Conterno's winery and vineyards are situated in the *comune* of Monforte, which, together with that of Serralunga, is where the really big, bold Barolos are produced. Here, the sandstone-rich soil gives the nebbiolo grape massive tannins and structure. The valley of Bussia in the western part of the *comune*, overlooking the village of Barolo itself, is where Aldo Conterno's most prestigious vineyards—Cicala, Colonnello, Romirasco, and Bussia Soprana—are located. All the wines from the different plots share the same fresh, intense scents.

In 1970, Aldo Conterno decided to produce Gran Bussia, the fruit of a painstaking selection of the grapes from vineyards he already owned in the area. Since then, every great vintage has been given recognition with the label, and the term Gran Bussia has now come to stand for a sort of seal of excellence, a "denomination within the denomination." The Bussia cru stands at an altitude of 980 to 1,150 feet above sea level and enjoys perfect southeast to south-southwest exposure and minimal wind—all factors that ensure the consistent high quality of the grape blends used to make the wine.

Bottled only in years deemed exceptional, Gran Bussia goes onto the market no earlier than six years after the grape harvest. Insofar as it's aged for thirty-six months in large Slavonian oak barrels, Barolo Gran Bussia counts as a great traditional wine. But stylewise it's timeless, at once inimitably classical, a wine of the future, and much more. You should never expect to come across two identical or even similar Gran Bussias. The basic breakdown of the cru sites from which the wine is sourced is Romirasco 70 percent, Cicala 15 percent, and Colonnello 15 percent, but the final blend all depends on the enologist's flair and the weather during the year. Whatever blend, Barolo Gran Bussia typically has earthy scents of truffle with notes of hazelnut and violet and an increasingly plush, velvety bouquet on aging.

Barolo Lazzarito Vigna La Delizia—
FONTANAFREDDA

FONTANAFREDDA AND Barolo Lazzarito are a winery and a wine that recount the story of the birth of Italy as a nation. Among the oldest branded wineries to produce Barolo, Fontanafredda was pivotal in thrusting Piemonte—and specifically the area of Alba—into the limelight and placing it among the greatest viticulture production areas in the world.

Although Toscana is Italy's most famous region (at least to Americans), Piemonte certainly offers the greatest experience to those who love to eat and drink. The wine and food of Peimonte, and specifically of the Langa Hills around Alba, are rooted in the area's history. Not only is there a rich peasant tradition of hunting and foraging, but these hills were also once home to dukes, lords, and even kings under the house of Savoy. Whereas the majority of Italian regional food developed from the peasant class, this area give birth to a cuisine fit for royal manors and noble banquets. The wealth and refined taste of the local gentry fostered the emergence of a more distinguished local cuisine. The finest local ingredients—such as rare game birds, ethereal white truffles, and exotic wild mushrooms—were combined with practiced cookery methods to create a new *cucina alta,* or high cuisine. With a well-financed demand for quality food, the Piemontese naturally sought out more dinstinguished and rarefied wines, like the ones they had tasted while traveling across the border to visit relatives in France. Fortunately, the vineyards that covered the hills around their castles contained what is perhaps the most noble varietal in the world: nebbiolo. Refined palates, swollen purses, and the great nebbiolo grape propelled the entire Alba wine production area, and specifically the *comuni* of Barolo, to the stage of great European wine production.

In 1858, Fontanafredda became the private estate of Victor Emmanuel II, King of Sardinia. The 250-acre estate was used as his private hunting lodge before being transformed into a viticultural estate in the 1870s. Most famous for his role in leading the *Resorgimento* (unification of Italy), Victor Emmanuel was fond of the Piemontese countryside. By handing the property over to his son, Emanuele Guerrieri—Count of Mirafiori and Fontanafredda, son of the king and his mistress, "la bella Rosina"—he facilitated the creation of the current viticultural estate. Emanuele Guerrieri started to produce important red wines and launched Fontanafredda's great tradition of sparkling wines. His passion for agriculture and land permeated the monolithic estate, and the wines he produced garnered a reputation for quality and a deep respect for their *terroir*.

The Fontanafredda estate is located in the heart of the Barolo production area. The headquarters of the operation is in Serralunga d'Alba, but there are Fontanafredda vineyards in Barolo and Diano d'Alba as well. One of the rare characteristics of this winery is that the vineyards are grouped together, whereas the rest of the estates in the Langa are fragmented. Fontanafredda's 220 acres of vineyard gently descend along the hills leading down from the estate offices—buildings that are recognizable by their characteristic yellow and red stripes. The winery is well known for its sweet moscato-based sparkling white wines, which make up a large share of the company's profit. However, if the whites talk in terms of numbers, the red wines count in terms of quality, as many of the crus that have made Fontanafredda famous include such reds as Vigna La Rosa, Lazzarito, and Vigna la Villa.

Lazzarito is the great Barolo from the *premier cru* vineyard of the greatest Barolo estate of Piemonte. In the Italy we love, where simple food and wine is made by people who are close to the earth, this is a regal Barolo. The "La Delizia" vineyard, located in the heart of Serralunga, produces grapes that go into a wine that stands as a testimony to the burly massiveness of Barolo's most powerful *terroir*. La Delizia has excellent exposure, and it is sheltered from the wind by a hill. The vineyard produces great results every year, with the help of the talented folks in the cellar. The resulting wine is a stellar representative of both nebbiolo and the *terroir*.

The grapes are then softly pressed and macerated for a short period of time to release the essence of the fruit and create a must that is rich in polyphenols and aromas. It is then aged first in large wooden barrels and then in barriques. On the nose, this wine is complex and alive, with perfumes of ripe red fruit, dried flowers, licorice, and spices. In the mouth, it is soft, almost silky, playing off the tannins and rich, extracted notes. Even though the wine is round and full-bodied, it is particularly elegant and complex. It has a very long, well-balanced finish that recalls the perfumes of the wine. With a garnet red hue slightly tinted orange at the edges, the wine is as pleasing to the eye in the glass as its elegant and complex flavors are in the mouth. With great structure and elegance, this wine is well balanced and extremely gratifying.

Barolo Monprivato—GIUSEPPE MASCARELLO E FIGLIO

FOR LOVERS of red wines of the Langa, Giuseppe is known as "the other Mascarello," in reference to Bartolo Mascarello, who passed away in 2005 (see page 170). Like this unforgettable champion of traditional winemaking, the family of Giuseppe Mascarello—no relation to Bartolo— has built its own fame, harvest after harvest, decade after decade, staying faithful to classic winemaking techniques.

First, let's get a few names straight. Bartolo Mascarello we know. Giuseppe Mascarello is the name of both the founder of the winery and of the winery itself. Giuseppe Mascarello's family is from Monchiero (a small town located just outside the Barolo production zone) and has produced wine for almost one and a half centuries. Like all the best Piemontese traditions, this close-knit family has passed first names down from generation to generation: There is the Giueseppe Mascarello from the late nineteenth century, another who lived through most of the twentieth (the one who founded the winery), and yet another Giuseppe, son of Mauro—the *figlio*, or son, of Giuseppe the founder.

Mauro and his son Giuseppe are known by everyone in the Italian wine world as the standard bearers of traditional winemaking. In the case of the Mascarello wines, quality comes from the vineyard and the soil, rather than from the provenance and character of the wood in which it is aged. In fact, the Mascarello family selects barrels based on capacity and how much wine they expect to produce from the grapes from a particular vineyard each harvest. The only certainty is that their wines will not be aged in barriques. (If a smaller barrel is needed, they prefer to use old 52-liter demijohns.) The same traditional approach holds true for maceration, another fundamental step by which Langa wineries are judged as "traditional" or not. In the case of Mascarello, their wines used to macerate for sixty days, then forty, and now they are at thirty, but they are not even close to the brief maceration times of local avant-garde winemakers. Everything moves according to nature in the Mascarello cellars. Mauro will talk with visitors for hours about their 1979 Barolo Rionda, which was so lacking in color that they stopped producing it altogether. And then there was the legendary 1971 Barolo Pugnane, a rosé made using a less noble nebbiolo clone. In the end, these stories set the stage for the pride of the Mascarello family, the Monprivato cru.

Based on this exceptional vineyard, located in the town of Castiglione Falletto, the Mascarello Monprivato cru is so extraordinary that the Mascarello di Monchiero family is known among locals and winemakers as Mascarello del Monprivato. Thanks to a series of important acquisitions during the last few decades, the Mascarello family is now the sole proprietor of the entire cru (almost). They have created a rare case of a virtual monopoly in the Langa. Compared with Burgundy, where monopolies are quite common (for example, Domaine de la Romanée Conti owns the entire La Tache cru), the top vineyards in the Langa were traditionally divided among a number of winemakers. In recent years, however, individual Piemontese wineries have begun to acquire more and more parcels of a single cru with the aim of arriving at sole ownership. Along with Conterno's Cascina Francia, Mascarello del Monprivato is the only sole owner of almost an entire cru (a small plot is owned by another farmer).

The aging cellar for Mascarello wines was carved out of an eighteenth-century building that was once used for producing and storing ice, whereas the center of wine production is a few miles away, toward the center of Barolo, where the company owns portions of the most noble and important vineyards in the entire denomination. The two towns in which the Mascarello family operates are Monforte, where the Santo Stefano di Perno vineyard is located, and Castiglione Falletto, where everything, or almost everything, revolves around Monprivato. The Mascarellos have owned a portion of the vineyard since 1904, when Maurizio, son of the first Giuseppe, bought a farmhouse on the edge of the vineyard. The family became the sole owner of the cru during the 1990s, after a series of small acquisitions from some old local farmers. Monprivato has become the symbol of the Mascarello winery and is synonymous with great Barolo (however, the family has also planted rows of barbera in the cru, with which they produce a Barbera d'Alba). At the heart of Monprivato, grapes are selected with great care and vinified separately to make the remarkable Barolo Monprivato Riserva Ca' d'Morissio.

Since this wine is so intrinsically tied to the Monprivato cru, it is only appropriate to begin our discussion with the vineyard itself. Monprivato stretches across the hills that head down from the center of Castiglione Falletto. The entire cru is less than 15 acres, all of which face southwest. In addition to benefiting from an excellent microclimate, Monprivato is also an extremely beautiful place; the summit of the vineyard boasts spectacular views of the valleys of Barolo. The soil comprises primarily white and gray marlstone. The fossils of fish and seaweed that have been upturned when tilling the vineyard are testament to the fact that this area was once submerged under the sea.

Monprivato, the wine, is a well-structured Barolo with great elegance and intense aromas. The long macerations and long, thirty-eight-month aging in Slavonian oak barrels of various sizes give Monprivato its austere character. The wine is light granite red in color and has perfumes of dried flowers, soil, tobacco, and truffles. In the mouth, the pronounced tannins are balanced and silky. The wine is tight and linear, but never heavy. It is actually a wine "for drinking," rather than "for tasting," which is often the case with Piemontese wines. Monprivato is not a wine you get tired of, especially if you drink it fifteen years after its production—when the unique characteristics of the *terroir* have completed their work, giving life to one of the greatest wines in the Langa.

Barolo Ciabot Mentin Ginestra—DOMENICO CLERICO

THE WINE THAT, in many ways, was responsible for changing the world's opinion of Barolo is Barolo Ciabot Mentin Ginestra. The talent and foresight of Domenico Clerico led to this extraordinary wine and the creation of an outstanding cru.

Domenico Clerico is the most charismatic and caring character in Barolo. In his youth, he decided to leave farming and his family farm because he found the agrarian lifestyle inhibitive. In the 1970s, country life in the Langa was quite different than it is today; the younger generation looked to escape from a life that seemingly had no future. Young Domenico was an excellent conversationalist and seduced everyone with his exuberant personality. He quickly found a job as an olive oil salesman, an occupation that required him to travel throughout Piemonte. After a couple of years, he realized that this was not the life for him, and he returned to the countryside and his family's property. In 1977, Domenico had the good fortune of being part of a group of friends who were interested in improving the quality of wine in Piemonte. This group, commonly referred to as the Barolo Boys, included Guido Fantino, Enrico Scavino, and Elio Altare, to name a few. After several trips to Burgundy and Bordeaux, these winemakers began to understand the techniques of the top French producers and imported the use of barriques to Piemonte.

The year 1982 was considered the turning point for Barolo, owing to the release of Ciabot Mentin Ginestra. This wine was an immediate success, unlike anything else that had come before it. Domenico Clerico's Barolo was elegant, clean, and captivating on the nose, intense and rich in the mouth—a far cry from the wines that had been made in the Langa until then. The Barolos of Domenico and a handful of other producers completely changed the region. Important German, Swiss, and American investors began to arrive. Then came 1990, and another turning point for the Barolo Boys: Wine critic Robert Parker Jr. awarded the vintage extremely high points. This was a first for a Piemontese wine. Within two or three years, the price of Barolo doubled, bringing wealth to the winemakers and notoriety to the wine.

Clerico continued to produce magnificent wine, focusing on modern winemaking techniques and using increasingly smaller wooden barrels like cigarillos (or 50-liter barrels) for aging his wine. Looking back, this may seem like a strange and less than positive decision, but at that time it was considered pioneering. Thanks to people like Domenico Clerico, Barolo kept progressing and people continued to believe in their work and in the land.

Monforte d'Alba is probably the town of Barolo that benefited the most from the changes that occurred in the 1980s. Some of the most famous wineries in Piemonte, and possibly in the world, are located here, including Clerico, Aldo and Giacomo Conterno, Conterno Fantino, Elio Grasso, Parusso, and Rocche dei Manzoni. These big names have homed in on Monforte because of the area's location and climate, which is ideal for growing nebbiolo. The wines made here have the power and tannins of the Barolos of Serralunga, and the grace and elegance of those from La Morra or Barolo.

Ciabot Mentin Ginestra gets its name from the cru from which it is made. In Piemontese dialect, *ciabot* means "tool shed" and refers to the stone cabins that can be found throughout the vineyards. Ginestra, on the other hand, is the name of the grand cru that has an optimal southwestern exposure. The slope of the vineyard causes the soil to absorb water quickly, leaving the grapes free of mold and other fungal diseases. The limestone and clay soil is ideal for nebbiolo and produces grapes that best express the character of the *terroir.*

In addition to Ciabot Mentin Ginestra, Domenico Clerico produces two other great Barolos: Pajana and Percristina. The first is extremely modern, while the second is produced only in the best vintages and is released two years later than the others. Ciabot Mentin Ginestra is the commanding Barolo made by Domenico Clerico that is responsible for changing the world's opinion of Barolo in general. Clerico's strong desire to experiment has resulted in perfect balance in this wine. It is a very modern Barolo, but the grapes still make more of a difference in the outcome than the wooden barrels used to age the wine. The *terroir* is still present in the wine, an aspect appreciated by traditionalists. Despite the twenty-four months the wine spends in barriques, its nose has notes of licorice, berries, mint, coffee, blackberries, currants, and jam. In the mouth, it is strong and full bodied, with strong tannins balanced by a refreshing acidity. Ciabot Mentin Ginestra is best drunk at least ten years after the harvest.

Barolo Rocche dell'Annunziata Riserva—PAOLO SCAVINO

THE SUCCESS OF this Barolo must be attributed to Enrico Scavino, one of the most forward-thinking and adaptable winemakers of his generation. Thanks to Enrico, this Barolo is one of the most magnificent in the world.

The story of Enrico Scavino can be considered a parable of

contemporary winemaking in the Langa. The wine made in this region is deeply rooted in tradition. The vineyards on the softly rolling hills of southern Piemonte have been around forever, and in the nineteenth century, wineries and wine companies were opened exclusively for the production of wine. However, in terms of approach to quality and viticulture, the Langa is certainly a young territory—if not compared with the rest of Italy, then at least compared with Burgundy.

In fact, much of the history of the Scavino winery parallels that of French winemakers. Paolo Scavino—father of the current owner, Enrico—founded his company in the beginning of the twentieth century, producing wine, among other things, from his *cascina* (farmhouse). At that time, it was common to cultivate a variety of crops to feed one's often large family. When things began to change in the 1970s, and growing grapes became enology, Paolo's children, especially Enrico, were open-minded enough to think ahead. The Scavino family became aware of the fact that they were in possession of a grand *terroir* and the extraordinary nebbiolo grape. They also realized that there was a market for new, modern products with a wider appeal. However, they lacked a reference point. In those years, many producers looked to Tuscan and Burgundian winemakers for a model. The first lesson Enrico and his fellow winemakers learned, though it seemed simple enough, was that you have to begin by studying the vineyard, and only from there can you start to build a future.

The first step these winemakers took to develop the vineyards they hoped for was to end the practice of blending grapes from multiple vineyards. Until this time, the blending of grapes in Piemonte was considered the most infallible method for covering up any flaws in the grapes from a single vineyard. Blending also meant that wines would, for the most part, be consistent from one harvest to another. In the 1980s, this practice was overturned: Willing to assume the risk, ambitious winemakers, like Enrico Scavino, began focusing on wines made from single vineyards. The result? A race to the cru! The most talented vignerons, including Scavino, began studying the Barolo production area in search of the best vineyards. They studied cadastral maps, they

spoke with the old-timers, they held on to the small parcels they inherited from their grandparents, and they purchased the best vineyards—often at outrageous prices—from farmers who preferred to live off their inheritance rather than cultivate it. The battery of Barolos that Enrico Scavino produces today is a demonstration of how well he made this transformation. The Scavino family now owns property in Cannubi, Fiasco, Bricco Ambrogio, Rocche di Castiglione, and Rocche dell'Annunziata: priceless vineyards that have turned the land in Barolo into a gold mine. Today, Enrico Scavino is one of the most well-regarded and most authoritative figures of "cru culture," a culture that has not only enriched the territory, but has decidedly changed the style and concept of Langa wines from those of twenty years ago.

By drawing a line from one Scavino vineyard to another, one can basically create a map of the grand crus of the Langa. Together with his wife, Anna Maria, and their young daughters, Enrica and Elisa, Enrico manages a hypertechnological and impressive cellar. The Scavino winery is based in Castiglione Falletto, one of the eleven towns south of the city of Alba legislated to produce Barolo. Fiasco, the cru that changed the course of the winery and which was vinified individually for the first time in 1978, is also located in Castiglione Falletto. Within the *comune* of Castiglione, Scavino owns a less valuable vineyard called Vignolo and another "super cru," known as Rocche di Castiglione—a long, narrow strip of hill containing parcels owned by other famous Piemontese wineries, including Oddero, Vietti, and Brovia. In the town of Barolo, the Scavino vineyards are located in one of the oldest crus of the area: Cannubi. The Vignane vineyard and the small cru of Via Nuova—which was once owned by the first president of the Italian Republic, Luigi Einaudi—round out the Scavino properties in Barolo. The family also owns a vineyard in Roddi, a small town on the outskirts of the territory. And in La Morra, another epicenter of Barolo production and home to the most celebrated vineyards, the Scavino family owns a marvelous vineyard in the center of the Rocche dell'Annunziata cru.

Rocche dell'Annunziata is an extremely beautiful, wide, and productive vineyard, at least in Langa standards: It is almost 74 acres in size and is located between 830 and 890 feet above sea level, facing south-southwest. The cru is positioned just south of the center of La Morra and almost at the center of a larger amphitheater of vineyards that you can see from the incredible lookout site, or *belvedere,* on the other side of town. The Scavino family purchased property in Rocche dell'Annunziata in 1990, and the grapes from this cru are treated with special care: Whereas the grapes from Cannubi, Fiasco, and their other top vineyards are made into single cru wines each year, those from Rocche dell'Annunziata are used to make a Riserva di Barolo that is released only in the best vintages. Riserva, in the world of wine in general, and specifically in Barolo, can be translated as "set aside," because it requires another two years of cellar aging in addition to the already-long four years mandated by the Barolo denomination. Producing a reserve wine is a major economic undertaking for a small- to medium-size winery. Add on the fact that the Riserva is not produced every year, and you will have a better understanding of why the prices for these bottles are so high. Barolo Rocche dell'Annunziata Riserva comes from a parcel of a vineyard that is little more than 1 acre in size and from which an average of 5,500 pounds of grapes are harvested annually. The plants are up to sixty years old and are located at an altitude of 1,100 feet; the soil is composed of marlstone and clay. The maceration time varies and the alcoholic fermentation occurs in temperature-controlled stainless steel vats. The malolactic fermentation takes place in barriques, where the wine rests for twelve months before aging for another twenty-four months in larger French oak barrels. After the blending of the barrels in stainless steel vats, the Barolo is bottled and aged for six to seven more months before it is released on the market.

Barolo Rocche dell'Annunziata Riserva is granite red in color, with intense aromas of wilted rose, tobacco, wet soil, vanilla, and ripe fruit. In the mouth, the wine's celebrated elegance shines. This is a far cry from your powerful, tannin-rich Barolo. That is not to say that this wine doesn't have force and strength, but these characteristics are softened by the wine's silkiness. The wine has a long, harmonious finish. It is no surprise that the top wineries in the Langa have competed for a part of Rocche. Scavino produces only 2,500 bottles of his Riserva—in the years that he actually produces it—making this wine a rare treat indeed.

Barolo Vigna Rionda Riserva—MASSOLINO

VIGNA RIONDA IS one of the most celebrated crus in Barolo, as is the wine produced by the owners of the vineyard, the Massolino family. The fact that the vineyard name appears before that of the Massolino family on the bottle suggests that the earth and the vine hold more significance than the people who work the land. In effect, when you have the good fortune of owning a cru like Vigna Rionda, or even the fortune to be based in Serralunga, the way you view the world changes.

You would be surprised to know how much has been said about a vineyard and a winemaking region that is far less famous than Cannubi or La Morra, for example. Serralunga always appears on the edges of the map of the great *comuni* of Barolo, revealing a shortcoming in wine writing, which is often focused more on the numbers than on actual quality. Serralunga represents 13 percent of the total Barolo production, compared with La Morra at 31 percent, or even Monforte at 17 percent. The reason that there are far fewer wineries in the territory of Serralunga is the presence of Fontanafredda, a large winery originally owned by the Savoy family. The company controls the commerce of grapes in the area, limiting the growth potential of small wineries. In absolute terms, however, Serralunga is a gem of the Barolo region—not only for the town itself, which radiates from one of the most beautiful medieval castles in southern Piemonte, but also for the large number of prized vineyards located within the *comune*. There are twenty-nine crus, distributed across a valley 4 miles long and 1 mile wide and characterized by its excellent exposure and excellent soil. Of the crus, Vigna Rionda is certainly the most well known, but only because the name of another exceptional Serralunga vineyard, Francia, does not appear on the label of Giacomo Conterno's legendary Barolo Monfortino. If you add Falletto, a historic cru whose grapes go into Bruno Giacosa's Barolo, we return to where we began: In Serralunga, the vineyards define the success of the wineries.

In addition to Barolo Vigna Rionda, which is produced only in the top vintages and released only after two additional years of aging—making it a Riserva—the Massolino family produces other single-vineyard Barolos: Margheria and Parafada are the most interesting and attest to the Burgundy-style approach of the winery. During the 1970s and '80s, wineries would commonly blend grapes from various vineyards into a single wine, except when it came to the so-called base wine of the winery. In recent years, things have changed, and winemakers are focusing on single-vineyard wine, a far more difficult task that ultimately affects the final price of the bottle. Single-vineyard wines have paved the path for better expression and control over production and quality. Yet, in some cases, production has been overly fragmented, creating a risk that single-vineyard production is too small to have any kind of market value or too difficult to communicate to the public. The greatest risk of all is that wines produced from lesser vineyards are marketed as great crus. Thankfully for the Massolino family, this is not the case. The Vigna Rionda Massolino is made up of three vineyards, all of which are top performers.

Serralunga gets its name from the unique shape of the *comune*, which is spread across a long *(lunga)*, thin strip of land completely covered in vines and located in the heart of the Barolo denomination. Serralunga is surrounded, if not overpopulated, by nebbiolo vineyards destined to produce the "King of Wines." The road that leads from the city of Alba toward Serralunga passes along a ridge of hills that provides the south-southwest-facing vineyards to the left of the ridge with a cool and ventilated microclimate. The south-southeast-facing vineyards get the afternoon sun. The characteristics of the territory are strongly felt in the wines of Serralunga, especially in the tannins and their ability to age well. Vigna Rionda dominates the right side of the aforementioned street at an altitude of 820 to 980 feet. The cru covers

5 acres, of which the Massolino family owns a little more than 5 acres—all with southern exposure. The soil is calcareous marlstone. Many Piemontese winemakers have made a name for themselves with grapes from Vigna Rionda, including Oddero, the prestigious family with a cellar in La Morra, and Bruno Giacosa, who produced a 1993 Barolo Collina Rionda that made this vineyard famous throughout the world.

Compared with Margheria and Parafada, which are made year after year (except in relatively bad vintages like 2003), Vigna Rionda is a Barolo Riserva: the word "Riserva" indicates that the wine has been aged further in wood and also in the bottle. Often, however, winemakers use the Riserva label for their top wines, which in addition to being very aged, are made with extreme care and in limited quantities. Massolino's Barolo Vigna Rionda Riserva, first produced in 1982, has had a series of excellent and memorable vintages, often acclaimed by international wine critics. This wine is a splendid example of traditional Barolo, even if the single-vineyard cru approach could be considered modern. The grapes macerate for twenty days on the lees, and then the wine spends three and a half years in large wooden barrels. During this time, the wine develops the characteristics that, once bottled, will continue to become more refined over the years.

Vigna Rionda has an attractive red granite color, with graceful and tight perfumes of dried rose, China root, raspberry, dark berries, wet earth, and tobacco leaves. In the mouth, you can taste the *terroir* of Serralunga and the vintage: The *terroir* gives the wine its power and tannin, while the vintage (depending on the year) gives the wine its grace and elegance, as well as its roundness and structure. This is a well-balanced wine with notable finesse. The finish is very long and is a sort of Rossini-worth crescendo that recalls the fruit aromas and best gusto-olfactory sensations. It is a jewel of the earth. Thankfully, the wise men of the Langa have not tried to intervene in the cellar, allowing the wine to truly taste of the earth.

Barolo Vigneto Arborina—ELIO ALTARE–CASCINA NUOVA

THE BEST TIME to go and visit Elio Altare in La Morra is during the morning on any given day in September. This is when the colors of the Langa are at their height: a veil of mist over the crus, green vineyards dotted with the occasional insolent red leaf, and ripe bunches of grapes ready to be picked. Elio's beautiful land gives life to a Barolo that speaks of its creator—a strong wine with a glorious aesthetic that expresses the exceptional earth from which it comes.

Elio's life can be counted in harvests. He is a man of the Langa, the last place on earth where seasons pass, not time. With the rough skin of a farmer, you can see he's a man who has breathed the air of the postwar years, when remaining on the land meant prolonging the resistance—not to a tangible enemy, but to poverty. High school was considered a luxury that his family couldn't provide, so young Elio took to the fields and vineyards. In 1975, Elio's father uprooted his nebbiolo vines to plant rows of dolcetto. This act was such a travesty to Elio that a year later he decided to leave his family's vineyard for Burgundy.

In France, Elio discovered that producers can work together as a community, that technology can successfully be used in the cellar, and that long-term investments can be rationalized. Upon his return, the situation began to change: In 1978, winemakers began to green-harvest (that is, they removed grape bunches a month before harvest to concentrate the maximum juice in the grapes that will be harvested) for the first time. The vision of grapes on the ground in Annunziata was like a Copernican revolution. Five years later, barriques took the place of imposing old casks for aging wine; however, the revolution was made complete with a third "sacrilege": the shortening of maceration times from sixteen days, to eight, to four, and finally to just forty-two hours in the case of Barolo Arborina 1994.

As extremely short macerations caught on quickly in the Langa, the rest of the wine world began to recognize that something was happening in these hills. The press coined the name Barolo Boys, naming Elio the leader of this group of young, impudent winemakers who were challenging the great legendary wines of the Langa, which until then had seemed untouchable. These were the years of the roaring 1990s, when Barolo was being heralded worldwide. While some producers began to flaunt their newfound fortune, Elio did not. Firm in his ways, today Elio Altare produces 50,00 bottles, the same number he made before the winemaking boom in Piemonte. In a place that seems like a workshop, his cellar has remained the humble setting of a working man.

Elio Altare is not alone in all this. He is tied to two other winemakers: Angelo Gaja and Bartolo Mascarello. Both in the market and in the cellar, Angelo was a mentor and friend to Elio. Bartolo, however, has always been portrayed as the fierce conceptual enemy of Elio: the modernist against the traditionalist, short macerations versus long. Deep down, however, Elio is closely bound to the image of Mascarello: Although their ideas about winemaking may differ, their stubbornness in their battles against industrial winemakers who have destroyed the Langa couldn't be more similar. They both fought against the men who bought up vineyards; built large, pharaonic wineries; and if things weren't looking good, abandoned the land to invest in the trend of the moment. People are born farmers, but only some remain so. Elio rarely smiles; he is a true farmer in the old-fashioned sense. The only thing that makes him proud is having reinstilled a sense of dignity to the profession of winemaking and its history to the territory. Elio is the true vigneron of the Langa.

La Morra is one of the eleven *comuni* in the Barolo denomination; however, it stands apart as one of the most famous due to its soil. It is also known for the many small winemakers who decided to start bottling grapes under their own name in the past twenty years, bringing about a winemaking revolution in the Langa. On the eastern side of the *comune*, where the hill peaks at 1,800 feet, there is a small suburb called Annunziata, where there are just a handful of houses surrounded by vines. This spot is where Elio Altare has built his little kingdom:

12 acres that he owns and 12 that he rents. This would be considered peanuts by some of the large Piemontese landowners, but it seems like a lot for Elio, who manages this land practically by himself. His eldest daughter, Silvia, is the only person who gives him a hand. Arborina is the oldest and best-positioned vineyard on his property. If it were in France, this area would definitely be called a *premier cru*. In Italy, however, it is referred to as a "grand cru." This is another particularity about Elio: He was able to create a vineyard out of nothing. Arborina was practically unknown until about twenty years ago. It has always had good positioning, but it was nothing exceptional compared with the many other vineyards in La Morra. Elio was able to complete the miracle of giving value to a piece of land that few would have considered of any worth.

What does it mean to be a modernist? We can say that Elio Altare, while being considered the leader of the Barolo Boys, has never sought to intervene directly in the cellar. In his winery, for example, the cigarillos (or 50-liter barrels) have never been used. The same goes for engineered yeasts; they have never entered the winery.

For these reasons, Vigneto Arborina, which can certainly be called a modern-style Barolo, is able to express the complex *terroir* of La Morra. In this area, nebbiolo grapes are not as tannic and muscular as those of Serraluna or Monforte. Here, the Barolo is characterized by its elevated elegance, grace, and a slight lack of structure, according to lovers of stronger tannins. Elio is probably the winemaker who was able to best interpret the feminine side of the grapes. He prefers the tannins in his Barolo to be caressing rather than muscular. On the nose, Arborina has nuances of nectarine, wild strawberry, dried flowers, and rosehip. In the mouth, the wine is smooth, velvety, and silky, with, however, a long and definite finish.

Another important characteristic of Elio's Arborina is that, strangely, it shows best in the worst vintages. His 1994 or even his 1993—a particularly bad year for wines from the Langa—are two excellent examples. At the same time, his 1982, 1985, and 1989 were unforgettable vintages. And there is no need to go looking for his 1997: Although

it was a great year, Elio did not release his Barolo because defective corks ruined his yearly production of Arborina. Elio Altare is the only one among the small wine producers who was able to successfully sue the multinational company that sold him the cork—just another incredible success story in the life of this intrepid *vignaiolo*.

Colli Tortonesi Bianco Costa del Vento—
VIGNETI MASSA

ONE OF the most recent stars to emerge onto the stage of the Italian wine world is, without a doubt, the timorasso grape variety. Although the word may mean little to the American wine-drinking public, that is sure to change soon. Timorasso is a miracle grape. It was once lost and has since been found, extant and revived in a far-off corner of Piemonte in the province of Alessandria.

Bordered by three regions of northern Italy—Liguria, Lombardia, and Emilia Romagna—Allessandria has grown timorasso for centuries. But the grape started to disappear at the end of World War II, when the market wanted only simple, standardized, profit-generating wines, leaving little room for a variety that requires special care in the vineyard and great attention in the cellar. Timorasso became less profitable compared with the more widely available grape varieties present in the zone, like cortese, barbera, freisa, and dolcetto. Slowly, people began to forget about timorasso and the vineyards where it was once planted. Then, suddenly, timorasso became popular again. In the 1990s, the market for white wines shifted. People started to look for wines with character from lesser-known regions. Old, native grape varieties became the rage, as did white wines with great acidity, strong aromas, and propensity for aging. Timorasso fit the bill.

Walter Massa is a winemaker from Monleale, a town in the territory of Colli Tortonesi, far east of the famed Langa hills. Until he found timorasso, Massa made modest red wines for the local market. In 2000, a little bit of fame came his way for his fantastic barrique-aged Barbera. Critics and wine lovers started to pay more attention to this tiny winery and discovered that Massa was making a praiseworthy effort to revive timorasso, which could be found only in the area around the city of Tortona. Massa, however, was not alone. Franco Martinetti, a well-known Piemontese winemaker, was producing a pure timorasso wine. Although Martinetti may have been the first to release his timorasso, Massa is certainly the person who relaunched the variety, reintroducing the wine to the wine world. Massa is a volcanic, passionate, and uncontrollable person who is almost eccentric in his personal vision and dedication to timorasso. Massa's winery became the flag bearer in the region, "forcing" his fellow winemakers to replant timorasso. He experimented with different styles of vinification, beginning with aging some of his grapes in stainless steel and others in barriques. Because of Massa's wines, people are talking about the Colli Tortonesi as a new, little Alto Adige, home to the most interesting white wines of the area. Thanks to the revival of timorasso, several research institutes, as well as individual wineries, began studying other grape varieties to save. The success of timorasso has also helped the wine to receive DOC status and to be exported to markets abroad.

Tortona is a small town in the province of Alessandria, where viticulture has been a part of life for centuries. Years ago, small family companies, passed down through the generations, produced wine for local markets. For a long time, the wine produced in this part of southern Piemonte was served at the tables of gentlemen in nearby Liguria, a region unable to produce enough wine to meet the demands of its local market because of its mountainous inland terrain. This area eventually become more famous for its sportsmen—Fausto Coppi, a champion cyclist, and Gianni Rivera, a former soccer player who scored the decisive goal in the Italy-Germany match during the semifinals of the 1970 World Cup in Mexico—than for its wines.

Massa has been able to champion a grape variety over a *terroir*. This corner of Piemonte certainly does not have the exposure, soil, and climate of the Langa, and for this reason, timorasso has distinguished the territory. Nowadays, the area of Alessandrino is known not only for its extraordinary whites, but also for excellent red wines, like Barbera and Dolcetto, which have finally been improved thanks to the introduction of more modern winemaking techniques.

Today, timorasso vineyards covers about 120 acres of land, a handful of which are owned by Walter Massa, who is able to produce around 40,000 bottles per year. Although timorasso is growing in popularity, it is still made in small quantities because of the need to respect the rhythms of nature and the difficulty of penetrating an already saturated wine market. Despite these obstacles, Massa continues to find converts willing to invest in this rediscovered grape. In the meantime, Massa has diversified his production, creating a sort of stylistic and conceptual pyramid. At the bottom, we have Derthona (the Latin name of the city of Tortona), a simple Timorasso made from grapes from the youngest vines. One step up is Sterpi, a single-vineyard Timorasso vinified exclusively in stainless steel, revealing some of the mineral notes that are the base of the wine's success. At the top of the pyramid is Costa del Vento, another cru also aged in small wooden barrels.

On the nose, Colli Tortonesi Bianco Costa del Vento recalls a Riesling and has notes of grapefruit, peach tree flowers, graphite, and musk. In the mouth, the wine shines: It is full, round with exceptional minerality, and juicy with fruit and floral notes on the finish. This is a wine of big impact. It is great drunk young and really great if aged for a few years, even if we will have to wait to see just how long it can evolve happily.

Langhe Nebbiolo Sorì San Lorenzo—GAJA

IT IS NOT easy to talk about the most famous Italian wine producer in the world without taking a tone of admiration, which he no doubt deserves, and of fascination with his unmatchable success with one of the most important types of Piemontese wines, Barbaresco. Over the years,

Angelo Gaja, a spirited public speaker, and his wines changed what the world thought about the wines of Italy.

The history of Gaja dates back to the middle of the nineteenth century, when Angelo's great-grandfather, the actual helmsman of the winery, decided to open a transportation company in Alba, leaving his farmhouse and its surrounding land to his five sons. Angelo's grandfather (also named Angelo) managed an *osteria* in Barbaresco with his wife, Clotilde Rey, a strong-willed and intelligent French woman who is credited with taking the first step to improving the quality of the wines produced in the family winery. We are talking the beginning of the twentieth century here. Real change began with Giovanni, Angelo and Clotilde's son and father to the current Angelo Gaja. A land surveyor, the mayor of Barbaresco, a successful building contractor, a grape broker, and a businessman popular throughout southern Piemonte, Giovanni spent enough time in the cellar to guarantee that his son Angelo would have a strong, growing business. Even if his Barbarescos were sold unbottled in demijohns, they were already being purchased by the most important families in Piemonte—from the Zegna textile family to the Angelli family, which owns Fiat. The wines were universally well received, commanded a great price, and were commercially diffused throughout the region. Eventually, the wine could age for ten years before being sold. Then the volcanic Angelo was born, and any calmness or steadiness the Gaja family had known seemed to vanish. In forty years of incessant work, the heir of the Gaja dynasty transformed the winery into the benchmark of great Italian wine.

Little of his success was due to good fortune; rather, the Gaja notoriety is based almost entirely on Angelo's intuition, commitment, and vision. To retrace the pivotal moments of Gaja's influence on the image of wine, we must begin in 1967, the year in which his first Barbaresco cru, the legendary Sorì San Lorenzo, was released. The decision to establish specific crus and to microvinify specific parcels of land, giving them a cru name, is a pivotal turning point in the entire world of Italian wine. In time, the Gaja crus did more to elevate Italian fine wine production on an international level than perhaps any other single decision in Italian viticulture and enology. After this point, the potential of Barbaresco's greatest crus would be known by the Italian wine world, and the reception of these vineyards would be put on a par with the great crus of Burgundy and the Mosel. In 1970, Guido Rivella, a top enologist, joined the winery and became a fundamental pillar of its development. That same year, Barbaresco Sorì Tildin, named in honor of Grandma Clotilde, was released. In 1978, Gaja created Costa Russi, the third wine in their Barbaresco trilogy, made from grapes harvested from fourteen vineyards.

In addition to the revolution of the cru, Angelo Gaja made at least two other changes in breaking away from the past and from his fellow winemakers. He was the first to grasp the importance of travel as a means of comparison, growth, exchange, and promotion of his own wines. His trips to the United States during the 1970s and '80s—where he is still received as a superstar (or, more fittingly, a king)—made quite an impression in the market. As a young boy in the late 1970s in Queens, I first got to meet Angelo. I still remember the encounter today; he had an incredible ability to communicate and transmit his message of quality and authenticity in Italian wine production. Later, in the late 1980s, I was lucky enough to live in Alba, and I spent some highly impactful moments with Angelo in the vineyard and the cellar. He continues to be a good friend, confidant, and mentor, and he has had a strong influence on my perspective on wine as a professional throughout my life.

Angelo Gaja spent his life working unremittingly to raise the perception of Barbaresco to that of Barolo. This portion of the Langa—located in southern Piemonte, with Barolo directly to the south-west and also close to Monferrato, and planted with barbera to the northeast—had felt, for a long time, the frustration of being Barolo's "younger" sibling. For years, or rather for decades, or perhaps even centuries, generations of grape growers and wine lovers had created a sort of hierarchy, placing Barolo a step above the more genteel, elegant, and immediate Barbaresco. The local agronomy, superficial knowledge of farming techniques, and historical factors all contributed to Barbaresco's being number two: Despite how amiable, elegant, sought after, and loved a wine it may be, it could never be Barolo. But then Angelo arrived. The Gaja family is responsible for having eliminated this secondary positioning, demonstrating that, with dedication, excellently positioned vineyards, and the greatness of the nebbiolo grape, the wines that could be made in the Barbaresco area are great and even sometimes greater than Barolo.

In 2000, in an attempt to challenge himself, Gaja bought land in Barolo to contrast the territories and measure himself against the great red of the Langa. Or perhaps, after working so long and hard in the world of Barbaresco, Angelo decided to abandon the single denomination of his wines in 2000, giving himself more flexibility with the Langhe Nebbiolo denomination.

In all fairness, there are two other famous Piemontese winemakers in addition to Gaja to whom this historic changing of the winds should also be attributed: Bruno Giacosa with his Santo Stefano cru, and Bruno Ceretto with his memorable vintages of Bricco Asili. Beyond what the production guidelines say—differences in aging, a minimum alcohol level, and even a different, less austere color—Barbaresco has become and has remained one of the greatest wines in the world. Its only remaining handicap with respect to Barolo is the considerable difference in production area and relative volumes: 10 million bottles of Barolo are produced a year from eleven *comuni,* while only 3 million bottles of Barbaresco are made from only three *comuni.* This is a fact that producers have had to deal with for years and which they have tried to use to their advantage when positioning the wine on the market.

Angelo Gaja has proved capable of excellence in everything he does and everywhere he goes, from Piemonte to Toscana (where he has recently purchased property). Every new initiative of his clearly bears his stamp, as do his wine labels, on which the brand awareness of his last name signifies both a sort of contradiction to tradition and at the same time a strong sense of history. But Gaja is king, and with the king there is no room for discussion—at least when it comes to wine.

Of course, the wine that is known far across Italy owes something of its royal bearing to the land on which the grapes are grown. Langhe Nebbiolo Sorì San Lorenzo, a Barbaresco produced from 1967 to 2000, comes from a vineyard called Secondine, located next to the town of Barbaresco. The Tanaro River runs through the lower valley, while the vineyard's position varies between 660 and 890 feet. Close by, there are two other famous crus of the denomination, Pajè and Moccagatta. The Gaja family purchased the heart of the Secondine area in 1964, renaming it San Lorenzo as homage to the saint after which the main church of Alba was named and the owner of the land before it was given to Gaja. "Sorì," in Piemontese, refers to the part of the cru with the best exposure, which is normally south-facing on a hill. This is a spectacular vineyard in all regards: for its landscape, for the care it is given, and for its regular yields of nebbiolo grapes of the highest quality. After the harvest, the grapes are macerated and fermented for three weeks in stainless steel. They are then aged for two years, first in *botti grandi* (big barrels) and then in barriques. According to the official production guidelines for the Langhe Nebbiolo (the current denomination of this wine), it is possible to add a small percentage of barbera grapes (5 percent) to Sorì San Lorenzo. This is a common practice with nebbiolo-based wines and is used to soften the tannins of the nebbiolo grape.

Of the five Gaja crus, Sorì San Lorenzo is the most austere and long lived, and certainly the most expressive of Gaja's powerful, masculine style. On the nose, the wine is an expression of concentrated fruit, especially black fruit and spices, with rich minerality and earthy notes. On the palate, it is the perfect balance between power, alcohol, tannins, and elegance. Its finish recalls leather and truffles, with a lingering promise of longevity and evolution.

Barbaresco Vigneti in Montestefano Riserva—
CANTINA PRODUTTORI DEL BARBARESCO

THIS IS the story of a great Italian winery, which, like many great Italian wineries, is credited with dramatically changing the course of Italian winemaking. In this case, we are talking about Cantina Produttori del Barbaresco, a cellar that, at a very early time, was able to understand the value of vineyard-designated crus. Made by the same winery, using the same grape variety and the same winemaking techniques, the Produttori del Barbaresco cru wines demonstrate the difference that the position of the vineyards can make on nebbiolo.

In the second half of the nineteenth century, in the far-off hills of the Langa, Domizio Cavazza, the founder of the winery, was able to demonstrate (as the French had already done in Burgundy) the impact that the precise location of a vineyard can have on the resulting wine. In fact, Domizio Cavazza is still considered a sort of hero in Piemonte today. Born in 1856—a year after Bordeaux classified its crus—into a noble family in Concordia sul Secchia, Cavazza grew up studying agronomy and traveling throughout Europe. He was invited by Italy's Ministry of Agriculture to create a viticulture and enology school in Alba in 1881, and to act as the school's first president. This was the beginning of an intense relationship with the area around Alba in southern Piemonte, an area known by few at that time.

Cavazza was a sharp observer, which allowed him to understand the potential of the vines cultivated on the hills surrounding Alba. He began to visit the small towns throughout the Langa and had a particular affinity for the hamlet of Barbaresco. He was quite taken by the character of the nebbiolo-based wines made there and decided to invest personally in the promotion of this "local red." He bought a farmhouse and some land and began to carefully study the soil and the grapes, looking to the French for inspiration. In 1884, together with another famous person of the time, Guido Rocca, he decided to start a Cantina Sociale, or winemaking cooperative, so that local winemakers could join forces. At the time, this idea came as a shock to the strongly individualistic Piemontese winemakers, who had always resisted commercial or economic "unions." However, Cavazza's charisma was convincing, and he was able to win over his fellow farmers, something many people before him had attempted but failed. The Cantina Sociale produced the first official bottle of Barbaresco, giving life to a new star in the Italian wine panorama.

When Cavazza died in 1913, he left behind a huge inheritance of values and know-how. The path for the Cantina had already been laid out: to produce consistent volumes of quality wine. Then Fascism came along, and with it came the end of the Cantina Sociale. The new political regime was intolerant of cooperatives, and therefore the Cantina was closed. In 1958, the winery was reopened, this time under the guidance of a priest, don Fiorino, and with a new name: Cantina Produttori del Barbaresco. The new Cantina originally brought together nineteen small producers; it has since grown to include sixty. The collective vineyards now cover 270 acres (about 20 percent of the entire denomination), and all are planted with nebbiolo destined to become Barbaresco. The winery produces 300,000 bottles a year, of which half are "base" (labeled simple Barbaresco, with no cru designation) Barbaresco aged in large casks and which are emblematic of the wine in terms of style, elegance, and balance. The other half are divided among nine labels corresponding to the nine different crus, or historic vineyards: Asili, Moccagatta, Montefico, Montestefano, Ovello, Pajè, Pora, Rabajà, and Rio Sordo. Acclaimed by critics, these wines are considered the symbol and pride of the city of Barbaresco itself, with fans across Italy, thanks also to their good price-to-quality ratios and their availability. The Cantina Produttori del Barbaresco is without a doubt the most famous cooperative in Piemonte, and, now in its third decade of activity, is likely to remain so.

Touring the Barbaresco crus owned by the members of the Cantina is truly an emotional experience because of the beauty of the surrounding landscape. The tiny town of Barbaresco is one of the best preserved in the Langa and is literally immersed among the vines. There are at least twenty-four crus worth mentioning that are responsible for almost 50 percent of the entire production of Barbaresco. The climate of the area is characterized by air currents that pass through the valleys, which are literally wedged between the vine-covered hills. Each valley has its own microclimate. The nine celebrated crus of the Cantina Produttori frame the city. Each one deserves an in-depth description because we are talking about the "best of the best" of Italian winemaking history and tradition. However, over the years, the Montestefano cru has produced great wines that on occasion can be extraordinary. Montestefano is formed by a very steep central area that faces directly south; it begins at the town of Barbaresco and extends down the hillside. The far sides of the vineyard stretch east and west, slightly losing that perfect southern exposure. The vineyard is located at 890 feet above sea level and covers 12 acres of land. The property is divided between five families—Gonella, Maffei, Marcarino, Rivella, and Rocca—all members of the Cantina. Montestefano was one of the first crus to be vinified with the name of the cru appearing on the label. This was back in 1961 and was the work of Beppe Colla of the Prunotto winery.

Montestefano can be considered "the most Barolo-like Barbaresco" as it has a traditionally powerful and tannic structure. It slightly steers one away from the classic idea of Barbaresco as a gentler red with respect to its "cousin" Barolo, while remaining in the same category of wine. Some of the more memorable vintages include 1971 and 1982: Tasted today, these bottles demonstrate the incredible longevity of the wines produced in Montestefano. Characterized by notes of leather and tobacco, the wine is considered one of the best expressions of the Langa. Made exclusively from nebbiolo grapes harvested in mid-October, Montestefano begins its life in the cellar, where it rests on the skins for twenty-four days. The wine is then aged for thirty-six months in small oak casks, followed by eight months in the bottle. The bottles labeled "Riserva" are left to age for an additional two years. The dark ruby red color and light hints of orange are the tradional signs of great classic nebbiolo. On the nose, the wine is typically spicy and earthy, with notes of licorice and the forest floor. Its flavor is strong, round, and powerful, yet refined, finishing on an unmistakable note of tobacco leaves.

Barbaresco Rombone—FIORENZO NADA

IT'S AMAZING to see how a man revered today for his brilliant Barbaresco wines was once considered lunatic for his seemingly idiotic winemaking methods. Fiorenzo Nada stubbornly pushed forward in spite of the resistance he faced, and we have him to thank for creating one of Italy's greatest wines.

The history of the Nada family of Treiso, a small village located in the area where Barbaresco is produced, is closely linked to that of the territory. Over the course of twenty years, the area has become one of the standouts on the Italian and European wine scene. Fiorenzo Nada is a lively eighty-seven-year-old who is young at heart. He does not leave out any details when recounting the difficult beginnings encountered by the region's winemakers. Born into a family of farmers, Fiorenzo grew up with the challenges and poverty of a world years away from knowing the comforts of modern life. The same manicured, rolling hills that today are known by wine lovers were once a place where people farmed for survival and where hunger was a constant threat. The land was cultivated with a variety of plants, of which grapes were certainly not the focal point. Things seemed destined to remain the same forever here in the Langa, but at the beginning of the 1980s, something changed for good. The young farmers' sons—including Bruno, son of Fiorenzo—began to notice what was occurring outside of Piemonte (in Toscana or Burgundy, for example). The new generation recognized that they were living in an extraordinary winemaking territory that had its own incredible grape variety. In other words, they realized they could make a living from wine but that they would have to make major investments to do so.

Bruno, in particular, was one of the first to pave his own way. Little did he know that in only a few years, the image of southern Piemonte would change completely. He began the practice of thinning out the nebbiolo grapes—his father reacted with disdain because he felt his son was "wasting" valuable raw material. Bruno also bought the first barrique, another sign of breaking tradition; in the past, regional wines were made in cement or in large wooden barrels. Based on these improvements, Bruno found the courage to market his wines outside of the usual client base. This may seem like a simple and relatively unimportant story, but it is a small example of what happened across the territory. In fact, we are talking about the birth of modern winemaking in Piemonte—a cultural and social phenomenon destined to have a major impact even on other regions in Italy. After having made this first step, Bruno Nada and his fellow winemakers did not stop there: The determination and the experience they had gained led them to compete with the most well-known Tuscan and French winemakers. Their work caused Barbaresco to grow in popularity and become "Barolo's brother." From here on, the life and pride of the farmer would change decisively.

Up to this point, the history of the Nada family is very similar to that of other families living nearby. However, what really sets them apart is that Bruno Nada had humility, passion, and a talent for making incredible, elegant wines that almost seemed "out of place and out of time." His wines were fascinating and had a strong character. Being welcomed into their small cellar at the top of the hill of Rombone and tasting their wines in the company of wise old Fiorenzo is truly a special experience. The Nada family demonstrated that it is possible to become a great winemaker while remaining true to yourself. Despite winning the Tre Bicchieri award in the *Vini d'Italia* wine guidebook, the family has steered clear of the press. With their dedication and hard work, they have a built a simple, essential, and uplifting history.

The production zone of Barbaresco wine borders, both geographically and "mentally," that of Barolo. It is located in southern Piemonte, near the dynamic city of Alba, in the swath of hills known as the Langa. Unlike Barolo—whose production zone is made up of eleven *comuni*—Barbaresco comprises only three: Barbaresco, Neive, and Treiso (besides a small area in Alba). Only recently has Treiso been confirmed as an important wine area. It boasts a magnificent location and is filled with vineyards with good exposure. For years, Treiso produced grapes for some of the most well-known winemakers in the Langa. Only recently, thanks to the example set by Bruno Nada, have the area's winemakers begun to keep the grapes with which nature and human tending have gifted them harvest after harvest. Today you can find many Barbarescos by producers from Treiso. Bruno Nada has some of the most beautiful vineyards in the area. One in particular, Rombone, has demonstrated an ability to produce very important nebbiolo-based wines and is now even considered a "grand cru" of the Langa. Built around the Nadas' property of the same name, the Rombone vineyard varies from 650 to 850 feet in altitude and has a southwest-facing exposure, allowing it to benefit from the day's last rays of light.

Barbaresco Rombone is named after the almost-fifty-year-old vines from which it is produced. The nebbiolo grapes are left to mature until mid-October, when the air cools and the first fog arrives, signaling harvest time across the hills. The maceration of the grapes occurs in stainless steel vats and continues for ten to twelve days. Then malolactic fermentation starts, which takes place in the same French oak barriques in which the wine will age for the next sixteen to eighteen months. The wine is then aged for another year in the bottle before the Barbaresco Rombone is ready. However, this wine is known to age well and can wait to be drunk.

With a brick-red core and deep orange ring, Rombone has a pretty nose, with spicy, earthy notes. It is more elegant than it is strong, even in regard to its aroma, in which you find elements of leather, cacao, and licorice; it is always well balanced, with fresh and lively sensations of red fruit. In the mouth, both the elegance and strength of the wine reach their peak—owing to the short period of time spent in small wooden barrels, which on one hand, rounds off the harshness of the nebbiolo, and on the other, exalts the tannic component of the varietal. Rombone has a long, silky finish, which recalls its aroma. It is a wine of brilliance, able to bring light to the Barbaresco zone like few others.

Barbaresco Vigneto Starderi—LA SPINETTA

THE RIVETTI BROTHERS—Carlo, Bruno, and Giorgio—who own the famous La Spinetta winery, have had a powerful and lasting impact on the Italian wine market. Their Barbarescos turned the wine world upside down with a confident and imaginative interpretation of tradition. Starderi Barbaresco shouts for attention with a fruit-forward style and technically rounded edges. In many ways, this wine brought the full potential of modern-style Barbaresco to the world.

The history of this Piemontese winery, however, begins on the opposite side of the world. Giovanni Rivetti, the brothers' grandfather, was a part of the huge wave of Piemontesi who emigrated to Argentina at the end of the nineteenth century (1890, in Giovanni's case) in search of fame and fortune. Having found neither, Giovanni returned to his native land and purchased a small farm. On his death, Giovanni left the property to his son Giuseppe, who began making wine commercially. The family bought property and vineyards in Castagnole Lanze, just a few miles from the area producing some of the top red wines of the Langa, where they began growing the nebbiolo grape, as well as the moscato grape, which is used to make a simple dessert wines. The Rivetti family was the first in the area to focus their attention on moscato, giving life to the crus of Moscato d'Asti by selecting and vinifying grapes from single vineyards. Back in 1978, the cru moscatos Bricco Quaglia and Biancospino wines represented a new way to interpret this popular white Piemontese wine.

In the years to follow, Giuseppe's three sons—Carlo, Bruno, and Giorgio—began working inside the winery, and in 1985, La Spinetta released its first red wine: Barbera d'Asti Ca' di Pian. Four years later, in 1989, came the birth of Monferrato Rosso Pin (dedicated to Giuseppe), a wine that once again had a tremendous impact on territory: This was the first-ever blend of barbera and nebbiolo. From here on out, there has been no end to the influence of the Rivetti brothers on Italian winemaking. Aware of their enormous potential, they decided, almost unconsciously at the beginning, to create a model winery focused entirely on quality. In just three years (1995–1997), they came out with three new wines: Barbaresco Gallina, Starderi, and Valeirano, each of which capture their interpretive spirit, style, and power.

The Rivetti brothers would certainly consider themselves modernists because of their decision to aggressively prune the vines and to use short maceration times and small wood casks, and beause of their dedication to the concept of cru wines. Compared with many other producers who have chosen to take the same road, La Spinetta has avoided strict definition or classification by exploring new stylistic territories, concentrating the wines (that, however, remain elegant), seeking out new flavors and sensations from traditional Piemontese red wines (which, however, still remain *terroir* driven), and giving a glamorous touch to the image of the winery. If we have to give the Rivetti brothers a label, the most fitting one might be "postmodernist." Giorgio, the leader of the *azienda,* is truly a man of the global wine world. Unlike many Italians who are extremely limited in their appreciation of wine, his palate has been developed by tasting throughout the world. The rhinoceros on La Spinetta labels has actually come to signify postmodern winemaking in Italy. And in recent years, a lion has been added to the portfolio of La Spinetta wine labels: Like the lion, their Barolo Campè is king of the jungle.

So far, nothing can stop the Rivetti brothers. They have purchased a property in Toscana, between Pisa and Volterra, where they are now producing sangiovese-based wines. Although this may seem like the course of a multinational brand, the company is growing and enlarging in a sustainable way, thanks to the familiar, generous, and informal style of the Rivetti family. Currently, the staff is focused on making the vineyards biodynamic—a potentially extremely effective mix of traditional and modern winemaking techniques.

In every place they set up camp—from Asti to Barbaresco to Barolo, all the way down to Toscana—the Rivetti brothers have made important contributions to the local management of the land, the promotion of native Italian wine varieties, and the implementation of forward-thinking production techniques and communication strategies. What they have brought to Barbaresco is a perfect example of this. Arriving in Neive during the 1990s, the Rivetti brothers divided their attention between two territories: the legendary Gallina vineyard, where they produced their first Barbaresco, and the semi-unknown and undervalued Starderi. (The third La Spinetta Barbaresco, Valeirano, comes from the *comune* of Treiso.) Starderi is a vineyard sheltered by a small town just outside of Neive and spreads down the valley toward the Tanaro River. The most prized part of the vineyard faces southwest at an altitude of about 890 feet. Vinified and bottled for the first time in 1996, the grapes from this vineyard have proved to have an explosive force, and it is being recognized as a grand cru of Barbaresco.

So why the rhinoceros and not another animal? Giorgio Rivetti loved the Albrecht Dürer woodcut of a rhinoceros, depicting an actual rhinoceros sent as a gift to the King of Portugal in 1515 from the governor of Portuguese India. The rhinoceros is undoubtedly a strong symbol, tenacious yet delicate since it is at risk of extinction. Giorgio and his brother must have thought of this when they had the image replicated for their wine labels. Starderi is strong, like the grape from which it is made (nebbiolo); tenacious, like the men who made it; and delicate, for it is ultimately a product of Mother Nature. The grapes of the vineyard (which covers 16 acres, with vines that have an average age of forty years) are harvested toward mid-October. The maceration lasts seven to eight days, and the malolactic fermentation occurs in small casks. The wine rests in barriques, of both old and new French oak, for twenty to twenty-two months before moving into stainless steel tanks for three more months. Once bottled, the wine is left to age for a year.

Barbaresco Vigneto Starderi has a deep, ruby red color and ethereal, toasty perfumes, as well as plenty of ripe fruit, with cherries, wild strawberries, currants, and sour cherries, then roses, wet earth, leather, and licorice. In the mouth, the wine is elegant, with a fine finish. In between is a cannon shot of power, flavor, sapidity, tannins, and round-ness. By tasting the 1996 Starderi, the first vintage produced, one can easily understand the astonishing effect the wine had, and still has, on the world of Barbaresco.

Barbera d'Asti Bricco dell'Uccellone—BRAIDA

FEW WINEMAKERS in Italy, or anywhere else for that matter, can be called "founders" of a wine and of a winemaking tradition. Giacomo Bologna, known as Braida (a nickname passed down—as names often are—from his grandfather, who was a local hero of a popular Piemontese sport called *pallapugno*), was a pioneer, an initiator, and a prophet who was capable of seeing into the future. Many years ago, Braida was responsible for making barbera, a grape once considered to be quite poor, into a global powerhouse. He turned it into a wine of excellence, recognized and awarded by wine critics from around the world. He was able to accomplish this feat thanks to an unshakable faith in the terri-tory, an atypical visionary talent, and an extraordinary love of life that made him an unforgettable person.

Born in Rocchetta Tanaro, a small town located between the hills of south-central Piemonte, in the area known as Monferrato Astigiano, Giacomo Bologna lived his childhood and youth to the fullest, slowly discovering the flavors, rites, and treasures of the rural landscape. He also discovered a love for *feste in piazza* (city fairs) and traditional music; a passion for eating well and for truffles (his family managed, and still manages, a trattoria that has become a destination spot for food lovers); and a strong sense of friendship and human relationships. These characteristics accompanied Braida throughout his life, and somehow eventually came to define the style of his wine.

Giacomo began to make his move into the farm of his father, Giu-seppe, in the 1960s. These were hard years. The economic boom was bringing Italy back to life, but the beneficiaries of the stimulus were primarily the city dwellers. The countryside was still considered backward and was often exploited by the large wholesalers. In 1964, in rebellion against one of these companies, known throughout Monferrato for buying grapes from the farmers at very low cost, Giacomo Bologna decided to bottle his own barbera grapes. This is how Monella—an exceptional wine at the time that to this day is still famous—was born, and how people began talking about this local varietal, barbera.

Braida realized that he was headed down the right path and put more effort into his work as a grape grower, winemaker, and communicator. He traveled to France and California, and he met with the top winemakers and chefs in Italy and abroad. He entered an elite cultural circle and was introduced to important figures like the wine critic and writer Gino Veronelli; the future founder of Slow Food, Carlo Petrini; and famous soccer players, musicians, and artists. Everyone was charmed by the infectious enthusiasm of this gregarious man. In 1982, he produced the first superquality Barbera in small French barrels, calling it Bricco dell'Uccellone. With the release of this wine, the history of this native varietal, which is grown on 50 percent of the Piemontese vineyards, changed forever. It finally distinguished itself as one of the great European reds. Giacomo, however, did not get to enjoy his success: He died prematurely in 1990, leaving his wife, Anna, and their children, Raffaella and Giuseppe, with the job of keeping his unique spirit alive. His mantra remains a spiritual testament among his fellow winemakers: "Build yourself a large, spacious, and well-ventilated cellar, liven it up with a lot of beautiful bottles, some standing straight up, others lying on their side, to consider with a friendly eye in the evenings of spring, summer, fall, and winter, smiling at the thought that a man without a song and without noise, without women and without wine, will supposedly live ten years longer than you." This was Giacomo Bologna.

Rocchetta Tanaro is a calm, tiny town immersed in the hills of the vast "green sea" of Monferrato. Less known than the neighboring Langa, this area boasts the same ancient tradition of winemaking, but with a different leading grape varietal: Here, barbera, not nebbiolo, reigns supreme. It seems as though the varietal comes from nearby Rocchetta, in the *comune* of Nizza Monferrato, where documents are kept that attest to its ancient origin and where some of the most important Barberas are made today. The varietal then spread throughout the region, to the point of becoming the most cultivated grape in Piemonte, forcing legislators to create three different Barbera denominations: Barbera d'Asti, Barbera d'Alba, and Barbera del Monferrato. Today, the Braida estates cover about 100 acres of vineyards that are located across the area but concentrated essentially in Rocchetta. In this specific town, you will find the Bricco dell'Uccellone vineyard, which over time has become the symbol of Barbera (and not only Barbera d'Asti). Located at the top of a hill composed of clay soil, not far from the city of Rocchetta, the vineyard gets its name from an old woman who used to live there. She used to always dress in black and was ironically referred to as "l'Uccellone," a local word meaning "crow" or "black magpie." Another interesting anecdote is that for years, the people of the area debated whether the gender of *barbera* was masculine or feminine, because in the Italian language, it could be either. In the end, as with any great compromise, it was established that the barbera grape would be considered masculine, while the wine, Barbera, would be feminine. And this is how the wine acquired the nickname "Lady in Red," referring to its seductive character.

The harvest of Bricco dell'Uccellone takes place in October. The yields are extremely low, owing in part to the fact that the vineyard is very old and not very productive. The maceration on the skins traditionally lasts for exactly twenty-two days and the pulp is pumped over the must a second time. The wine is then placed primarily in new oak, where it rests for at least twelve months. The Barbera d'Asti Bricco dell'Uccellone is bottle-aged for another year before it is released.

Bricco dell'Uccellone has a relatively high alcohol content (13.5 percent to 14.5 percent, depending on the vintage) and an intense ruby red color with a violet tinge, characteristic of barbera grapes grown in this area. On the nose, it has a joyful mix of red fruit and spices, with strawberries, cherries, sour cherries, blackberries, and blueberries. In the mouth, it is both elegant and powerful, as only the best reds are: The typical acidity of the grape varietal is rounded off thanks to the taming effect of oak aging. The wine is full on the palate, with great equilibrium. After Bricco dell'Uccellone, other producers have come out with other successful and well-liked Barbera wines. However, the wine of Braida is still the quintessential wine of the area.

Gattinara Vigneto Osso San Grato—ANTONIOLO

FROM THEIR VINEYARDS in Gattinara, the Antoniolo family brings us a taste of the other Piemonte. In many ways, these wines are the antithesis of a great Barolo. They are an inverse wine experience, drawing you in rather than shouting out at you. Osso San Grato is a Gattinara that in its own quiet way can be more demostrative than the great wines of Alba.

Piemonte is a region of many varietals and diverse *terroirs*. The southern part of the region, where the great Barolos and Barbarescos are made, has certainly become famous worldwide, and for good reason, but there are also other interesting wine production areas in Piemonte that are slowly gaining the attention of wine critics and wine lovers. One such microregion is Gattinara, where an eponymous wine is made with the nebbiolo grape.

Located about 50 miles north of Torino, Gattinara is not well known for its viticulture, even though it has had periods of notoriety over the centuries. After a golden age in the beginning of the twentieth century until the 1950s, wine and agriculture in general slowed because of internal emigration from the countryside to the cities. In the 1960s, during the so-called economic boom, there was a mass exodus from rural towns to the metropolitan, industrial cities. In Piemonte, for example, Fiat hired around a hundred thousand farmers, at the price of a patrimony of knowledge and know-how related to caring for the land that were gone for good. The triangle between Vercelli Novara, and

Biella, at the center of which you will find a very high concentration of vineyards and cellars, was turned on its head and became an industrial center, considered avant-garde for its time and referred to as the "Manchester of Italy." Luckily, not everyone in the country decided to give up their rural ways. The Antoniolo family, a close-knit group of vignerons known in the winemaking community since the 1940s, remained on their land, even when it became financially unsustainable.

Rosanna Antoniolo, the daughter of the founder of the cellar and doyenne of Italian winemaking for her sixty-plus years of experience, played witness to an important historical passage for Italian society. Called to manage her family's company at a young age after the early death of her father, Rosanna, a woman in a man's world, led the winery forward with the goal of making quality wines and introducing people to the "nebbiolo of the north." Despite her geographical distance from the epicenter of Piemontese winemaking, Rosanna Antoniolo knew how to build a company on long-term goals. She employed the concept of cru wines—wines made with grapes from a single vineyard, a practice that came into use in the 1970s, even before her fellow winemakers down in Alba. She also focused on a traditional winemaking style, allowing for the maximum expression of the particular characteristics of the northern soil. Today Antoniolo is synonymous with Gattinara, and Gattinara is synonymous with an enological renaissance. The real work of the Antoniolo family, however, has been their defense of local biodiversity. Although many wineries have embraced modernity, at Antoniolo, winemaking is culture, memory, and faith in tomorrow.

When talking about the wines from Gattinara, one often uses a simple, perhaps simplistic, expression to get the idea across: "northern Piemonte." This term oversimplifies the wines because it places Gattinara in a larger geographical context, which includes all the microwinemaking regions found north of Torino. Gattinara is a vast area and difficult to define because it is not flat, it is not exactly hilly, and it is still not mountainous, even though the area has climatic and morphological characteristics of all three. It has a strong winemaking culture that was briefly interrupted mid-twentieth century and that had to be rebuilt in recent years. Thankfully, the region had two things going for it: nebbiolo and the *terroir*. There is little to be said that hasn't already been said on the first: "Her majesty," the grape itself, has lent her adaptive grace and quality to the wines of Gattinara. The *terroir* is what remains—not having been consumed by the artisanal, industrial, and commercial human activities—a very little amount, but enough to give the landscape its character. The soil is made up of volcanic rock, which shouldn't be surprising after the recent discovery of Valsesia (the valley beginning at the base of Monte Rosa and leading down to Gattinara), a so-called supervolcano that was active a couple of million years ago and that is considered by geologists to be the largest of its type.

In 1974, when Antoniolo released their two selections of Gattinara, Vigneto Osso San Grato and San Francesco, a wave of praise arrived from critics and fellow winemakers. The company made a decidedly innovative choice in a time when wines were generally categorized by type, and not by specific vineyard. The Antoniolo family was looking ahead and knew that sooner or later, the concept of the cru would come to define modern taste and wine culture. They also began producing a third cru wine, Vigneto Castelle.

The Osso San Grato comes from an 11-acre vineyard above the town of Gattinara; it is made of volcanic soil and able to produce around 5,000 bottles a year. The vinification methods are focused on bringing out the character of the soil. The must is left to rest on the lees for fourteen days, and the wine is then transferred to large 3,000-liter oak barrels, where it remains for at least thirty-six months.

The resulting wine is unique. The color is an intense granite red. The aromas are austere and earthy, recalling the humidity of the forest floor, dried violet, and sour cherry. In the mouth, the wine is strong, but incredibly elegant, a real symphony of acidity, tannins, and pleasure.

Roero Mombeltramo Riserva—MALVIRÀ

THE DAMONTE BROTHERS, Massimo and Roberto, never seem to stop. After having opened an elegant farmhouse hotel just outside the town of Canale, Piemonte, and having become leading producers of Roero wine—which was awarded a DOCG denomination in 2005—the men are now focused on enlarging their winery and vineyards. If you ask the brothers why they haven't decided to slow down, they will respond, in unison, that Roero is a young *terroir*. It is gaining fame and has the chance of establishing itself as Italy's next great wine region.

The history of Roero, and of Malvirà, is actually quite interesting. The winemaking district defined as Roero is located just a few miles from the world-famous crus of Barolo and Barbaresco. Although nebbiolo is grown in all three regions, Roero remained outside the important national and international wine circuits, selling most of its wine unbottled to merchants from nearby Torino. In the 1950s, even Massimo and Roberto's father would transport demijohns to the city or welcome Sunday day-trippers into their old farmhouse, located in the center of Canale. The Damonte *cascina*, or farmhouse, was famous among locals for being *mal girata*, or "turned strangely," because the courtyard of the home faced north, not south as was the tradition. In fact, this is where the name of the winery, Malvirà, comes from. With Italy's economic boom came a new generation of *vignaioli*, or farmer/winemakers, who took over the family business and decided to focus on producing quality wine. The youngsters of Roero began looking more carefully at the Langa wines from across the Tanaro River, and they began to travel and select the grape varieties best suited for the territory. They also discovered that the principal difference between Roero and the Langa is that the soil is far sandier on the left bank of the river—in Roero. Because Roero is at a lower altitude than the Langa, it spent much more time under the marine waters that covered much of northern Italy centuries ago. The water caused limestone sediments and sand to deposit in the soil: As you walk through the Malvirà vineyards, it is not uncommon to find a shell or a fossil of a fish. In the 1980s, the Malvirà family decided to divide their vineyard between two grape varieties: arneis, a native white wine grape (whose name comes from a vineyard owned by the Damonte brothers called Renesio), and nebbiolo, the most famous grape of southern Piemonte. Since the 1990s, Malvirà is, together with Matteo Correggia, the most famous brand in Roero: The two wineries are 100 yards from each other, and together, the ambitious young winemakers have turned Roero into an internationally recognized wine zone.

Do not attempt to look for Roero on a map of Piemonte, because it will not be there! The recognition of the territory—not only in terms of wine, but also in respect to the region's history and culture—is so recent that people are still getting accustomed to the name. For a long time, Roero was simply referred to as the left bank of the Tanaro River, which separates the clay-soiled crus of the Langa from the sandy vineyards of the Roero. Today the *rive gauche* is creating a fame of its own, thanks to the work and intelligence of its more forward-thinking wine producers. The Damonte brothers were the first winemakers to identify which vineyards were best suited for which types and varieties of grapes. For over ten years, Massimo and Roberto have produced three different single-vineyard types of Arneis, and the same philosophy goes for their top two reds: Roero Trinità and Roero Mombeltramo. The latter comes from a 4-acre east-facing vineyard located at around 1,100 feet above sea level, with characteristically sandy, calcareous soil. In their 104-acre property, the majority of which is located around the winery, forming a large, natural amphitheater, Malvirà has begun experimenting with so-called light production methods: Organic certification is just a matter of time, but the company is currently involved in protecting the health of the soil and the grapes with natural manure fertilizer, careful pruning, and general reduction of stress on the plant. Even in this respect, the winery is on the forefront for the region, improving the quality of the environment that weighs heavily on the final quality of their wines.

Roero Mombeltramo Riserva is a relatively new wine for the company, but the concept behind the wine can be traced back much further in history. It comes from the recent split from Malvirà's famous Roero Superiore, with which the company made its name at the beginning of the 1990s. Now Malvirà produces two red Roero Reserves: Trinità and Mombeltramo. Both wines cannot be released, according to regulation, until three years after harvest, putting them in line with Barbaresco in terms of aging time.

Mombeltramo Riserva is a nebbiolo with extreme elegance and measured power. It is the perfect testimony of the land it comes from. The soft, calcareous soil gives the grapes their unique character, which in turn gives the wine its fruity aroma. When drunk young, the wine can be enjoyed for its delicate tannins and finesse. After a couple years of aging, the earthy, austere notes of this wine become harder, and harder to find.

It is difficult to classify Malvirà in a precise category of winemaking—given that there still are any—because its wines are modern in their conception, but the use of tonneaux for aging their wines is quite original, compared with the methods of their fellow winemakers in Roero and the Langa. The Damonte brothers' decision to focus on quality has also allowed them to define their own style based on the grace, harmony, and attention paid to this special territory.

~VALLE D'AOSTA~

Valle d'Aosta Chardonnay Cuvée Bois—LES CRÊTES

VALLE D'AOSTA CROWNS the region of Piemonte, transitioning from Italy into France. A former province of the great House of Savoy, the now autonomous region sets the limits of extreme high-altitude vineyards for all of Europe. The postwar generation had all but abandoned quality winemaking, and the wines of Valle d'Aosta had sunk to an all-time low. Only the rise of Costantino Charrère, owner and winemaker of Les Crêtes, unified this divided and neglected wine region and reprioritized quality wine production.

Charrère, a world-class skier and mountaineer, inherited tiny plots of vineyards that straddled mountain ridges and streaked up sky-bound peaks. Because of the limited (only 870 acres) and fragmented vineyards, winemaking was done at home or in a few cooperatives. Charrère's decision to focus on multiple varietals, experimentation, and extreme quality caused many locals to view him as heretical and his lofty ambitions as unachievable. Les Crêtes winery was set up as a partnership among Charrère, the Vai brothers (local restaurateurs), and the Grosjean family, who had also been growing grapes for generations in the nearby village of Quart. A full-time winemaker by the early 1990s, Charrère cut his teeth on the indigenous and familiar varietals of his father's vineyards, but he constantly peered over the Alps at white wine nirvana: Burgundy, home of the world's most noble white grape. Charrère believed that his own mountain soil could also yield a world-class Chardonnay of racy minerality, firm acidic structure, and gentle time-proven evolution. The great white wines of Burgundy and their proximity provided inspiration, yet he never sought to duplicate the style of Bonne. Respecting the style of small-barrel fermentation and aging, Charrère and his wines gave a newfound voice to the great white wine *terroir* of Valle d'Aosta. Now boasting 45 acres of vineyards and having left his founding partners behind, Charrère and his family are the beacon of quality viticulture in the entire region and represent the undying spirit that is the independent vigneron of Valle d'Aosta.

The Valle d'Aosta is situated in the extreme northwest part of the Italian peninsula. The Dora Baltea River splits the region in half on the rising valley floor from the town of Donnas, rising past Aosta and scaling the heights of Morgex. Mountain tributary streams of snowmelt from the pure and lofty peaks of Mont Blanc and the Matterhorn are the source of glacial moraine *terroir* (pulverized glacial rock from the ice age) and are the life-giving arteries to this extreme mountaintop viticulture. A terraced patchwork of vineyards guides the river north and is accented by the ramparts of once dominant castles. As the river wraps around Aosta, the 2,100-foot tower of Coteau la Tour rises in the east. This medieval watchtower sits atop the vineyard-shrouded hill that provides the chardonnay used to make Cuvée Bois. The colonists of the Roman Empire were the first to carve vineyards into the steep hills by grading small, level vineyard sites, using stones to divide the parcels and to adjust for the changing elevation. The effort to farm these vineyards is nothing short of heroic. Yet over the years, these stone walls have not only maintained vineyards but have saved the very *terroir* of the Valle d'Aosta from being washed away into the valley by the unrelenting annual snowmelt. The patchwork of vineyards created by these ancient stone walls have come to represent the Aosta people, as they cling to the steep hills they call home and as they coax world-class wine from dirt that walls and men have held in place for thousands of years.

Costantino Charrère's unwavering belief in the potential of chardonnay to create world-class wine in his native *terroir* of Valle d'Aosta gave birth to Cuvée Bois. Employing the nontraditional farming techniques of ultralow yields and vinifying in barriques with extended lees contact, Charrère uprooted the long-standing winemaking methods of his forefathers. The gentle and integrated use of oak gives this Chardonnay a rich sweetness that, when combined with the acidity and racy minerality of the soil, makes a wine of evolving complexity and utter satisfaction.

SOUTHERN ITALY
AND THE MEZZOGIORNO

CROATIA

Viterbo

VATICAN
CITY

Roma

Fiume Tevere

Rieti

L'Aquila

Teramo

Pescara

Chieti

A

B

*Mare
Adriatico*

LAZIO

ABRUZZO

Latina

Frosinone

MOLISE

Isernia

Campobasso

I

Benevento

Caserta

Avellino

G **E**
F **H**

Foggia

Napoli

D

MONTE
VESUVIO

Salerno

C

Bari

PUGLIA

CAMPANIA

Potenza

Matera

BASILICATA

Brindisi

K

Lecce

*Mare
Tirreno*

Cosenza

CALABRIA

Vibo Valentia

Crotone

*Mare
Ionio*

Catanzaro

Reggio
Calabria

Southern Italy
and the
Mezzogiorno

Abruzzo

A *Trebbiano d'Abruzzo* Valentini

B *Montepulciano d'Abruzzo Villa Gemma* Masciarelli

Basilicata

C *Aglianico del Vulture Titolo* Elena Fucci

Campania

D *Costa d'Amalfi Furor Bianco Fiorduva* Cantine Gran Furor Divina Costiera di Marisa Cuomo

E *Fiano di Avellino* Colli di Lapio

F *Irpinia Aglianico Serpico* Feudi di San Gregorio

G *Taurasi Radici Riserva* Mastroberardino

H *Taurasi Vigna Cinque Querce* Salvatore Molettieri

I *Terra di Lavoro* Galardi

Lazio

J *Grechetto Latour a Civitella* Sergio Mottura

Puglia

K *Le Braci* Azienda Monaci

~ABRUZZO~

Trebbiano d'Abruzzo—VALENTINI

FOUNDED IN 1650, Valentini di Loreto Aprutino is the oldest winery in Abruzzo. The company's history is full of fascinating and charismatic people. In the 1960s, Edoardo Valentini emerged on the world wine scene as a producer of great Italian wine. A nobleman from Abruzzo, Valentini became an important player in the history of Italian wine-making, thanks to his intelligence and his unordinary character. Only a few wine lovers have had the privilege to visit his cellar and learn about the production methods of this baron of Abruzzo. He has only ever produced three wines: Cerasuolo (Edoardo's favorite), Montepulciano, and Trebbiano.

His winemaking friends and many enologists who loved his wines asked him what his secret was. Very candidly, he would reply that to make his wines, he had to read the writings on wine found in the ancient pre-Socratic texts of Thales, Pythagoras, Parmenides, Zeno, and Heraclitus. In these texts, the authors, who had a pantheist vision of the world that centered on Mother Earth, described nature as a living being composed of animals, minerals, stars, planets, plants, and even humans. After having read the texts, the enologists and wine producers went back to him to ask for an explanation. He said that his words were meant to be interpreted: The texts describe not a precise recipe for winemaking but rather a vision of the universe as a whole, including the vines, the fields, and the casks for aging wine. Edoardo was quite a personality. For example, Edoardo never showed up for public wine tastings and press conferences, instead always sending his psychiatrist in his place! In the last years of his life—he died in 2006—Edoardo would instead send his son Francesco Paolo, a man of about fifty, tall, aristocratic in the ways of his father, but a farmer through and through.

The Valentini wines have received innumerable awards and are among the most sought after and difficult to find on the market because their limited production does not even come close to the incredibly high demand. In the past decade, only the 2002 and 2006 vintages of Montepulciano have been bottled to date. With minimal intervention in the vine and the cellar, production variability can be high, and Edoardo was very selective. To truly understand the rebellious and anarchic spirit that fills the air in Loreto Aprutino, home to the Valentini cellar, just consider this: The Valentini family owns 160 acres of vineyards, and rather than producing 400,000 bottles, which would be the norm, they produce a maximum of 50,000, and only when it is an excellent vintage. A fun anecdote from the 1970s, when the Valentini wines were still exported to the United States, captures the spirit of Edoardo and Francesco. Someone, possibly an informer, told the American authorities about the anarchic sympathies of the family and the authorities ordered the American importer to write a letter to Edoardo asking him to kindly deny the accusations. So what did Edoardo do? He stopped selling to the States! Even so, the top wine stores and restaurants in America still serve his great Trebbiano; somehow they are able to get their hands on it.

Edoardo was first and foremost a farmer, and so is his son Francesco. Francesco has continued to make wine for two reasons. First, through winemaking he is able to cultivate his yearning and passion for nature, in particular for grapevines and olive trees, and he has the chance to be in direct contact with the kingdom of the plants and that of the animals. He can directly observe and study the changes in the seasons. Second, when immersed in the beating heart of nature, he can stay as far away as possible from so-called modern society.

The Valentini vineyard is a sort of miracle that few agronomists can explain. For decades now, winemakers have been promoting the system of training vines vertically with the *cordone speronato* technique. However, the Valentinis have continued to arbor their vines, planting them with a density of 490 to 570 plants per acre, keeping them carefully cropped so the bunches can reach optimal ripeness. In this case, contrary to what their malicious and ill-speaking competitors would like to believe, the Valentini family did not choose this method just to be antimainstream: *Tendone* (a system of training the vines on high, flat trellises) is actually quite suitable for the areas, like theirs, that have a hot climate and little rain. Therefore, the choice was not an act of snobbery, but rather the perfect understanding of the land and use of the proper training system, even if the production costs are higher.

Valentini Trebbiano is a wine that polarizes wine lovers. Some turn their noses up at the imperfections that can sometimes be present in this wine. The Trebbiano has been known to referment in the bottle and develop bubbles. But this is barely a defect: Leave the wine in the glass for a couple of seconds to breathe, and it will recompose itself. The other special characteristic of this wine is its extreme longevity; it is among the only Italian white wines with such a long lifespan. In fact, many of the bottles produced in the 1980s are drinking perfectly.

To describe the Trebbiano, people often compare it with some of the great French wines like a Chablis Premier Cru of excellent vintage, or a Chassagne-Montrachet, or a Corton-Charlemagne. In reality, the Trebbiano di Valentini is unique because of the warm notes that come from the latitude at which the wine is produced. However, the scent can be deceiving, since its freshness and minerality are completely out of the ordinary. When the wine is tasting well, it is without rivals, thanks to its fine, elegant aromas of ginestra (broom), yellow apple, and resin, with underlying notes of flint, rust, and, often, bacon. In the mouth, it has good sapidity, almost like that of a red wine. It is acidic, fresh, and juicy, and quite raw when tasted young. It should be drunk at least four years after the harvest.

Montepulciano d'Abruzzo Villa Gemma—
MASCIARELLI

SAN MARTINO sulla Marrucina is a small town of about one thousand people located in the heart of the province of Chieti, in southern Abruzzo. To one side of the city rise the large mountains of the Majella range, while to the other is the flat Adriatic Sea, which keeps the area fresh and well ventilated throughout the year. However, the city is known for more than just its enviable climate. First of all, San Martino has been known for more than a century as the *paese della polvere,* or the "town of powder"—specifically, of gunpowder—because of the number of companies that produce explosives in the area. In more recent history, San Martino has become famous for one name in particular: Masciarelli, an international superstar of Italian wine.

The founder of the company, Gianni Masciarelli, entered the world of wine late, in 1981, but was able to grow both the quantity and the quality of its production like few others in Italy. Based on well-calculated and well-targeted acquisitions, Gianni built a patrimony of 740 acres of vineyards located in all of the principal winemaking zones of the region. He also focused production on the two main grape varieties of Abruzzo: trebbiano and montepulciano. Concurrently, he built a magnificent cellar, outfitted with the most advanced technologies, and converted an ancient castle into the headquarters of the company. And to top it all off, Gianni has provided financial backing to the *comune,* enabling them to pass an ambitious environmental-protection plan. In 1987, Gianni joined forces (both in life and in work) with Marina Cvetić, an extremely charismatic woman who is directly responsible for the eponymously named line of wines that are among the most important in the portfolio. Keeping in mind the natural rhythms of the earth and of the vineyards, Gianni was able to achieve great success in relatively little time. The region has looked on in amazement as Masciarelli became the beacon of Abruzzo.

Gianni Masciarelli created a modern version of Trebbiano d'Abruzzo,

shaped the Montepulciano d'Abruzzo that we think of today, and built up the image of Cerasuolo, or Montepulciano vinified without spending time on the skins to produce a rosé. Masciarelli's vision, however, extends beyond production: He has created a successful company and a large commercial network. He travels across the globe to build new relationships, open new markets, and introduce his wine and his homeland to a new and larger wine-drinking public. Today, however, we can only describe him with memories and by the fantastic wines he left behind. Sadly, Gianni passed away suddenly on July 31, 2008, at only fifty-two years of age. Up until now, we have intentionally described Gianni as if he were still alive. In Italy, it is a tradition to *parlare da vivi*—that is, to refer to people who have passed away but have left an important mark on their territory as if they were, and always will be, alive. And this certainly holds true for Gianni Masciarelli, an atypical winemaker, genuine in his progressive political ideas, generous to the point of sacrifice for Abruzzo, and a genius in terms of his intuitions. Today his vision continues to unfold under the direction of Marina, whose ability and inexhaustible strength are testimony to the unshakable high quality of Masciarelli wines.

Like a game of chess, Gianni Masciarelli and Marina Cvetić's company advanced one step at a time until it finally owned property in every province in Abruzzo, of which there are four: Chieti, Pescara, Teramo, and Aquila. With each move, the company added value to the territory, revitalizing old professions and literally creating new ones. Everything, as always, starts with the vineyard or, in this case, the vineyards: The Masciarelli company is very focused on agronomy and invites visitors and clients into the vineyards to touch the soil with their hands before tasting the resulting wines in the cellar. Masciarelli wines are a perfect mix of modern and traditional elements. The grapes are trained using both the more modern *cordone speronato* system, characterized by high density (up to 3,600 plants per acre) and the outdated *pergola abruzzese* system, traditionally used in the region. The soil in the vineyards is composed primarily of calcareous clay and is rich in minerals. In the plots closest to the Majella range, the soil tends to be drier compared with that of the coastal areas. In addition to trebbiano and montepulciano, Gianni Masciarelli, like any good experimentalist, has planted other grape varieties, some of which are rare varieties from Abruzzo, like cococciola, and some of which are international varieties, like chardonnay and cabernet sauvignon.

It is not clear where the montepulciano grape comes from, and its name doesn't help to clarify the situation. Montepulciano is the name of a small Tuscan town, in the province of Siena, famous for its sangiovese-based wine, called Vino Nobile. The grape of Abruzzo may come from Toscana and the area around Siena; however, it is in no way related to sangiovese. One of the most exemplary expressions of the montepulciano is Masciarelli's Villa Gemma. The grapes come from a vineyard located at 1,300 feet above sea level in the area of San Martino sulla Marrucina. Here, the soil is composed of calcareous clay. The vines are planted at a density of almost 3,600 plants per acre and are trained using the Guyot system. The average age of the vines is sixteen to eighteen years. Harvest occurs at the end of October, after which the grapes are left to ferment for fifteen to twenty days. The maceration takes about a month. Since 1997, the wine is fermented in wood barrels of varying size and is then left to age in new barriques for eighteen to twenty-four months. The wine is then aged for a year in the bottle before it is released to the market.

Villa Gemma is dark ruby red in color with dark blue tones. On the nose, it is dominated by fruity aromas, especially ripe red fruit and elegant spices. The bouquet is complex, penetrating, and very evocative. In the mouth, the wine is concentrated and surprisingly strong, while balanced and elegant at the same time. Villa Gemma wine is soft and round, with notes of vanilla and fruit. It has a noteworthy finish, and the flavor corresponds perfectly to its perfumes.

~BASILICATA~

Aglianico del Vulture Titolo—ELENA FUCCI

IF I WERE to bet on which region in Italy will be the next to make a leap in quality, I would put my money on Basilicata. Many signs point to the potential of this small region in southern Italy: its excellent *terroir,* beautiful exposures, and long winemaking tradition are just a few. Basilicata, however, has been hindered by the limited number of entrepreneurial winemakers interested in taking their farmhouse wines to the next level. At least on two fronts, the situation is changing: Investors from outside the region have chosen Basilicata as a new frontier for growth, and young, local wineries are taking the first steps toward modernizing their winemaking process.

Another telltale sign that Basilicata is positioned to come out on top is that the region is blessed with a strong, adaptable, and trustworthy grape variety: aglianico. This red wine grape is the backbone of southern Italian winemaking; from Molise to Campania to Basilicata, aglianico has produced great results in a myriad of wineries. It has assumed an important role in the economy of a large part of southern Italy, and for this reason, aglianico is often described as the nebbiolo of the south. The primary production zones are Campania, on the slopes of Vesuvio, the area of Taurasi, and in Basilicata, especially in the area around Mount Vulture, which is not far from the capital city of Potenza. Aglianico is strangely attracted to the volcanic rock soil that is present in these two zones. Another way in which aglianico is compared with nebbiolo is that it has the ability to age for a long time. Aglianico can age longer than all the other great red wine grapes of southern Italy—longer than montepulciano in Abruzzo, primitivo in Puglia, and nero d'Avola in Sicily. In Basilicata, the winery that is truly paving the way for aglianico is Elena Fucci.

Elena is very young (twenty-eight years old with a degree in enology), she produces only one wine (Aglianico di Vulture), and she is dedicated to natural winemaking practices. In other words, she is the future of this area. Leveraging what her grandfather and father had taught her about growing grapes, Elena modernized the winemaking process by increasing vineyard density and aging in barriques. Elena's approach allowed her to bring out the characteristic aspects of aglianico while improving the wine. Currently the winery produces a few thousand bottles of pure Aglianico from a single cru. Italian critics are happy with Elena's wine, and the public is slowly coming to recognize her name. Only time will tell what is to become of Basilicata, but I am ready to bet on it—and her.

The Fucci family winery is located in the small town of Barile, in the province of Potenza, in the northernmost section of Basilicata, not far from the borders with Puglia (to the north and east) and Campania (to the west). The landscape is dominated by the ancient volcano of Vulture, which lends its name to a vast area of more than 111,000 acres. This subregion is known for its low number of inhabitants, its unspoiled countryside, and its long agricultural tradition: Grapes and olives have been grown on the mountain slopes in the nearby valleys since time immemorial. The volcanic soil and favorable climate—cool, ventilated summers; not particularly harsh winters; and an abundance of water—set the stage for quality agriculture. Barile is the main production center of Aglianico del Vulture and is home to many of the most famous wineries in Basilicata. Titolo, the name of Fucci's wine, comes from a vineyard in the district of Solagna, just outside the town's center. The vineyard is 9 acres in size and is planted with very old vines that are cared for naturally, without the use of chemical fertilizers.

In the past, the Vulture basin has witnessed difficult times because of its isolation and delayed industrialization compared with other areas of southern Italy. In recent years, Fiat, Italy's largest car manufacturing company, built one of the biggest factories in Europe in Basilicata, breathing life back into the local economy and creating conditions for the future growth of the region. When guided by farsighted entrepreneurs like Fucci, even local agriculture has a chance of becoming an important part of the future of Basilicata. Aglianico and the Grande Punto—the most famous car manufactured in the Fiat factory in Menfi—are destined to become the two symbols of Basilicata, representing a balance between rural activity and industrial development.

For the moment, Elena Fucci produces one wine from one grape variety: Aglianico del Vulture Titolo from aglianico. All the family's resources and attention are focused on this type of wine and this cultivar. Elena's approach to winemaking seems to be working. Titolo could easily be at the top of the list of "second generation" Aglianico wines, or those that began to be made in the past ten to fifteen years with modern winemaking techniques. In terms of modern winemaking, however, we should be more clear: The Fucci wine is certainly modern in terms of conception (barriques are used to age the wine because of the limited space in the cellar for large barrels), but it fully respects the classic canons of Aglianico.

Aglianico del Vulture Titolo is dark ruby red in color with garnet tones. On the nose, it is an explosion of ripe red fruit, sweet spices, and dried flowers, with notes of oak. In the mouth, the wine is a real gem and is the key to understanding Aglianico deep down. Strong, round, and slightly austere, Titolo has serious tannins that, paired with its acidity, allow the wine to age for years and years. The long, perfectly balanced, and fruity, floral finish of the wine is another one of its strengths. A rising star in southern Italian enology, Aglianico del Vulture Titolo pleases wine drinkers both when it's in its youth and when it's in its old age.

~CAMPANIA~

Costa d'Amalfi Furor Bianco Fiorduva—CANTINE GRAN FUROR DIVINA COSTIERA DI MARISA CUOMO

ONE OF the most fascinating parts of Itailan winemaking is trying to understand where grapes are able to grow. For the most part, vineyards in Italy can be divided into two large categories: the "classics," or vineyards located on rolling hills (like those of the Langa, Chianti, or Valpolicella), and the "extremes," or those where the vines have, for centuries, fought against nature to survive. There are even places (many of which have been touched upon in this book) that we can define as "miraculous," like the Cinque Terre, Valtellina, Valle d'Aosta, and Etna. There are few areas, however, that are as beautiful, and at the same time as difficult to cultivate, as the Amalfi coast.

An idyllic corner of Italy, the Amalfi coast can be reached either by boat or by the narrow, curvy road that links the Amalfi cathedral to the colorful hillside of Positiano, where the views of Capri are certain to seduce any tourist passing through. Ravello, a tiny little town poised on the summit of the hill leading down to the coast, is one of the many gems hidden along the coast. Half the population of Ravello is made up of Americans who have fallen in love with the city and its famous villas. Wagner found his inspiration to write *Parsifal* here in Ravello, and Greta Garbo looked longingly out at the sea from the famous terrace of Villa Cimbrone. Even President John F. Kennedy spent time in this enchanting town.

As is true of most of Italy's most picturesque villages, Ravello was originally home to a community of farmers. The little orchards and fields planted along the coast have been responsible for the survival of many types of native fruit and vegetable varieties. The community cultivated and produced what it needed to survive, for the steep and curvy roads leading to Ravello discouraged any commercial traffic. Your average Amalfi coast farmer must have had a mighty will and great skill to find and cultivate the fertile areas of an otherwise rock-solid terrain. The land had to be tilled, terraced, and practically turned upside down before becoming the beautiful garden that it is today. Most of the land is still covered in fruit trees (especially the famous lemons of Sorrento used to make Limoncello), but more and more vineyards have been planted alongside the almond and walnut trees, the branches of which were once used to support the vines. At a later time, poles were used in the place of the tree branches, and later still, the poles were replaced by pergolas made of chestnut stakes. Monoculture has never been a major risk here on the Amalfi coast, because the grapes literally hang over the vegetable beds, suspended by these stakes. In fact, wine was the only good to be sold at market; the farmers consumed the rest of the harvest.

This was more, or less, the situation that Marisa Cuomo and Andrea Ferraioli encountered in 1980 when they created Cantine Gran Furor Divina Costiera. The challenge facing these two crazy young winemakers was to build a successful winery focused on quality and not just the praiseworthy defense of the old ways. The Amalfi coast was a jewel box of native grape varieties, with which Marisa and Andrea created their own distinctive style. In 1995, the Amalfi Coast DOC, an appellation that includes wines exclusively from the microzones of Furore, Ravello, and Tramonti, recognized the hard work at Gran Furor. Since then, the legendary Fiorduva has become a symbol of this unique, miraculous coastline.

The Amalfi Coast is the long strip of land and rock that extends out into the Tyrrhenian Sea from just south of Napoli and the basin of Mount Vesuvius. Castellammare di Stabia and Salerno are considered to be the main cities at the start and finish of the coastline, while the most panoramic part of the stretch is believed to begin in Sorrento and end in Amalfi—31 miles of hairpin curves along the Lattari mountain roads, overlooking the water. Sant'Agata sui Due Golfi, home to the famous restaurant Don Alfonso, is located halfway along the winding road. Frequent landslides cause the road to be closed from time to time and force both locals and tourists to adapt to nature's whims. The coastline is a unique and difficult environment, and companies like Gran Furor play an important role in its maintenance. Cuomo and Ferraioli tend 25 acres of vineyard in the *comune* of Furore, 9 acres of which they own and the remainder of which they rent. The winery's vineyard is at 1,600 feet above sea level and has an incredible view. The soil is made up of rocks and hard, friable limestone. The grapes are trained with arbors and often climb into the vertical, rocky walls. Fenile, ginestra, ripoli, and tintore are some of the rare grape varieties that grow here and that are cultivated by Marisa and Andrea, together with the great Italian enologist Luigi Moio.

Of the many wines produced at Cantine Gran Furor Divina Costiera, Costa d'Amalfi Furore Bianco Fiorduva is certainly the most renowned. For the past few years, it has been placed at the top of many wine rankings. The wine is made from a blend of native grape varietals—fenile (30 percent), ginestra (30 percent), and ripoli (40 percent)—grown on neighboring vineyards on terraces located 660 to 1,800 feet above the sea, with excellent southern exposure. The soil is composed of rocky, dolomitic limestone, and the vines are vertically trellised using the pergola system. The vineyard density is between 2,000 and 2,800 plants per acre. Chemicals for disease prevention are not needed because of the extreme growing conditions, which act as a natural defense. The average yield is around 5,300 pounds per acre (about 3 pounds per plant), and the harvest occurs in the third week in October, fairly late in the season. The grapes are brought to the winery, slightly underripe, and are softly pressed. The must is fermented in barriques at 54 degrees Fahrenheit with naturally occurring yeasts for about three months.

The result is a rich, yellow-colored wine with golden tones. On the nose, apricot, broom flower, dried fig, and candied fruit prevail. In the mouth, the wine is soft, juicy, and perfectly balanced between sweetness and acidity. It has a long, aromatic finish that comes full circle to the initial fruity notes.

Fiano di Avellino—COLLI DI LAPIO

COLLI DI LAPIO has only just come to light in the past decade. Angelo and Clelia Romano are winemakers who own 15 acres in Irpinia, an area that until recently was renowned for producing opulent, full-bodied reds made from aglianico. Not that Irpinia—at the center of the region of Campania—was unknown to wine lovers: Names such as Feudi di San Gregorio and Mastroberardino have done much in the last twenty years to affirm its reputation to even international markets. But that reputation has been, as noted, predominantly one for reds. Colli di Lapio, however, is a game changer, as it demonstrates that Irpinia can produce impressive white wines. The secret was actually held within a grape that had been cultivated in the area at least ever since the Romans had written admiringly of its virtues: fiano.

Originating with all likelihood in Irpinia (and some say it may have even come from the diminutive *comune* of Lapio), for decades the grape was neglected, considered good enough for the winemaker to drink himself or for direct local sale. But in the 1990s, it dawned on producers that the fiano grape, if carefully cultivated and vinified with the help of modern technology (which is indispensable for giving life to great white wines), can produce wine with impressive strength and extraordinary aging ability. At the same time, producers were researching and experimenting with the other white grape from this region, greco di tufo. With both grape varieties, they achieved results unheard of just a short time ago: mineral wines of fantastic drinkability, both elegant and able to evolve with time. Most surprising, from a socioeconomic and perhaps also a cultural point of view, is that the wineries most welcoming of these qualities were the small—if not the smallest—ones, rather than the largest. The most significant fiano- and greco-based wines you're likely to taste today are certainly those produced by the tiny wineries sunk into the cold and slightly wild areas of Irpinia.

The addition of Fiano di Avellino and Greco di Tufo to the pantheon of Italian whites has been remarkable. The borderline for great whites has been moved a little south, into that area that the collective imagination considers hot, sunny, and Mediterranean—that is, a climate more suited to producing structured, heavy reds. While the white wine boundary once ended at Trebbiano, in Abruzzo (the rest lay farther north, with Soave in Veneto, the "Superwhites" of Friuli, Verdicchio in Marche), there's now a white-wine movement in the south, with growing production of spectacular bottles, each more compelling than the last. Though currently only a few of the 30,000 bottles of Fiano di Avellino produced by Colli di Lapio reach the United States, this is just the beginning. The wine will soon find a deserved market following.

In 2003, the Italian legislature instituted the DOCG for Fiano di Avellino. The defined area lies in Campania on the shoulders of Vesuvius, an inland region with a severe climate, dotted with many small hamlets boasting a strong tradition of agriculture. Only recently has high-quality winemaking gained traction here. The soil is primarily composed of volcanic rock, and along with the particular microclimate and the intrinsic characteristics of the vines, the region is capable of giving the wine pronounced freshness and minerality. Lapio in particular is a kind of unique *grand cru* for Fiano. Names such as Stazzone, Scarpone, and Arianello are not yet known, but you will do well to take note of them: They're the vineyards from which Colli di Lapio obtains the grapes for its best white.

Colli di Lapio's Fiano di Avellino comes from the aforementioned vineyards within the *comune* of Lapio. The altitude is about 1,600 feet above sea level, and the predominantly south and southwest exposure is very good. The production protocol of the DOCG allows for other varietals, especially greco di tufo, to a maximum of 15 percent of the total. However, the best producers, notably Angelo and Clelia Romano, have opted to make wine solely from fiano to best express the potential of this varietal. The very first bottlings were notable for their extraordinary fragrance, but they always lacked the body and length to make the wine memorable. Now that those aspects have been addressed, we have a masterpiece.

Fiano di Avellino is straw yellow with notes of musk, stone, grapefruit, candied fruit, pine, and an interesting lingering smokiness. It offers striking finesse, combined with the acidity that is typical of whites from the far north and also typical of the grape, and it is round, soft, and fascinating. The finish is never-ending and recalls the wine's whole olfactory range. Fantastic for drinking right away, this wine is still better with some age—five, or even ten, years. Colli di Lapio's Fiano di Avellino is a milestone in the new frontiers of Italian winemaking.

Irpinia Aglianico Serpico—FEUDI DI SAN GREGORIO

LOCATED IN the heart of Campania, in a age-old winemaking area, Feudi di San Gregorio has been able to produce top-quality wines and a successful brand in just two short decades. The company is known as a beacon for southern Italian wines and has conquered the international markets with ease.

The best way to start telling the history of the winery is simple: Irpinia, 1986. Irpinia is a remote region in central Campania. It is mountainous, difficult to reach, cold, and dotted with small villages hanging on the sides of valleys. Not exactly the sun-soaked coastline one normally associates with southern Italy. In addition to isolation and daily challenges, the people of Irpinia have suffered from considerable disaster. At 7:30 p.m. on Sunday, November 23, 1980, the earth began to shake and continued shaking for ninety long seconds, destroying entire towns, turning lives upside down, and devastating the economy of about 40 square miles. The earthquake caused almost 3,000 deaths and left 300,000 people without homes. Irpinia was the epicenter of the quake and remained in a state of shock, like a punch-drunk boxer, for years.

In 1986, a regional law was established governing new entrepreneurial activity in southern Italy, in the hope of encouraging young people to rebuild. The Capaldo family saw this as an opportunity for redemption. Although they had to build their winery from scratch, they decided to give it an ancient and resonant name: Feudi di San Gregorio. (Granted, the first grapevines they purchased were once owned by the church during the time of Pope Gregory I.) The debut of the Capaldo family on the Italian winemaking scene did not go unnoticed: Their notable business and financial sense—particularly that of Pellegrino Capaldo, a banker and important figure on the national level—helped the winery to grow. By aligning the land, production methods, and communication, the Capaldo family formed a powerful vision for the company. Thanks to innovative advertising campaigns, sophisticated cultural events, an effective marketing strategy, and captivating packaging, the Feudi wines quickly spread across the world, proving that there is more to Campania winemaking than Mastroberardino (see page 252). The winery's success even rivals that of Planeta (see page 99). Feudi di San Gregorio built its success by researching native grape varietals and the adaptability of international ones by mapping the best vineyards in the area, by promoting biodiversity and environmental awareness, and by the intentionally modern style of their wines. In addition, many of the top names in winemaking have worked at Feudi: Riccardo Cotarella as a consultant; Enzo Ercolino as a communication and sales director, who was responsible for introducing the wines to the American market; Pierpaolo Sirch, a well-known agronomist and pruner; and Anselme Selosse, the master of Champagne and partner in Feudi's sparkling wine project. The convergence of this incredible talent has helped Feudi become what it is today: 618 acres of vines and gardens; a portfolio of wines representing southern Italian winemaking; 4 million bottles; a farmhouse/hotel for guests to stay overnight in; and a Michelin-starred restaurant overlooking all of Irpinia. Not bad for so little time. At this pace, who knows what the future might hold?

Irpinia is a land of struggle: between man and nature, between the will of the city's inhabitants and an arid, at times wild, environment.

The coast of Campania is not far away, but a series of hills and winding valleys prevent the Mediterranean breezes from reaching Irpinia. As a result, the winters are harsh, and the summers are pretty mild and fairly long. Grapes have been grown here for centuries. Historically, the grapes were consumed locally rather than exported abroad because of the poor roads and poor transportation network. The land is optimal for grapes: The structure, porousness, and drainage of the volcanic soil is good for the rooting of the plants. The soil also provides important nutrients to the grapes, like potassium and magnesium. Never planted as a monoculture, the grapes in Irpinia do not define or dominate the landscape as in other regions of Italy. Although 250 acres of vineyard were planted for wine production at Feudi di San Gregorio, the Capaldo family is well aware of the importance of the woods, which still cover the valleys and the hills, as well as the value of agricultural diversity. Olives are grown throughout the region to make some of Italy's best extra virgin olive oil. Feudi is also known to have created a local "cru" culture, producing wines made from grapes from a single vineyard, following the success this philosophy has had in northern Italy.

The first wine produced at Feudi di San Gregorio was not Serpico, but Pàtrimo, a wine made from merlot grapes and which embodied the modernist approach to winemaking that was popular in Italy during the 1990s. Then came the aglianico grape, native to Campania and Basilicata, commonly referred to as the "nebbiolo of the south." Like nebbiolo, aglianico is harvested last in the season and is long lived and quite austere. Serpico comes from hundred-year-old aglianico vines and is named after the *comune* where Feudi di San Gregorio is located (rather than after the New York City police officer made famous in Italy by the 1973 Al Pacino film of that name). The altitude of the vineyard is fairly high, at over 1,600 feet, and it has a fairly cool microclimate, even in the warmest months of the year. To keep the grapes from burning, the winery has converted its training method from the *cordone speronato* to the Guyot system. This is not the only new aspect of this wine. Given the late harvest, between October and November, the fermentation and barrique aging processes have been modified: not in respect to the time—they still ferment and age for twelve to fourteen months and bottle-age for another six—but in relation to the toasting of the wood itself.

To bring out the distinctive side of aglianico, in the past, winemakers aged the grapes in highly toasted new oak. In recent years, Serpico has been only partially aged in new wood, which results in nice notes of cherry, spices, licorice, and chocolate on the nose. In the mouth, the wine is at the same time smooth and powerful, round and edgy, sweet and austere—a true symphony of harmonies and contrasts. Serpico is produced in the tens of thousands of bottles each year and is considered the pearl of the Feudi di San Gregorio porfolio.

Taurasi Radici Riserva—MASTROBERARDINO

THE HISTORY OF Campania as a quality viticultural zone is closely tied to the history of the Mastroberardino family. As far back as I can remember, Mastroberardino family members have been traveling the world to promote the wines of Campania, a winemaking area that was once on the verge of extinction.

When the winery was founded at the end of the nineteenth century, the family had already been involved in the wine trade for more than ten generations. Their mission was clear: plant native grape varieties, and work in the vineyards. The Campania of the Mastroberardino estate is not the sunny seaside resort people tend to associate with the region, but a cold, shady inland zone that is difficult to cultivate and that is threatened by frequent seismic activity. In this area called Irpinia, Mastroberardino established the foundation for the great comeback of an entire region. The winery is in many ways responsible for the popularity of Fiano d'Avellino, Greco di Tufo, and Taurasi, and for the revival of the grapes that make up these wines: fiano, greco, and aglianico, respectively. The fact that these three types of wines have all been awarded DOCG status, the top classification given by the Italian government, and the fact that these wines are known and appreciated abroad, is due to the relentless work of Mastroberardino. In terms of innovation, the company has invested in 870 acres of vineyards located throughout the top areas of production of Campania, a supertechnological cellar, and a forward-thinking marketing strategy.

Today the winery is run by Piero Mastroberardino, a well-respected and charismatic winemaker. The style of his wines has changed dramatically from when he took over. Prior to this regime change, the winery was making extremely traditional wines that did not quite live up to his expectations. They were wines typical of the 1950s, '60s, and '70s and were perceived to be outdated and static. Now Mastroberardino wines are a more modern expression of the land, and have been well studied and improved on by technology and artistry. Their vineyards are still planted with native, traditional grape varietals but are now being vinified into better, more precisely constructed wines. The outcome can be measured in the production numbers. The winery produces almost 2.5 million bottles a year while staying true to its roots, to technological progress, and to the needs of the market. Mastroberardino not only produces great wines, but has strengthened the historic and cultural value of an entire region.

Mastroberardino, together with Feudi di San Gregorio (see page 249), are the indisputable symbols of winemaking in Irpinia. While Feudi is fairly new, Mastroberardino has been tied to this part of Campania for centuries. Like a large part of the entire Avellino province, located in southeast Campania, Iripinia is the winemaking center of the region. Grapes have grown here since before the Romans arrived and have always represented an important economic reality for the local people. The entire enological architecture of the territory was built on three grape varieties: fiano, greco, and aglianico. These grapes have adapted perfectly to the rigid climate of this mountainous area, which is often bathed in rain and cold air. Local winemakers have revived these grapes to the point of their becoming symbols of rebirth, not just in Irpinia, but in all of Campania. At the beginning of the 1980s, the area suffered from a devastating earthquake that destroyed entire communities and crippled the economy of Avellino. The rebirth of the wine industry took some time, but it has managed quite a comeback. Today Campania places ninth in Italy's regional ranking by volume of wine produced, accounting for 4 percent of the national total. Mastroberadino and Campania represent the soul of Italy that people around the world love so dearly.

Taurasi is a small center within Irpinia with ancient origins. It is located 1,300 feet above sea level and is home to a Lombard castle built during their occupation of the area. Were it not for the wine produced here, this town of two thousand people would probably have been forgotten by the world. Taurasi is the historical center of wine production in Campania, and its viticultural importance led to the naming of a DOCG denomination. According to the designation guideline, Taurasi must be made with at least 80 percent aglianico, but the best producers tend to make it exclusively with aglianico, as is the case with Mastroberardino's Radici Riserva. This wine is made from a vineyard in Montemarano 1,600 feet in altitude that faces south. The soil comprises clay and rock. The vineyard is only ten years old, but it is already mature and yields over 5,300 pounds per acre.

Because of the microclimate of Irpinia, the harvest occurs closer in time to that of northern Italian vineyards than to that of southern ones. It is not surprising for harvest to start at the end of October and continue through November. After a long period of maceration, the Taurasi ages in both French oak barriques and large Slavonian oak barrels for no less than thirty months. The result is a complex red wine, with perfumes that recall tobacco, cherry, dark berries, and herbs. In the mouth, the wine is welcoming and elegant, yet austere and modern while remaining faithful to the traditional aglianico-based wines produced in the area. The wine can be drunk after three or four years, but improves with age. Today, Taurasi Radici Riserva is among the best-aging red wine from southern Italy.

Taurasi Vigna Cinque Querce—SALVATORE MOLETTIERI

THE SMALL TOWN of Taurasi in the province of Avellino, Campania, about 50 miles from Napoli, hides beneath its surface hundreds of tunnels and a maze of cellars. If you walk around the city in heels, you will quickly discover this secret, as you'll hear the hollow city echo beneath your feet. These cellars are testament to the fact that Taurasi is the heart of a very important, centuries-old winemaking region.

In this region, the aglianico grape reigns supreme. The red wine made from aglianico, produced in the seventeen towns in the mountain community of Terminio Cervialto, is known as Taurasi, named after the capital of the subregion. In 1993, Taurasi became the first denomination in southern Italy to be recognized as a DOCG. This important red wine became the symbol of the enological rebirth of the south, thanks to its complex aromas of fruit and spices, and its power and potential for long aging. Important wineries like Mastroberardino and Feudi di San Gregorio were the first to introduce Taurasi, both the wine and the *terroir,* to the rest of Italy and the international wine-drinking world. These exemplary wineries caused a number of local farmers to push themselves to become wine producers. This is certainly the case of Salvatore Molettieri and his five children. Given the commercial and critical success of Taurasi around the world, the family decided to produce and bottle its own wine in 1995. In ten short years, Molettieri has become a phenomenon.

Taurasi is nothing like postcard-perfect southern Italian beach towns. There are no palm trees, no sand, no orange groves, or tropical plants here. Taurasi has a cool climate, and the winters can be absolutely frigid. The wine that is made in this subregion is completely different from any other from southern Italy. Vigna Cinque Querce, the vineyard where Molettieri's grapes are grown, should be considered a cru. The vineyard is located at 2,000 feet above sea level, and the difference in daytime and nighttime temperatures is dramatic, giving the wine complex aromas and a strong personality. The vineyard is located in an area commonly known as Agro di Montemarano, one of the best zones for growing aglianico. The vines are planted on the slopes of the hills leading down to the valley formed by the Calore River. The soil here comprises limestone and clay. Because of the cool temperatures, the harvest occurs very late in the season, usually at the end of October or the beginning of November.

The Molettieri winery is truly a boutique enterprise: Total production rarely exceeds 30,000 bottles. Because of the limited production, Molettieri's wines are not widely known, yet passionate aficionados are growing in number. The rarity of this wine also has something to do with the fact that Salvatore started to produce wine just about fifteen short years ago, meaning that there are fewer vintages to drink from. The Molettieri family employs the consultation of Attilio Pagli, an experienced and serious consulting enologist who looks after the cellar along with Giovanni. Vigna Cinque Querce is a wine of the vineyard. Little work has to be done in the cellar because the quality of the grapes is top-flight. This wine has very interesting organolectic qualities. It is refined, elegant, and graceful, backed by a powerful, muscular body. The vinification process is both traditional and modern, based on the use of wooden barrels of varying size (both large and small). On the nose, the wine has nuances of blackberry and cherry, as well as aromas of damp soil and graphite, followed by leaves and dried fruit. In the mouth, the wine has ripe tannins, which are pronounced but not aggressive. The tannins give this wine its juiciness and long finish. Vigna Cinque Querce packs a punch, but it is also incredibly smooth—both velvet and silk at the same time.

Terra di Lavoro—GALARDI

TERRA DI LAVORO is an extremely evocative area of Italy. Located in Campania, Terra di Lavoro is the part of the region that is closest to the Tyrrhenian Sea. The capital of the subregion is Capua. In Roman times, this area was particularly fertile, a sort of large garden with big, open skies where vegetables and grains grew in abundance. Its inhabitants were rich and envied by the other members of the Roman Empire. In fact, the coat of arms that was given to Terra di Lavoro consists of two cornucopias, a symbol of abundance as well as social and economic welfare. Currently, this symbol is used in the coat of arms of the provinces of Frosinone and Caserta. In the twentieth century, this area experienced a drastic growth in population as a result of the repopulation policies imposed by the Fascist regime—laws created to reclaim the Pontine marshes, a territory located to the north of Terra di Lavoro.

Galardi is a small winery that was started by a partnership between two couples: Dora and Arturo Celentano and Maria Luisa Murena and Francesco Catello. The couples joined forces in 1991 to create what is a model winery. The first vintage dates back to 1993, but the real turning point was in 1994 with the release of Terra di Lavoro, a unique wine strongly tied to the territory that it comes from. Thanks to the gushing reviews and strong sales, we can say without any doubt that it did not take long for this wine to become legendary. A great deal of the credit should be attributed to the winemaker Riccardo Cotarella, who has had a profound influence on the viticulture of southern Italy. This controversial winemaker is accused of having fueled the planting of merlot in vineyards that were once home to indigenous varietals, making for wines that tasted the same all over Italy. Terra di Lavoro rebuts this accusation: It is a wine that is completely original and that has no counterpart in the entire region of Campania. To his credit, Riccardo Cotarella was working in quite a challenging territory and was able to adapt his knowledge to the needs of this *terroir*. He did not try to mold the wine into a wine to everyone's liking but instead managed to allow the characteristics of the two native grape varietals, aglianico and piedirosso, to resonate in this wine.

The small Galardi property rests on volcanic soil that gradually slopes toward the sea. Vineyards, olive groves, and chestnut trees cover the slopes of the Roccamonfina volcano, which offer an extraordinary view of the local countryside. Friends get together to harvest the fruits of the earth and to make extra virgin olive oil, in addition to wine. The region is also known for its famous *mozzarella di bufala* and San Marzano tomatoes, two products that come together in another of the world's greatest foods: pizza. The Galardi winery is focused on caring for nature and preserving the land. The vines are planted at an altitude of between 1,300 and 1,600 feet above sea level and face the enchanting Gulf of Gaeta.

Terra di Lavoro is a blend of two important and indigenous grape varietals of Campania: aglianico and piedirosso (also known in the local dialect as *palummo*). Aglianico is quite possibly the most noble grape varietal of southern Italy and is often referred to as the "nebbiolo of the south" because of its similar characteristics of strong tannins, elegance, and great aging potential. Piedirosso, although a less noble variety, is certainly more popular. It also blends very well with aglianico because of its acidity, freshness, and abundance of fruit. From these two varietals, a wine was created with a very distinct personality. When young, Terra di Lavoro is edgy and sometimes underdeveloped, leaving discerning wine tasters stopped in their tracks. But this experience only occurs when the wine is young, like a child throwing a tantrum.

Over time, Terra di Lavoro matures, and both the nose and palate mellow so the wine becomes pleasent to drink while still maintaining its extremely original characteristics. The nose gives off notes of red fruits, sweet spices, leather, and fur with a consistent sense of wet earth and dried leaves. Notes of chocolate and vanilla result from aging the wine for ten months in French barriques—although the process leaves no other traces of wood in the wine. On the palate, the wine is powerful, intense, and full bodied. It is truly an example of the power of the sun in southern Italy. The finish is rich, persistent, and very long. Terra di Lavoro gives us authenticity and power in the glass. It is a wine that will lead the charge of great southern Italian wines.

~LAZIO~

Grechetto Latour a Civitella—SERGIO MOTTURA

THERE IS A white heart that beats strongly in the center of Italy: Sergio Mottura, undisputed master of Grechetto. The center of Italy is Lazio, the region located halfway down the boot, where you find the country's capital, Roma. In truth, Sergio Mottura is a winemaker on the frontier. His winery is indeed technically within the confines of Lazio, but only by a few miles. Just north is Umbria, and not far away is the wonderful *comune* of Orvieto, world renowned for its spectacular duomo.

The land on which Sergio Mottura works is not known for its wine. A thoroughfare between the regions north of Roma, this part of Italy has long remained unexplored apart from commercial trade, relegated to a kind of rural isolation that has maintained the area's slow rhythms and traditions. The sharecropper held the purse strings until a little more than thirty years ago, and the Mottura family winery has had to deal with this unusual, static system of land management. In the 1960s, the sharecropping system changed when Sergio's increasing involvement in operations shook everything up. The young winemaker had bet on the vines, with odds that were far from promising. The vines were already in place, but in the most marginal sense. And then there was the question of which vineyards to plant: those in Lazio? Umbria? Sergio found himself at a crossroads, far from the great Italian vineyards in a place where anything was possible but nothing was certain. In speaking with old sharecroppers, consulting books and maps, and experimenting in the field, Sergio found in grechetto the means for realizing his winemaking aspirations. This grape, as its name indicates, is part of the group of varieties (such as greco campano or calabrese) that originated in the Hellenic peninsula and was introduced to Italy when the ancient Greeks colonized the the land in the first centuries A.D. How grechetto managed to travel up the peninsula and take root in Lazio—much less in Umbria—remains a mystery. Very old farmers recall the cultivar being widespread in these areas of central Italy from time immemorial. The grape is strong, robust, resistant, and versatile, and for decades it was used in combination with other varietals both native (procanico especially) and international (the renowned Cervaro della Sala made by Antinori is a blend of chardonnay and grechetto grapes) wines.

Sergio Mottura decided not to vinify grechetto on its own. The Grechetto Latour a Civitella is a clear homage to the masters on the opposite side of the Alps, in particular Louis-Fabrice Latour, the renowned *négociant* of Burgundy wines and head of one of the most famous producers of barriqued wines. (Sergio acquired his first five small barrels from Latour.) Mottura didn't quit at the first discouraging results. In fact, in all these years, he has never ceased experimenting, studying clones of his beloved grechetto, trying new grafts and pruning methods, varying the use of wood. A sacred flame kindles his passion and has made him into the Italian emblem of the winemaker who from nothing has achieved something truly incredible. Today, apart from the inconsistent quantity of some wines made with grechetto, you might say that the grape has been delivered from its uncertain past and placed firmly among the noble Italian white varieties. And Sergio, from his magnificent subterranean cellar in the center of the village of Civitella d'Agliano, has become the grechetto ambassador and an authoritative voice among Italy's top makers of white wines.

Sergio Mottura's property covers 320 acres (91 of which are dedicated to organic grape cultivation) and is situated in the area surrounding the small center of Civitella d'Agliano. A region little known to the public and still far from the waves of tourists that stop in neighboring

Orvieto, it boasts unique geomorphological traits. The environment is ravinelike; a kind of canyon with river origins gives the landscape a severe appearance—rough and somewhat disquieting. The land peaks in Bagnoregio, birthplace of one of the great Catholic saints, the philosopher and theologist Bonaventura. East of Civitella, the panorama opens up toward the wide valley of the Tiber, the legendary river that reaches and crosses the capital, Roma. The soil here is calcareous, and the microclimate is favorable, owing to the mild temperatures of the seasons and regular precipitation throughout the year. Mottura's vineyards are numerous and spread throughout the Civitella countryside. The antiquated planting and pruning methods have given way to the Guyot traning system, with a density of 2,000 plants per acre.

Grechetto Latour a Civitella is made from carefully selected grechetto grapes grown in the five top vineyards of the property. Productive, precocious, and resistant to disease, grechetto's Achilles' heel is its rough tannins. Sergio Mottura has had to work hard in the vineyards (density of plantings, yields, choice of clones) and the cellar (maceration, getting the wood just right) to transform this potential flaw into a strength. I'd say Mottura's bets have paid off, as his Latour a Civitella is an assertive wine of aesthetic importance. Once harvested, the grechetto grapes are gently pressed and the must is decanted at a low temperature as a preventive measure. Fermentation begins in stainless steel vats and ends in barriques of French oak, where the wine remains nine months in the ancient tufa caves that provide the soul—as well as the scenic aspect—of Mottura's winery. After six months' aging in the bottle, the Latour a Civitella is ready to be released.

A straw-yellow color, the wine offers a bouquet of white pepper, grapefruit, fresh flowers, and candied fruit on a smoky and characteristically mineral base. Its tannins prove to be well tamed by an acidic backbone, while oak provides the right amount of roundness. Mottura has created a wine of significance and pleasure from the previously untested grechetto.

~PUGLIA~

Le Braci—AZIENDA MONACI

AZIENDA MONACI IS the fruit of two fathers: the first is the owner of the winery, Severino Garofano, and the second is Salento, home to this splendid estate. Born in San Potito Ultra, in the province of Avellino, Severino is also one of the main players in the rebirth of southern Italian winemaking. Thanks to his brilliance, at least two wine areas truly emerged on the wine scene during the 1990s: Cirò, with Severino's Gravello di Librandi and Duca San Felice, and Salento, with his Patriglione, Notarpanaro, and Graticciaia. Severino can be considered a genius, not so much for having produced excellent wines, but for having made them in areas that not long ago were considered incapable of producing quality.

At the beginning of Severino's career, improving the quality of the wine in this region was a fairly difficult mission because wine was still considered to be a drink of the *osterie* and *cantine,* where it was poured in smoke-filled rooms. Wine was sold unbottled, in bulk, valued for its alcoholic content. This was a time when grapes traveled across Italy in baskets, and wine was produced in large factories built by northern Italian entrepreneurs. The wine was loaded on cargo trains and sent up north along the railroads departing from Capo di Leuca and San Severo. This was the wine route of the time. People talked very little about the bottlers of the south, and even less about their winemaking skill. Wine from Puglia only began to be recognized in the 1980s, thanks in part to the many enological consultants who started to take trips down south. Local entrepreneurial winemakers also had the far-sightedness to impose rigid rules for growing and vinifying their grapes, creating quality and thereby attracting the attention of the wine market for the first time. The international press and curious wine lovers recognized the potential of Pugliese wines.

After having worked as a consultant for a lifetime and after having produced great wines, Severino Garofano decided at age seventy, to go off on his own. He founded Azienda Monaci in 1995, after having read what the Baroness de Rothschild had written about wine: "Making great wine is easy. It's just the first several hundred years that can be difficult." Severino realized that he wanted to create something of his own that would last beyond his lifetime. Convinced that Puglia had an enormous amount of untapped potential, he decided to focus on the most important indigenous grape of the region: negroamaro.

In Puglia, there is a vineyard that begins in Gargano al Capo di Leuca and stretches for 190 miles. It is planted with vines trained using the old *alberello* system. Because the vineyard is located between two seas, its climate is defined by ocean winds that create many microclimates within it. This holds true not only for Salento, but also for the part of the vineyard that runs along the Adriatic, backed by the Murge highlands. The grapes here have adapted to the natural ecosystem and are for the most part the product of the grape and wine trade. The vineyards of Puglia are planted with a number of varieties, many of which are new and difficult to identify. The various zones are increasing because of the market interest and the choices that winemakers have made to be able to offer wines of a certain price. The *terroir* is gaining fame, not only for its wine, but also for the beauty of the Salento countryside. The southernmost part, practically the heel of the Italian peninsula, is covered with splendid century-old olive trees and *alberello* (treelike) grape vines. There are also beautiful farmhouses with stark white walls, commonly called *masserie*. Puglia has become a major tourist destination and is being invaded by English and American investors.

With Le Braci, Severino Garofano has created his ultimate masterpiece. Made from negroamaro grapes, the wine expresses and embraces its southern origins. The grapes are grown at sea level. The vineyard practices are traditional, with the use of the *alberello* training system, requiring that many hours be dedicated to the care of each vine. In a region as hot as, and with such strong sunlight as, Salento, it is vital to use the *alberello* system; its fundamental function is to encourage the roots of the vines to stretch deep below the ground and maintain a consistent level of humidity. The grapes are harvested at the end of October, when they are intentionally overripe. The dried grapes ferment for several days in steel and then make a second pass in barriques, where they remain for about ten days.

Le Braci has great elegance on the nose, with clear scents of prune marmalade and black cherries. There are also nuances of rhubarb and aromatic herbs like rosemary. In the finish, there is the essence of vanilla and chocolate. On the palate, the tannins are mature and smooth, with a long fruity finish.

~WINE LIST~

A NOTE ON production methods: the Italian government recognizes
upward of twenty agencies that certify agricultural products as "organic" and "biological." Whereas "conventional" wineries are free to
use fertilizers, pesticides, and other synthetic chemicals, wineries that
have been certified "organic" avoid all synthetic chemicals. Biodynamic
winemaking is even more extreme in its regulation of chemical inputs:
A kind of homeopathic, almost mystical approach to viticulture, it
stresses the importance of a self-sustaining ecosystem and relies on the
cycles of the moon. Certified in Italy by the Demeter Association, biodynamic agriculture not only eschews chemicals but replaces them
with a diet of "preparations" ranging from medicinal herbs and minerals to manures and even the horns and skulls of domesticated livestock.
Some wineries practice organic or biodynamic viticulture without
going to the expense of certification. Those are listed herein as
"organic" and "biodynamic"; those that have been certified are noted
as such.

CENTRAL ITALY

EMILIA ROMAGNA

Sangiovese di Romagna Superiore Avi Riserva *San Patrignano*
DENOMINATION: Sangiovese di Romagna Superiore Riserva DOC
WEBSITE: www.sanpatrignano.org
FIRST VINTAGE: 1997
GRAPE VARIETAL: 100% sangiovese
ANNUAL PRODUCTION: 60,000 bottles
AGING: 12 months in large oak
PRODUCTION METHOD: Conventional

MARCHE

Kurni *Oasi degli Angeli*
DENOMINATION: Marche IGT
WEBSITE: www.kurni.it
FIRST VINTAGE: 1997
GRAPE VARIETAL: 100% montepulciano
ANNUAL PRODUCTION: 6,000 bottles
AGING: 14–16 months in small oak
PRODUCTION METHOD: Natural

Verdicchio dei Castelli di Jesi Classico Villa Bucci Riserva *Bucci*
DENOMINATION: Verdicchio dei Castelli di Jesi Classico Riserva DOC
WEBSITE: www.villabucci.com
FIRST VINTAGE: 1983
GRAPE VARIETAL: 100% verdicchio
ANNUAL PRODUCTION: 20,000 bottles
AGING: 18 months in large oak
PRODUCTION METHOD: Certified organic

Verdicchio dei Castelli di Jesi Classico Superiore Podium *Gioacchino Garofoli*
DENOMINATION: Verdicchio dei Castelli di Jesi Classico Superiore
WEBSITE: www.garofolivini.it
FIRST VINTAGE: 1992
GRAPE VARIETAL: 100% verdicchio
ANNUAL PRODUCTION: 42,000 bottles
AGING: 15 months in stainless steel, 4 months in glass
PRODUCTION METHOD: Conventional

TOSCANA

Alceo *Castello dei Rampolla*
DENOMINATION: Toscana IGT
FIRST VINTAGE: 1996
GRAPE VARIETALS: 85% cabernet sauvignon, 15% petit verdot

ANNUAL PRODUCTION: 14,000
bottles
AGING: 21 months in small
oak
PRODUCTION METHOD:
Biodynamic

Bolgheri Superiore Grattamacco Rosso *Podere Grattamacco*

DENOMINATION: Bolgheri
Superiore Rosso DOC
WEBSITE: www.collemassari.it
FIRST YEAR OF PRODUCTION:
1982
GRAPE VARIETALS: 65% cabernet
sauvignon, 20% merlot, 15%
sangiovese
ANNUAL PRODUCTION: 20,000
bottles
AGING: 18 months in small oak
PRODUCTION METHOD: Certified
organic

Brunello di Montalcino *La Cerbaiola*

DENOMINATION: Brunello di
Montalcino DOCG
FIRST VINTAGE: 1985
GRAPE VARIETAL: 100% sangiovese
ANNUAL PRODUCTION: 9,000
bottles
AGING: 28 months in large oak
PRODUCTION METHOD:
Conventional

Brunello di Montalcino Cerretalto *Casanova di Neri*

DENOMINATION: Brunello di
Montalcino DOCG
WEBSITE: www.casanovadineri
.com
FIRST VINTAGE: 1986
GRAPE VARIETAL: 100% sangiovese
ANNUAL PRODUCTION: 18,000
bottles
AGING: 27 months in small oak
PRODUCTION METHOD:
Conventional

Brunello di Montalcino Tenuta Il Greppo Riserva *Biondi Santi*

DENOMINATION: Brunello di
Montalcino Riserva DOCG
WEBSITE: www.biondisanti.it
FIRST VINTAGE: 1888
GRAPE VARIETAL: 100% sangiovese
ANNUAL PRODUCTION: 7,300
bottles
AGING: 40 months in small oak, 30
months in large oak
PRODUCTION METHOD:
Conventional

Brunello di Montalcino Riserva *Poggio di Sotto*

DENOMINATION: Brunello di
Montalcino Riserva DOCG
WEBSITE: www.poggiodisotto.com
FIRST VINTAGE: 1995
GRAPE VARIETAL: 100% sangiovese

ANNUAL PRODUCTION: 5,000
bottles
AGING: 48 months in large oak
PRODUCTION METHOD: Certified
organic

Camartina *Querciabella*

DENOMINATION: Toscana IGT
WEBSITE: www.querciabella.com
FIRST VINTAGE: 1981
GRAPE VARIETALS: 70% cabernet
sauvignon, 30% sangiovese
ANNUAL PRODUCTION: 18,000
bottles
AGING: 24 months in small oak
PRODUCTION METHOD:
Biodynamic

Cepparello *Isole e Olena*

DENOMINATION: Toscana IGT
WEBSITE: www.isoleolena.it
FIRST VINTAGE: 1980
GRAPE VARIETAL: 100% sangiovese
ANNUAL PRODUCTION: 43,000
bottles
AGING: 18 months in small oak
PRODUCTION METHOD:
Conventional

Chianti Classico Riserva Castello di Fonterutoli *Castello di Fonterutoli*

DENOMINATION: Chianti Classico
DOCG
WEBSITE: www.fonterutoli.it
FIRST VINTAGE: 1995

GRAPE VARIETALS: 90%
sangiovese, 10% cabernet
sauvignon
ANNUAL PRODUCTION: 80,000
bottles
AGING: Sangiovese aged for 16
months in small oak (70%
new); 18 months for the
cabernet sauvignon
PRODUCTION METHOD:
Conventional

Chianti Classico Riserva Rancia *Fèlsina Berardenga*

DENOMINATION: Chianti Classico
DOCG
WEBSITE: www.felsina.it
FIRST VINTAGE: 1983
GRAPE VARIETAL: 100% sangiovese
ANNUAL PRODUCTION: 38,000
bottles
AGING: 15 months in large oak
PRODUCTION METHOD:
Conventional

Chianti Classico Vigneto Bellavista *Castello di Ama*

DENOMINATION: Chianti Classico
DOCG
WEBSITE: www.castellodiama.com
FIRST VINTAGE: 1978
GRAPE VARIETALS: 90%
sangiovese, 10% malvasia
nera
ANNUAL PRODUCTION: 9,000
bottles

AGING: 15 months in small oak
PRODUCTION METHOD:
Conventional

Flaccianello della Pieve *Tenuta Fontodi*

DENOMINATION: Toscana IGT
WEBSITE: www.fontodi.com
FIRST VINTAGE: 1981
GRAPE VARIETAL: 100% sangiovese
ANNUAL PRODUCTION: 50,000
bottles
AGING: 18 months in small oak
PRODUCTION METHOD: Organic

Masseto *Tenuta dell'Ornellaia*

DENOMINATION: Toscana IGT
WEBSITE: www.ornellaia.it
FIRST VINTAGE: 1987
GRAPE VARIETAL: 100% merlot
(Masseto)
ANNUAL PRODUCTION: 30,000
bottles
AGING: 24 months in small oak
PRODUCTION METHOD:
Conventional

Nobile di Montepulciano Nocio dei Boscarelli *Boscarelli*

DENOMINATION: Nobile di
Montepulciano DOCG
WEBSITE: www.poderiboscarelli
.com
FIRST VINTAGE: 1991
GRAPE VARIETAL: 100% sangiovese

ANNUAL PRODUCTION: 10,000
bottles
AGING: 24 months in small and
large oak
PRODUCTION METHOD:
Conventional

Percarlo *Fattoria San Giusto a Rentennano*

DENOMINATION: Toscana IGT
WEBSITE: www.fattoriasangiusto.it
FIRST VINTAGE: 1983
GRAPE VARIETAL: 100% sangiovese
ANNUAL PRODUCTION: 17,000
bottles
AGING: 22 months in small oak
PRODUCTION METHOD: Certified
organic

Le Pergole Torte *Montevertine*

DENOMINATION: Toscana IGT
WEBSITE: www.montevertine.it
FIRST VINTAGE: 1977
GRAPE VARIETAL: 100% sangiovese
ANNUAL PRODUCTION: 25,000
bottles
AGING: 18 months in large oak, 6
months in small oak
PRODUCTION METHOD:
Conventional (without the use
of chemical fertilizers or anti-
mold products)

Redigaffi *Tua Rita*

DENOMINATION: Toscana IGT
WEBSITE: www.tuarita.it

FIRST VINTAGE: 1996
GRAPE VARIETAL: 100% merlot
ANNUAL PRODUCTION: 7,000
  bottles
AGING: 18 months in small oak
PRODUCTION METHOD:
  · Conventional

Sassicaia *Tenuta San Guido*
DENOMINATION: Bolgheri DOC
WEBSITE: www.sassicaia.com
FIRST VINTAGE: 1968
GRAPE VARIETALS: 85% cabernet
  sauvignon, 15% cabernet
  franc
ANNUAL PRODUCTION: 180,000
  bottles
AGING: 24 months in small oak
PRODUCTION METHOD:
  Conventional

Tenuta di Valgiano *Tenuta di Valgiano*
DENOMINATION: Colline Lucchesi
  Rosso DOC
WEBSITE: www.valgiano.it
FIRST VINTAGE: 1999
GRAPE VARIETALS: 60%
  sangiovese, 20% syrah, 20%
  merlot
ANNUAL PRODUCTION: 9,000
  bottles
AGING: 15 months in small oak
PRODUCTION METHOD:
  Biodynamic

Tignanello *Marchesi Antinori*
DENOMINATION: Toscana IGT
WEBSITE: www.antinori.it
FIRST VINTAGE: 1970
GRAPE VARIETALS: 85%
  sangiovese, 10% cabernet
  sauvignon, 5% cabernet franc
ANNUAL PRODUCTION: 330,000
  bottles
AGING: 12 months in small oak
PRODUCTION METHOD:
  Conventional

Vin Santo Occhio di Pernice
Avignonesi
DENOMINATION: Vin Santo di
  Montepulciano Occhio di
  Pernice DOC
WEBSITE: www.avignonesi.it
FIRST VINTAGE: 1970
GRAPE VARIETAL: 100% prugnolo
  gentile
ANNUAL PRODUCTION: 1,130 0.375
  liter bottles
AGING: 10 years in small oak
PRODUCTION METHOD:
  Conventional

UMBRIA

Montefalco Sagrantino 25 Anni
Arnaldo Caprai
DENOMINATION: Montefalco
  Sagrantino DOCG
WEBSITE: www.arnaldocaprai.it

FIRST VINTAGE: 1993
GRAPE VARIETAL: 100% sagrantino
ANNUAL PRODUCTION: 30,000
  bottles
AGING: 24 months in small oak
PRODUCTION METHOD:
  Conventional

Cervaro della Sala *Castello della Sala*
DENOMINATION: Umbria IGT

WEBSITE: www.antinori.it
FIRST VINTAGE: 1985
GRAPE VARIETALS: 85%
  chardonnay, 15% grechetto
ANNUAL PRODUCTION: 192,000
  bottles
AGING: 6 months in small oak
PRODUCTION METHOD:
  Conventional

THE ISLANDS

SARDEGNA

Carignano del Sulcis Superiore Terre Brune *Cantina Sociale di Santadi*
DENOMINATION: Carignano del
  Sulcis Superiore DOC
WEBSITE: www.cantinadisantadi.it
FIRST VINTAGE: 1970
GRAPE VARIETALS: 95% carignano,
  5% bovaleddu
ANNUAL PRODUCTION: 80,000
  bottles
AGING: 16–18 months in small oak
PRODUCTION METHOD:
  Conventional

Tenores *Tenute Dettori*
DENOMINATION: Romagnia IGT
WEBSITE: www.tenutedettori.it

FIRST VINTAGE: 2000
GRAPE VARIETAL: 100% cannonau
ANNUAL PRODUCTION: 5,000
  bottles
AGING: 30 months in cement
PRODUCTION METHOD: Natural

Turriga *Argiolas*
DENOMINATION: Isola dei Nuraghi
  IGT
WEBSITE: www.argiolas.it
FIRST VINTAGE: 1990
GRAPE VARIETALS: 80% cannonau,
  10% carignano, 5% bovale
  sardo, 5% malvasia nera
ANNUAL PRODUCTION: 50,000
  bottles
AGING: 18–24 months in small oak
PRODUCTION METHOD:
  Conventional

SICILIA

Rosso del Conte *Tasca d'Almerita*

DENOMINATION: Contea di Sclafani DOC
WEBSITE: www.tascadalmerita.it
FIRST VINTAGE: 1991
GRAPE VARIETAL: 100% nero d'Avola
ANNUAL PRODUCTION: 56,000 bottles
AGING: 18 months in small oak
PRODUCTION METHOD: Conventional

Etna Bianco Pietramarina *Benanti*

DENOMINATION: Etna Bianco Superiore DOC
WEBSITE: www.vinicolabenanti.it
FIRST VINTAGE: 1991
GRAPE VARIETAL: 100% carricante
ANNUAL PRODUCTION: 12,000 bottles
AGING: 12 months in stainless steel
PRODUCTION METHOD: Conventional

Faro Palari *Palari*

DENOMINATION: Faro DOC
WEBSITE: www.palari.it
FIRST VINTAGE: 1995
GRAPE VARIETALS: 50% nerello mascalese, 30% nerello cappuccio, 10% nocera, 5% tignolino, 5% galatena
ANNUAL PRODUCTION: 25,000 bottles
AGING: 12–18 months in small oak
PRODUCTION METHOD: Conventional

Marsala Superiore Riserva 10 Anni *Marco De Bartoli*

DENOMINATION: Marsala Superiore Riserva DOC
WEBSITE: www.marcodebartoli.com
FIRST VINTAGE: 1983
GRAPE VARIETALS: 50% grillo, 50% inzolia
ANNUAL PRODUCTION: 10,000 bottles
AGING: Aged using the solera method for more than 10 years
PRODUCTION METHOD: Conventional

Passito di Pantelleria Ben Ryé *Donnafugata*

DENOMINATION: Passito di Pantelleria DOC
WEBSITE: www.donnafugata.it
FIRST VINTAGE: 1989
GRAPE VARIETAL: 100% moscato d'Alessandria (zibibbo)
ANNUAL PRODUCTION: 80,000 bottles

AGING: 10–12 months in stainless steel

PRODUCTION METHOD: Conventional

Santa Cecilia *Planeta*
DENOMINATION: Sicilia IGT
WEBSITE: www.planeta.it

FIRST VINTAGE: 1997
GRAPE VARIETAL: 100% nero d'Avola
ANNUAL PRODUCTION: 105,000 bottles
AGING: 12 months in small oak
PRODUCTION METHOD: Conventional

NORTHEAST ITALY

ALTO ADIGE

Alto Adige Terlano Pinot Bianco Vorberg Riserva *Cantina Terlano*
DENOMINATION: Alto Adige Terlano Pinot Bianco Riserva DOC
WEBSITE: www.cantina-terlano.com
FIRST VINTAGE: 1995
GRAPE VARIETAL: 100% pinot bianco
ANNUAL PRODUCTION: 50,000 bottles
AGING: 12 months in large oak
PRODUCTION METHOD: Conventional

Alto Adige Sauvignon Sanct Valentin *San Michele Appiano*
DENOMINATION: Alto Adige DOC
WEBSITE: www.stmichael.it
FIRST VINTAGE: 1993

GRAPE VARIETAL: 100% sauvignon blanc
ANNUAL PRODUCTION: 150,000 bottles
AGING: 6 months in stainless steel
PRODUCTION METHOD: Conventional

Alto Adige Valle Isarco Kaiton Riesling *Peter Pliger Kuenhof*
DENOMINATION: Alto Adige Valle Isarco DOC
FIRST VINTAGE: 1995
GRAPE VARIETAL: 100% riesling
ANNUAL PRODUCTION: 3,500 bottles
AGING: 8 months in stainless steel and large oak
PRODUCTION METHOD: Natural

Alto Adige Valle Isarco Kerner Praepositus *Abbazia di Novacella*

DENOMINATION: Alto Adige Valle
Isarco DOC
WEBSITE: www.abbazianovacella.it
FIRST VINTAGE: 1994
GRAPE VARIETAL: 100% kerner
ANNUAL PRODUCTION: 27,000
bottles
AGING: 8 months vinification and
maturation in stainless steel
PRODUCTION METHOD:
Conventional

Alto Adige Valle Venosta Riesling *Falkenstein*

DENOMINATION: Alto Adige Valle
Venosta DOC
WEBSITE: www.falkenstein.bz
FIRST VINTAGE: 1995
GRAPE VARIETAL: 100% riesling
ANNUAL PRODUCTION: 18,000
bottles
AGING: 12 months in stainless
steel
PRODUCTION METHOD:
Conventional

FRIULI–VENEZIA GIULIA

Ribolla Gialla *Josko Gravner*
DENOMINATION: Friuli Bianco IGT
WEBSITE: www.gravner.it
FIRST VINTAGE: 1999
GRAPE VARIETAL: 100% ribolla
ANNUAL PRODUCTION: 18,000
bottles

AGING: 12 months in amphora, 36
months in large oak
PRODUCTION METHOD: Organic

Collio Bianco *Edi Keber*
DENOMINATION: Collio Bianco
DOC
FIRST VINTAGE: 2008
GRAPE VARIETALS: 70% tocai
friulano, 15% ribolla gialla,
15% malvasia istriana
ANNUAL PRODUCTION: 55,000
bottles
AGING: 10 months in glass
PRODUCTION METHOD: Natural

Vintage Tunina *Silvio Jermann*
DENOMINATION: Friuli Bianco IGT
FIRST VINTAGE: 1975
GRAPE VARIETALS: sauvignon,
malvasia istriana, picolit,
ribolla gialla (percentages vary
with each vintage)
ANNUAL PRODUCTION: 65,000
bottles
AGING: 10 months in large oak
PRODUCTION METHOD:
Conventional

TRENTINO

Giulio Ferrari *Ferrari*
DENOMINATION: Trento Bianco
Spumante DOC
WEBSITE: www.ferrarispumante.it
FIRST VINTAGE: 1972

GRAPE VARIETAL: 100%
chardonnay

ANNUAL PRODUCTION: 28,000
bottles

AGING: Up to 10 years on the lees

PRODUCTION METHOD:
Conventional

San Leonardo *Tenuta San Leonardo*

DENOMINATION: Vigneti delle
Dolomiti IGT

WEBSITE: www.sanleonardo.it

FIRST VINTAGE: 1982

GRAPE VARIETALS: 60% cabernet
sauvignon, 30% cabernet franc,
10% merlot

ANNUAL PRODUCTION: 48,000
bottles

AGING: 24 months in small oak

PRODUCTION METHOD:
Conventional

VENETO

Amarone della Valpolicella di Monte Lodoletta *Romano Dal Forno*

DENOMINATION: Amarone della
Valpolicella DOC

WEBSITE: www.dalforno.net

FIRST VINTAGE: 1983

GRAPE VARIETALS: 60% corvina,
20% rondinella, 10% croatina,
10% oseleta

ANNUAL PRODUCTION: 8,000
bottles

AGING: 25 months in small oak

PRODUCTION METHOD:
Conventional

Amarone della Valpolicella Classico *Giuseppe Quintarelli*

DENOMINATION: Amarone della
Valpolicella DOC

FIRST VINTAGE: 1961

GRAPE VARIETALS: 55% corvina,
25% rondinella, 20% cabernet,
nebbiolo, croatina, sangiovese

ANNUAL PRODUCTION: 10,000
bottles

AGING: 7 years in large oak

PRODUCTION METHOD:
Conventional

Amarone della Valpolicella Classico Vigneto Monte Ca' Bianca *Lorenzo Begali*

DENOMINATION: Amarone della
Valpolicella DOC

WEBSITE: www.begaliwine.it

FIRST VINTAGE: 1995

GRAPE VARIETALS: 40% corvina,
35% corvinone, 20%
rondinella, 5% oseleta

ANNUAL PRODUCTION: 7,000
bottles

AGING: 4 years in small and large
oak

PRODUCTION METHOD:
Conventional

Recioto della Valpolicella Classico TB *Tommaso Bussola*
DENOMINATION: Recioto della Valpolicella Classico DOC
WEBSITE: www.bussolavini.com
FIRST VINTAGE: 1995
GRAPE VARIETALS: 70% corvina, 15% rondinella, 15% cabernet franc
ANNUAL PRODUCTION: 4,000 bottles
AGING: 30 months in small oak
PRODUCTION METHOD: Conventional

Soave Classico Calvarino *Leonildo Pieropan*
DENOMINATION: Soave Classico DOC
WEBSITE: www.pieropan.it
FIRST VINTAGE: 1971
GRAPE VARIETALS: 70% garganega, 30% trebbiano
ANNUAL PRODUCTION: 40,000 bottles
AGING: About 2 months in stainless steel and glass
PRODUCTION METHOD: Conventional

Soave Classico Monte Fiorentine *Ca' Rugate*
DENOMINATION: Soave Classico DOC
WEBSITE: www.carugate.it
FIRST VINTAGE: 1986
GRAPE VARIETAL: 100% garganega
ANNUAL PRODUCTION: 40,000 bottles
AGING: 6 months in stainless steel
PRODUCTION METHOD: Conventional

NORTHWEST ITALY

LIGURIA

Cinque Terre Sciacchetrà *Walter De Batté*
DENOMINATION: Cinque Terre Sciacchetrà DOC
FIRST VINTAGE: 1997
GRAPE VARIETALS: 80% bosco, 20% albarola
ANNUAL PRODUCTION: 1,000 bottles
AGING: 12 months in small oak
PRODUCTION METHOD: Natural

LOMBARDIA

Franciacorta Cuvée Annamaria Clementi *Ca' del Bosco*
DENOMINATION: Franciacorta DOCG

WEBSITE: www.cadelbosco.it
FIRST VINTAGE: 1979, release of
first vintage Franciacorta; 1989,
release of Cuvée Annamaria
Clementi
GRAPE VARIETALS: 50%
chardonnay, 25% pinot bianco,
25% pinot nero
ANNUAL PRODUCTION: 45,800
bottles
AGING: 7 months in small oak,
about 2 years in glass
PRODUCTION METHOD:
Conventional

Valtellina Sfursat 5 Stelle *Nino Negri*
DENOMINATION: Valtellina DOCG
WEBSITE: www.ninonegri.it
FIRST VINTAGE: 1983
GRAPE VARIETALS: 100% nebbiolo
(chiavennasca, local name of
the nebbiolo grape in
Valtellina)
ANNUAL PRODUCTION: 45,000
bottles
AGING: 16 months in small oak
PRODUCTION METHOD:
Conventional

PIEMONTE

Barbaresco Vigneto Brich Ronchi *Albino Rocca*
DENOMINATION: Barbaresco
DOCG

WEBSITE: www.roccaalbino
.com
FIRST VINTAGE: 1993
GRAPE VARIETAL: 100% nebbiolo
ANNUAL PRODUCTION: 2,500
bottles
AGING: 9 months in small oak, 9
months in large oak
PRODUCTION METHOD:
Conventional

Barbaresco Santo Stefano Riserva *Bruno Giacosa*
DENOMINATION: Barbaresco
Riserva DOCG
WEBSITE: www.brunogiacosa.it
FIRST VINTAGE: 1964
GRAPE VARIETAL: 100% nebbiolo
ANNUAL PRODUCTION: 12,000
bottles
AGING: 32 months in large oak
PRODUCTION METHOD:
Conventional

Barolo *Bartolo Mascarello*
DENOMINATION: Barolo DOCG
FIRST VINTAGE: 1918
GRAPE VARIETAL: 100% nebbiolo
ANNUAL PRODUCTION: 20,000
bottles
AGING: 24–30 months in large oak
PRODUCTION METHOD:
Conventional

Barolo Brunate *Roberto Voerzio*
DENOMINATION: Barolo DOCG

FIRST VINTAGE: 1988
GRAPE VARIETAL: 100% nebbiolo
ANNUAL PRODUCTION: 2,000
bottles
AGING: 24 months in small oak
PRODUCTION METHOD:
Conventional

Barolo Brunate–Le Coste
Giuseppe Rinaldi
DENOMINATION: Barolo DOCG
FIRST VINTAGE: 1993
GRAPE VARIETAL: 100% nebbiolo
ANNUAL PRODUCTION: 10,000
bottles
AGING: 36 months in large oak
PRODUCTION MENTHOD:
Conventional

Barolo Cannubi Boschis *Luciano Sandrone*
DENOMINATION: Barolo DOCG
WEBSITE: www.sandroneluciano
.com
FIRST VINTAGE: 1985
GRAPE VARIETAL: 100% nebbiolo
ANNUAL PRODUCTION: 9,000
bottles
AGING: 24 months in small oak
(tonneaus)
PRODUCTION METHOD:
Conventional

Barolo Ginestra Vigna Casa Maté *Elio Grasso*
DENOMINATION: Barolo DOCG

WEBSITE: www.eliograsso.it
FIRST VINTAGE: 1978
GRAPE VARIETAL: 100% nebbiolo
ANNUAL PRODUCTION: 14,000
bottles
AGING: 24 months in large oak
PRODUCTION METHOD:
Conventional

Barolo Gran Bussia Riserva
Aldo Conterno
DENOMINATION: Barolo Riserva
DOCG
WEBSITE: WWW
.poderialdoconterno.com
FIRST VINTAGE: 1970
GRAPE VARIETAL: 100% nebbiolo
ANNUAL PRODUCTION: 9,600
bottles
AGING: 36 months in large oak
PRODUCTION METHOD:
Conventional

Barolo Lazzarito Vigna La Delizia—*Fontanafredda*
DENOMINATION: Barolo DOCG
WEBSITE: www.fontanafredda.it
FIRST VINTAGE: 1971
GRAPE VARIETAL: 100% nebbiolo
ANNUAL PRODUCTION: 23,000
bottles
AGING: 12 months in small oak,
12 months in large wooden
barrels
PRODUCTION METHOD:
Conventional

Barolo Monprivato *Giuseppe Mascarello e Figlio*
DENOMINATION: Barolo DOCG
WEBSITE: www.mascarello1881
.com
FIRST VINTAGE: 1970
GRAPE VARIETAL: 100% nebbiolo
ANNUAL PRODUCTION: 25,000
bottles
AGING: 38 months in large oak
PRODUCTION METHOD:
Conventional

Barolo Ciabot Mentin Ginestra *Domenico Clerico*
DENOMINATION: Barolo DOCG
FIRST VINTAGE: 1982
GRAPE VARIETAL: 100% nebbiolo
ANNUAL PRODUCTION: 19,000
bottles
AGING: 24 months in small oak
PRODUCTION METHOD:
Conventional

Barolo Rocche dell'Annunziata Riserva *Paolo Scavino*
DENOMINATION: Barolo Riserva
DOCG
WEBSITE: www.paoloscavino.com
FIRST VINTAGE: 1990
GRAPE VARIETAL: 100% nebbiolo
ANNUAL PRODUCTION: 2,500
bottles
AGING: 12 months in small oak, 24
months in large oak

PRODUCTION METHOD:
Conventional

Barolo Vigna Rionda Riserva *Massolino*
DENOMINATION: Barolo Riserva
DOCG
WEBSITE: www.massolino.it
FIRST VINTAGE: 1982
GRAPE VARIETAL: 100% nebbiolo
ANNUAL PRODUCTION: 8,400
bottles
AGING: 40 months in large oak
PRODUCTION METHOD:
Conventional

Barolo Vigneto Arborina *Elio Altare-Cascina Nuova*
DENOMINATION: Barolo DOCG
WEBSITE: www.elioaltare.com
FIRST VINTAGE: 1982
GRAPE VARIETAL: 100% nebbiolo
ANNUAL PRODUCTION: 9,000
bottles
AGING: 24 months in small oak
PRODUCTION METHOD: Natural

Colli Tortonesi Bianco Costa del Vento *Vigneti Massa*
DENOMINATION: Colli Tortonesi
Bianco DOC
FIRST VINTAGE: 1992
GRAPE VARIETAL: 100% timorasso
ANNUAL PRODUCTION: 10,000
bottles

AGING: 6 months in small
oak

PRODUCTION METHOD: Natural

Langhe Nebbiolo Sorì San Lorenzo *Gaja*

DENOMINATION: Langhe Nebbiolo
DOC

FIRST VINTAGE: 1967 (with the
denomination Barbaresco;
changes to Langhe Nebbiolo in
2000)

GRAPE VARIETALS: 95% nebbiolo,
5% barbera

ANNUAL PRODUCTION: 12,000
bottles

AGING: 12 months in large oak, 12
months in small oak

PRODUCTION METHOD:
Conventional

Barbaresco Vigneti in Montestefano Riserva *Cantina Produttori del Barbaresco*

DENOMINATION: Barbaresco
Riserva DOCG

WEBSITE: WWW
.produttoridelbarbaresco.com

FIRST VINTAGE: 1978

GRAPE VARIETAL: 100% nebbiolo

ANNUAL PRODUCTION: 15,000
bottles

AGING: 36 months in small oak

PRODUCTION METHOD:
Conventional

Barbaresco Rombone *Fiorenzo Nada*

DENOMINATION: Barbaresco
DOCG

WEBSITE: www.nada.it

FIRST VINTAGE: 1997

GRAPE VARIETAL: 100% nebbiolo

ANNUAL PRODUCTION: 4,000
bottles

AGING: 16–18 months in small oak

PRODUCTION METHOD:
Conventional

Barbaresco Vigneto Starderi *La Spinetta*

DENOMINATION: Barbaresco
DOCG

WEBSITE: www.la-spinetta.com

FIRST VINTAGE: 1996

GRAPE VARIETAL: 100% nebbiolo

ANNUAL PRODUCTION: 15,500
bottles

AGING: 22 months in small oak

PRODUCTION METHOD:
Conventional

Barbera d'Asti Bricco dell'Uccellone *Braida*

DENOMINATION: Barbera d'Asti
DOC

WEBSITE: www.braida.it

FIRST VINTAGE: 1982

GRAPE VARIETAL: 100% barbera

ANNUAL PRODUCTION: 55,000
bottles

AGING: 12–15 months in small oak
PRODUCTION METHOD: Natural

Gattinara Vigneto Osso San Grato *Antoniolo*
DENOMINATION: Gattinara DOCG
FIRST VINTAGE: 1974
GRAPE VARIETAL: 100% nebbiolo
ANNUAL PRODUCTION: 5,000 bottles
AGING: 36 months in large oak
PRODUCTION METHOD: Conventional

Roero Mombeltramo Riserva *Malvirà*
DENOMINATION: Roero Riserva DOCG
WEBSITE: www.malvira.com
FIRST VINTAGE: 1999
GRAPE VARIETAL: 100% nebbiolo

ANNUAL PRODUCTION: 20,000 bottles
AGING: 24 months in small oak
PRODUCTION METHOD: Natural

VALLE D'AOSTA

Valle d'Aosta Chardonnay Cuvée Bois *Les Crêtes*
DENOMINATION: Valle d'Aosta Chardonnay DOC
WEBSITE: www.lescretes.it
FIRST VINTAGE: 1988
GRAPE VARIETAL: 100% chardonnay
ANNUAL PRODUCTION: 18,000 bottles
AGING: 12 months in small oak
PRODUCTION METHOD: Conventional

SOUTHERN ITALY AND THE MEZZOGIORNO

ABRUZZO

Trebbiano d'Abruzzo *Valentini*
DENOMINATION: Trebbiano d'Abruzzo DOC
FIRST VINTAGE: 1988
GRAPE VARIETAL: 100% trebbiano
ANNUAL PRODUCTION: 15,000 bottles

AGING: 12 months in large oak
PRODUCTION METHOD: Natural

Montepulciano d'Abruzzo Villa Gemma *Masciarelli*
DENOMINATION: Montepulciano d'Abruzzo DOC
WEBSITE: www.masciarelli.it

FIRST VINTAGE: 1984
GRAPE VARIETAL: 100%
montepulciano
ANNUAL PRODUCTION: 30,000
bottles
AGING: 36 months in small oak
PRODUCTION METHOD:
Conventional

BASILICATA

Aglianico del Vulture Titolo
Elena Fucci
DENOMINATION: Aglianico del
Vulture DOC
WEBSITE: www.elenafuccivini.com
FIRST VINTAGE: 2000
GRAPE VARIETAL: 100% aglianico
ANNUAL PRODUCTION: 18,000
bottles
AGING: 12 months in small oak
PRODUCTION METHOD: Natural

CAMPANIA

Costa d'Amalfi Furore Bianco
Fiorduva *Cantine Gran Furor*
Divina Costiera
DENOMINATION: Costa d'Amalfi
Furore Bianco DOC
WEBSITE: www.granfuror.it
FIRST VINTAGE: 1995
GRAPE VARIETALS: 30% fenile,
30% ginestra, 40% ripoli
ANNUAL PRODUCTION: 5,000
bottles

AGING: 3 months in small oak
PRODUCTION METHOD: Natural

Fiano di Avellino *Colli di Lapio*
DENOMINATION: Fiano di Avellino
DOCG
FIRST VINTAGE: 1994
GRAPE VARIETAL: 100% fiano
ANNUAL PRODUCTION: 50,000
bottles
AGING: 6 months in stainless steel
PRODUCTION METHOD:
Conventional

Irpinia Aglianico Serpico *Feudi*
di San Gregorio
DENOMINATION: Irpinia Aglianico
DOC
WEBSITE: www.feudi.it
FIRST VINTAGE: 1990
GRAPE VARIETAL: 100% aglianico
ANNUAL PRODUCTION: 50,000
bottles
AGING: 12–14 months in small oak
PRODUCTION METHOD:
Conventional

Taurasi Radici Riserva
Mastroberardino
DENOMINATION: Taurasi Radici
WEBSITE: www.mastroberardino
.com
FIRST VINTAGE: 1997
GRAPE VARIETAL: 100% aglianico
ANNUAL PRODUCTION: 8,000
bottles

AGING: 30 months in small oak, 30 months in large oak
PRODUCTION METHOD: Conventional

Taurasi Vigna Cinque Querce
Salvatore Molettieri
DENOMINATION: Taurasi DOCG
WEBSITE: www.salvatoremolettieri.it
FIRST VINTAGE: 2000
GRAPE VARIETAL: 100% aglianico
ANNUAL PRODUCTION: 8,000 bottles
AGING: 30 months in small and large oak

Terra di Lavoro *Galardi*
DENOMINATION: Campania IGT
WEBSITE: www.terradilavoro.com
FIRST VINTAGE: 1994
GRAPE VARIETALS: 80% aglianico, 20% piedirosso
ANNUAL PRODUCTION: 25,000 bottles
AGING: 10 months in small oak
PRODUCTION METHOD: Certified organic

LAZIO

Grechetto Latour a Civitella
Sergio Mottura
DENOMINATION: Grechetto di Civitella d'Agliano IGT
WEBSITE: www.motturasergio.it
FIRST VINTAGE: 1993
GRAPE VARIETAL: 100% grechetto
ANNUAL PRODUCTION: 13,000 bottles
AGING: 9 months in small oak
PRODUCTION METHOD: Certified organic

PUGLIA

Le Braci *Azienda Monaci*
DENOMINATION: Salento IGT
WEBSITE: www.aziendamonaci.com
FIRST VINTAGE: 2000
GRAPE VARIETAL: 100% negroamaro
ANNUAL PRODUCTION: 20,000 bottles
AGING: 10 months in small oak
PRODUCTION METHOD: Conventional

INDEX

Manetti, Martino, 53
Manetti, Sergio, 52–53
Manfredi, Alberto, 52
Marche
  Kurni (Oasi degli Angeli), 8–11
  Verdicchio dei Castelli di Jesi Classico
    Superiore Podium (Gioacchino Garofoli),
    14–16
  Verdicchio dei Castelli di Jesi Classico Villa
    Bucci Riserva (Bucci), 11–14
Marchesi Antinori (Toscana), 61–63
Marchesi Mazzei family, 36–37
Marco de Bartoli (Sicilia), 93–96
Marsala Superiore Riserva 10 Anni (Marco de
  Bartoli), 93–96
Martinetti, Franco, 204
Martini di Cigala, Enrico, 50
Martini di Cigala, Franceso, Luca, and
  Elisabetta, 50
Mascarello, Bartolo, 170–72, 188, 201
Mascarello, Franca and Maria Teresa, 173
Mascarello, Giulio, 171, 172
Mascarello, Giuseppe, 188–90
Mascarello, Maria Teresa, 177
Mascarello, Maurizio, 190
Mascarello, Mauro, 189
Masciarelli, Gianni, 238–39
Masciarelli (Abruzzo), 238–40
Massa, Walter, 203–5
Masseto (Tenuta dell'Ornellaia), 45–47
Massolino family, 198
Massolino (Piemonte), 197–99
Mastroberardino, Piero, 253
Mastroberardino (Campania), 252–54
Maule, Casimiro, 163
Mazzocolin, Giuseppe, 38–39
merlot grapes, 37, 46, 54, 55, 59, 60, 99, 130,
  131–32, 251
methanol scandal, 174
mezzandria system, 12, 32, 34, 36
minnella grapes, 88
Moio, Luigi, 246
Molettieri, Salvatore, 255
molinara grapes, 134, 139
Mondavi, Robert, 45
Montefalco Sagrantino 25 Anni (Arnaldo
  Caprai), 66–68
Montepulciano d'Abruzzo Villa Gemma
  (Masciarelli), 238–40
montepulciano grapes, 9, 10, 238, 240
Montevertine (Toscana), 52–54

moscato d'Allessandria grapes. *See* zibibbo
  grapes
moscato grapes, 159, 216
Mottura, Sergio, 259–61
Muccioli, Vincenzo, 5
Murena, Maria Luisa, 257

Nada, Bruno, 213–14, 215
Nada, Fiorenzo, 213, 214
nasco grapes, 79
nebbiolo grapes
  in Lombardia wines, 162, 163
  in Piemonte wines, 165–66, 168, 175, 177,
    185, 187, 192, 193, 194, 198, 202, 209,
    210, 211, 212, 214, 215, 216, 217, 222,
    226, 227
Negri, Carlo, 162
Negri, Nino, 162
negroamaro grapes, 263, 264
nerello cappuccio grapes, 88
nerello mascalese grapes, 88, 93
Neri, Giacomo, 25
Neri, Giovanni, 24–25
nero d'Avola grapes, 86–87, 89, 97, 101
Nino Negri (Lombardia), 161–64
Nobile di Montepulciano Nocio dei Boscarelli
  (Boscarelli), 47–49
nuraghe (stone towers), 83
nuragus grapes, 79

Oasi degli Angeli (Marche), 8–11
organic operations, 44, 50, 58, 226, 265
oseleta grapes, 134, 140, 142

Pagli, Attilio, 256
Palari (Sicilia), 90–93
Pallanti, Marco, 40, 41, 42
Palmucci, Piero, 30–31
Paolo Scavino (Piemonte), 193–97
Parker, Robert, Jr., 25, 192
Passito di Pantelleria Ben Ryé (Donnafugata),
  96–98
Percarlo (Fattoria San Giusto a Rentannano),
  49–51
pergola abruzzese vine training system, 239
pergola veronese vine training system, 147
pergola vine training system, 108
Perini, Moreno, 58
Peter Pliger Kuenhof (Alto Adige), 112–14
petit verdot grapes, 19
Petrilli, Saverio, 58–59

sagrantino grapes, 66
Salvatore Molettieri (Campania), 255–56
Salvioni, Giulio, 22, 23–24
Sandrone, Luciano, 179–81
Sangiovese di Romagna Superiore Avi Riserva
   (San Patrignano), 5–7
sangiovese grapes
   in Emilia Romagna wines, 6
   in Toscana wines, 17, 23–24, 26, 30–31, 32,
      35, 37, 38–39, 42, 44, 49, 51, 52, 53, 59,
      60, 61, 62, 63, 217
sangiovese grosso grapes, 28, 29
San Leonardo (Tenuta San Leonardo),
   129–32
San Michele Appiano (Alto Adige), 109–11
San Patrignano (Emilia Romagna), 5–7
Santa Cecilia (Planeta), 99–101
Sardegna
   Carignano del Sulcis Superiore Terre Brune
      (Cantina Sociale di Santadi), 77–79
   Tenores (Tenute Dettori), 79–81
   Turriga (Argiolas), 82–84
sauvignon blanc grapes, 110, 111, 123–24
Scavino, Anna Maria, Enrica, and Elisa, 195
Scavino, Enrico, 192, 193–96
Scavino, Paolo, 194
schiava grossa grapes, 115
Sebasti, Lorenza, 40, 42
Seghesio, Renzo, 183
Selezione Fattorie, 40
Selosse, Anselme, 250
Sergio Mottura (Lazio), 259–61
Settesoli (wine cooperative), 99
Sicilia
   Etna Bianco Pietramarina (Benanti),
      87–90
   Faro Palari (Palari), 90–93
   Marsala Superiore Riserva 10 Anni (Marco
      de Bartoli), 93–96
   Passito di Pantelleria Ben Ryé
      (Donnafugata), 96–98
   Rosso del Conte (Tasca d'Almerita), 85–87
   Santa Cecilia (Planeta), 99–101
Silvio Jermann (Friuli–Venezia Giulia),
   123–25
Sirch, Pierpaolo, 250
Soave Classico Calvarino (Leonildo Pieropan),
   145–47
Soave Classico Monte Fiorentine (Ca' Rugate),
   147–50
solera method, 94, 95

sparkling wines
   Franciacorta Cuvée Annamaria Clementi
      (Ca' del Bosco), 158–61
   Giulio Ferrari (Ferrari), 126–29
   Lambrusco, about, 6
Spumante, 159
Stocker, Sebastian, 107
Super Tuscans
   Bolgheri Superiore Grattamacco Rosso
      (Podere Grattamacco), 20–22
   Camartina, 32–33
   Cepparello (Isole e Olena), 33–35
   Le Pergole Torte (Montevertine), 52–54
   Sammarco, 18
   Sassicaia (Tenuta San Guido), 20, 21, 46,
      56–58
sylvaner grapes, 113
syrah grapes, 60

Tachis, Giacomo, 17–18, 32, 56, 61, 78, 82–83,
   131
Tasca d'Almerita (Sicilia), 85–87
Taurasi Radici Riserva (Mastroberardino),
   252–54
Taurasi Vigna Cinque Querce (Salvatore
   Molettieri), 255–56
tendone vine training system, 237
Tenores (Tenute Dettori), 79–81
Tenuta dell'Ornellaia (Toscana), 45–47
Tenuta di Valgiano (Tenuta di Valgiano), 58–60
Tenuta di Valgiano (Toscana), 58–60
Tenuta Fontodi (Toscana), 43–45
Tenuta San Guido (Toscana), 56–58
Tenuta San Leonardo (Trentino), 129–32
Tenute Dettori (Sardegna), 79–81
Terra di Lavoro (Galardi), 256–58
Terzer, Hans, 110, 111
Tessari, Amedeo, 148
Tessari, Amedeo and Giovanni, 148
Tessari, Fulvio, 148
Tessari, Michele, 148
Tignanello (Marchesi Antinori), 61–63
timorasso grapes, 203–5
tintore grapes, 246
tocai friulano grapes, 121
Tomasi, Giuseppe, 96
Tommaso Bussola (Veneto), 142–44
Toscana
   Alceo (Castello dei Rampolla), 17–20
   Bolgheri Superiore Grattamacco Rosso
      (Podere Grattamacco), 20–22